Advance Praise
for *American Daughter*

"Much more than a story of a rape and its aftermath, *American Daughter*—in the tradition of classics like *The Glass Castle*, *The L.A. Diaries*, and *White Oleander*—explores in unsparing detail the complex interplay between intimate family ties, generational abuse, cataclysmic losses, and the extraordinary and limitless power of compassion and self-discovery. Stephanie Thornton Plymale is often asked, throughout this riveting and powerful memoir: How? How did you emerge from that wreckage powerful and whole? But *American Daughter* resists such easy binaries and instead gives us a portrait of coming together stronger at the broken places as Plymale interrogates both her own survival and her fragile, damaging and compelling mother's. A story by turns feral and transcendent, *American Daughter* illustrates the enormous strength and will it takes for anyone to choose love."

—**GINA FRANGELLO,** author of *Every Kind of Wanting* and
A Life in Men, editor of *The Coachella Review*

"Stephanie Plymale brings readers of her well-written memoir into the complex process of attempting to understand, reconcile, and forgive adult family members who failed her. When she looks at her accomplishments in deep relationships and a powerful career, she asks the poignant question, 'Why am I the resilient one?' Ultimately unanswered, it is gratifying to follow her on the journey to redemption. She leaves us with hope for every individual and every fraught family relationship."

—**JANIS AVERY,** former CEO of Treehouse

"*American Daughter* is a deeply compelling page-turner of a memoir, beautifully written, and insightful. The reasons some of us survive chaotic childhoods and go on to lead happy productive lives, to even thrive, are complex and seemingly random. Yet we long to discover a secret formula for resilience. *American Daughter* does not give us facile answers. We follow Stephanie's journey from horrific childhood to successful businesswoman, mother, and wife, and are captivated by her inner strength, her kindness, her desire to seek truth, and most poignantly, her desire to find her place in the world, to belong. This memoir does not pretend that scars of a traumatic childhood can be erased, but it shows us happiness is still possible. Stephanie's investigation into family history leads to a truth many abuse victims eventually discover, that our abusers have often survived their own hellish childhoods, and that we all carry the trauma of our ancestors."

—**KAREN LYNCH**, author of *Good Cop, Bad Daughter: Memoirs of an Unlikely Police Officer*

"*American Daughter* is a riveting page-turner that has the reader looking forward to each chapter with a mix of anticipation and unease; given that it inevitably means another heartache lay just around the corner for the author, her mother, and siblings. The book is both a haunting memoir and Cinderella story that has you rooting for this family until the end. The writing is exquisitely vivid and poetic, making it easy to conjure up images of mother and daughter throughout the many decades of their lives together, and apart. In the end, *American Daughter* is one woman's triumphant tale of determination and hope to create a truly beautiful life for herself against all odds."

—**TRACY KLINKROTH**, founder of ChickChat and The Power of She

"The story of *American Daughter* has affected my life forever! Stephanie's story minimizes what being a survivor is: Does a victim really have a choice or in their journey do some just get luckier than others? The people they meet, the breaks they get—bottom line, those who can survive the most horrific, unimaginable things actually can break the cycle of such a terrible life. And if they do, then to me they are nothing short of a living saint! My heart is so heavy for Stephanie's unimaginable story, but I have learned so much about love—even if it's too late—and about forgiveness even if it seems impossible.

"I want to help share Stephanie's story to inspire others! We have many surface similarities including a life in the Northwest, tennis, adopting a baby girl from Guatemala, running from things in life, family secrets revealed late in life, ancestry surprises, and life perceptions. Her book reminds me that we are all connected at some level and all of us have a story. Ten percent of life is what happens to us and 90 percent is really how we react to it! God bless her bravery in sharing her well written book with many intricate details of her life! You have a fan, a friend, and a real admirer in me."

—**KAREN PHELPS MOYER,** founder of Good Morning Gorgeous, LLC; Emmy award winner; founder of Moyer Foundation

"This book takes the reader along on a journey that is equal parts heart-rending, shocking, and uplifting. It may be surprising to describe a story of homelessness, child abuse, and mental illness as uplifting, but Plymale's open and thoughtful consideration of her life story gives hope to those who have struggled through adversity. She does not shy from describing those challenges, creating a sense of profound empathy for both her and, shockingly, for the mother who was the catalyst for so much suffering. But the heart and humanity at the core of her story ultimately leave the reader with a sense of the redemption that is possible and an abiding appreciation for what we have."

—**CHRIS SHORTELL,** author of *Rights, Remedies, and the Impact of State Sovereign Immunity*; political science professor at Portland State University

"The story is never less than compelling as the reader learns how her mother's grandiose statements have a basis in truth. The trauma Plymale discovers is so horrible it was recorded in the newspapers. Stephanie Plymale is honest about her family's failings and her own, but ultimately forgiving, reminding me that hope is not: 'the conviction that something will turn out well, but the certainty that something makes sense regardless of how it turns out.' (Vaclav Havel, *Disturbing the Peace*, 1985)"

—**MARTHA CRITES,** author of *Grave Disturbance*, mental health counselor

STEPHANIE THORNTON PLYMALE

with ELISSA WALD

American Daughter

A Memoir

HarperOne
An Imprint of HarperCollinsPublishers

The names and identifying characteristics of persons referenced in this book, as well as identifying events and places, have been changed to protect the privacy of the individuals and their families.

For permission to reproduce copyrighted material, grateful acknowledgment is made to the following sources:

HarperCollins books may be purchased for educational, business, or sales promotional use. For information, please email the Special Markets Department at SPsales@harpercollins.com.

First published in 2020 by River Grove Books.
First HarperCollins edition published in 2021.

Design adapted from the River Grove edition designed by Greenleaf Book Group

Library of Congress Cataloging-in-Publication Data has been applied for.

ISBN 978-0-06-305433-2
ISBN 978-0-06-308310-3 (Intl)

21 22 23 24 25   LSC   10 9 8 7 6 5 4 3 2 1

To my mother, Florence. In the most
untraditional way, you gave me what I needed.

American Daughter

Prologue

ON THAT JANUARY morning, I woke up in a car. Isabella and the baby were beside me in the back of our station wagon, still asleep. Allan and Pablo were outside, lying on the ground in their sleeping bags. Our mother was gone.

The year was 1974. I was six years old. We were in Mendocino Headlands State Park on a bluff overlooking the ocean. The car had been our home for many months, and it would be our home for many months to come. It was the car of someone who had come to the end of the line—the car of a driver who'd driven as far as she could go.

I was warm beneath the wool blanket, pressed against my sister with the sun slanting through the back windshield. Every morning I lingered in the shelter of the station wagon for as long as I could, until hunger and the need to relieve myself drove me up and out of our makeshift bed.

It was always cold outside the car. A bitter wind came hard off the water, whipping my hair in every direction and making the bones of my face ache. Each morning began with the same ritual: First I crouched to urinate in the brush, and then I went to the cardboard box in the back of the car in the hope of having some semblance of breakfast. Whatever was inside that box was what we had to eat that day.

On a good day there might be hempseed bread and fresh-ground peanut butter, Tiger's Milk bars, or apricot granola.

On other days, there might be nothing but bran cereal. The bran pellets were hard and dry and tasted like dust, and they made my stomach hurt.

Or there might be nothing but brown sugar, which I'd eat straight from the container. My mother said brown sugar was good for us because it had molasses in it.

Or there might be nothing at all.

On the nothing-at-all days, the empty days, my brothers collected seaweed for us to eat. They climbed down the cliffs to the cove where the kelp was most abundant, and they would gather armfuls of it—as much as they could carry. Allan, who at ten was the oldest of us, went first, with nine-year-old Pablo following close behind. Each time they descended into that canyon of rock and moss and pounding surf, I felt afraid that they'd be swept away to sea or dashed against the jagged black boulders. The ocean was a fury; to live beside it was to know this well. Evidence of its violence was everywhere we turned. The sand was littered with broken things: dismembered claws, gutted shells, the shards of clams dropped from the sky and eviscerated by gulls.

But Allan and Pablo always reappeared beside the car with the seaweed. They spread it on a blanket to dry in the sun, a process that took several hours. Even then, the seaweed was nearly impossible to swallow—slick and oily, hard to chew, with a lingering aftertaste like dead fish. I held my breath while forcing it down, and gulped water after each bite.

Our mother worked as a maid at a motel several miles away. She left the car before first light to hitchhike to her job and didn't come back until early evening. For months on end—for most of that year—we were on our own every day, fending for ourselves, aimless and feral and free.

We didn't go to school that year, and this drew no notice from anyone. Mendocino was a hippie refuge where a passel of half-wild children wandering around unattended struck no one as unusual and aroused no concern. Every afternoon we ran and capered and played on the beach like a pack of stray puppies.

Each morning brought the same set of difficulties: the hunger and the cold, the relative lack of shelter, the long stretch of unstructured hours. And yet each morning the world was new. The sky was pink like the inside of a shell. The shoreline was studded with treasure: sea glass, shards of abalone, intricate sticks of driftwood, and the occasional fisherman's float.

I loved just to look at all the marvels of the ocean. I would crouch down to peer for long minutes at the skeletal underside of a horseshoe crab, the elegant twist of a whelk, the clear blue bodies of jellyfish washed up on the sand. The beach was as much our home as the station wagon. Years later I would hear the phrase "sea urchins," and although the reference was to a marine creature, my first thought was: *That was us.*

We spent our days roaming the same two-mile stretch again and again. On any given afternoon, we could be found beside the bluffs, on the outskirts of the village, on the winding trails along the cliffs, or down by the water.

It was a relief to see our mother each time she returned in her pale blue uniform dress, and to trail her to the neighborhood store. We never had more than a few dollars to spend on dinner for the six of us. My mother's scant pay had to cover diapers for the baby, the cost of washing our clothes at the laundromat, soap and shampoo, cigarettes by the carton, the little squares of paper she ate every morning, and the pungent green clusters of buds she called herbs. At the local grocery, we picked out random items: grapes or tangerines, carob bars, halvah, dried slices of persimmon or papaya.

Sometimes a kind cashier gave us hot water in cardboard cups. On these blessed evenings, we would divide the contents of a Top Ramen package among the cups and sit on the curb outside the store to eat it. That soup was the best dinner I'd ever had, the best dinner I could imagine having.

After this, we would go to the public showers at Fort Bragg, an event that rivaled dinner as the best of the day. Hot water was a benediction, however it came.

That January day began like any other: shivering, driftless, dreaming of heat, wandering the headlands with my sister and baby brother. Allan and Pablo were back at the car, drying seaweed. On a distant bluff was a bus—one we had never seen before—like a school bus but bleached white on the outside with blue-green trim. The novelty of it pulled us

xiv   STEPHANIE THORNTON PLYMALE

near and somehow, though we moved through the world with a kind of wary insularity (we did not talk to strangers; we tended not to even go near them), I found myself knocking at its door.

I'll never know what led me to knock, and I'll never know why the man inside swung open the door to admit us. I only know that I climbed the steps that day and beheld a sight that seared itself into my mind, an image that never dimmed, that carried me through the weeks and months and years ahead. It's an image that's still with me now: a vision of sanctuary, of a haven, ensconced within the metal shell of a battered old vehicle. It was a home on the road just as ours was, but inside it was as enchanted and exquisite as a Fabergé egg.

It was warm inside the bus. There were cream-colored café curtains on all the windows, and each pane of glass was clouded with steam. There was a stove with a cooking pot and a red teakettle. There was bench seating built in along the sides, covered with brightly colored pillows and a batik throw. A macramé owl hung on one wall.

The air was fragrant with cooking spices. The man stirred whatever was in the pot with a wooden spoon. I had never imagined a space like this: orderly, cheerful, cozy and snug, a world unto itself. It was like a cottage in a fairy tale.

I looked at Isabella in wonder, and she looked back at me with nothing in her face. The indifference in her eyes filled me with bewilderment. *She doesn't see it*, I thought.

I would think about that bus every single day for years and years. I'd conjure the memory of it just before falling asleep at night. I would draw pictures of it, embellish it in my mind, and add whimsical touches like a jeweled curtain, woven rugs, and paper flowers. I'd imagine it with different drapes and fixtures and furniture. I would hold it close to me.

But at the moment, I could only stand as if rooted in the middle of the room, overwhelmed by a desire so fierce it was like a revelation.

This, I thought. *I want this. And one day I'll have it.*

Chapter 1

IN HER BRONX apartment on that March afternoon in 1967, my mother was listening to the wind. It had a message for her. She was ready to let it blow her west, blow her all the way across the country.

It was spring, not winter, but the world around her was as drab as in the song. She didn't belong here among these brick-box apartment buildings, the charmless storefronts—the drugstores and nail salons and bodegas with their dirty windows and weathered awnings. She hated the dreary stretch of Ogden Avenue and the swamp-green swath of the Harlem River. She didn't care if she never saw any of it again. It was time to leave it all behind.

Birds don't think about flying south, they just fall into formation. They yield to the great pull, the directive written into their wings. What she felt now was like that, and it wasn't just her. What was happening now was a great migration.

She could almost hear the rustling across the country as the bards and muses and dreamers and seekers and poets and mystics and flower children came forth from their former places to heed the call. She saw them hitchhiking on the highway, driving VW buses, riding in makeshift caravans and gypsy wagons, walking with rucksacks and blankets and musical instruments, shawled and beaded and embroidered and feathered and fringed. All of them were tuned into the same frequency and heading west.

California was the gathering place, the mecca. It was where she belonged. The people making their way there were her rightful tribe. She was one of them—anyone could see that. She had waist-length hair the color of sunflower honey and light blue eyes like an invitation.

Not everyone heard the call, of course. The country was still full of establishment types with no interest in expanding their consciousness. The war was still going on, and plenty of people were still into working for The Man. She refused to be left behind with them. She was going.

Louie, her husband, knew this. Or rather, he was willing to defer to her certainty. He had gone there ahead of her, to find them a place and himself a job, and that was a good thing, because she could take care of her problem while he was away.

The problem wasn't that she was unexpectedly pregnant for the fourth time. No, that would have been fine under ordinary circumstances. She had three kids already, what difference would one more make? She liked being pregnant and she didn't mind babies. The problem was that she couldn't be sure who its father was.

Of course it could be Louie, which would be the best thing. He had already given her Pablo and Isabella, and he treated Allan—her first baby—just the same as them.

Allan's father was a bartender at McSorley's Old Ale House. He had stepped outside for a smoke one autumn evening when my mother happened by and asked him for a light. The moment she heard his brogue, she decided to go to bed with him. She never saw him again, and by the time she learned she was pregnant, she didn't even remember his name.

At that time, she was a waitress in a pancake house. She had moved to New York City to be an actress, but so far the only roles she'd been offered were in blue movies. She was staying uptown with her Aunt Lily, but she knew she would never be forgiven an illegitimate pregnancy. She would surely lose her waitressing job for the same reason, but she had some time before that would happen. She was naturally slender and would not start to show beneath her loose peasant blouses until the sixth or seventh month.

Louie worked at the pancake house too. He was the Puerto Rican short-order cook. He winked at her from the kitchen whenever she picked up her plates. He was handsome and muscular and she liked his ease at the stove. She liked the cigarette he kept tucked behind his ear and the slash of a scar beneath his left eye. By the time she was eight months along, she was living in his Bronx apartment and he was smitten with her, willing to treat her baby as his own. He wouldn't do that with this baby, though. Not unless he believed it was his.

Of course he might believe it was his, even if it wasn't. If the father were William, for instance, Louie would never suspect a thing. William was her childhood friend, her first love. His hair was dark and his eyes were similar to her own. Everyone would say the child took after her and leave it at that.

She and William had met when he was fourteen and she was only ten. Unlike any of the other men in her life, he had known her Before, and when he looked at her, he still saw purity and girlishness and innocence. *Lovely*: His word for her was *lovely*. He looked at her the way a sailor might look at a mermaid: as an otherworldly creature he could never really have.

William was special. Once when she was on acid, it came to her that he had a lifelong knowledge of *her very essence*—that for him, she was like one of those burned-out stars whose glow is purely residual. It didn't matter what she did for the rest of her life; to William, there would always be a light around her. For this reason, she went all calm and peaceful inside whenever she was with him, and she slept with him whenever he came through town.

Of course it was also possible the father was Giuseppe, the dapper and handsome man who sold diapers in the maternity ward of Morrisania

Hospital. All the new mothers were sweet on him. They called him the "Italian Stallion."

Giuseppe's wife had once been beautiful but now she had short hair and a ruined figure: the most disastrous fate that could befall a woman. Because of this, my mother felt sorry for him. Whenever he came over, she offered him coffee and cookies and then, almost as a natural extension of her hospitality, a half hour in her bedroom. A hardworking man like that deserved a little treat every now and then.

Giuseppe wore a suit every time he came to see her, and he splashed on a light, clean cologne that she liked. A few times a week, he stopped by during his lunch break—a perfect time because her children were napping. He was always warm and appreciative. He held her face in both of his hands afterward and called her *cara, bella, bellissima*: his darling, his beauty. She never ran low on diapers.

Giuseppe looked as if he could be a cousin of Louie's. A baby with him would raise no more suspicion than a baby with William. If the father were either one of them, then everything would be all right.

But the father could also be Ron, her best friend's husband, who was black, and this would not be all right. At least it would not be all right with Louie; it would be a shock to him. He might even kill her, or Ron, or both. Louie didn't understand about free love.

Ron was tall and handsome and college-educated. He knew about things like wine and classical music. He and her best friend Judy lived five blocks away, in an apartment filled with art and records and books. They had two little boys close in age to Allan and Pablo and Isabella. She and Judy met at the playground sometimes, shared a smoke on the benches while the children climbed on the monkey bars and rode the seesaws.

My mother adored Ron, but if the baby were his then of course her husband and everyone else would know she'd been with another man. Louie would go crazy, and Judy would never forgive her. No, if Ron were the father, it would not be all right.

The rape had happened on her way home from Ron's apartment, on a Saturday in late October. She told Louie that Ron and Judy were having a party, and she went over to their apartment by herself. The truth was that Judy was upstate with the two little boys, visiting her mother, which meant she and Ron could be alone in the apartment.

My mother knew Louie wouldn't want to come with her. Judy and Ron were intellectuals; both of them had graduated from Fordham. When they really did have parties, a bunch of their college friends crowded into their cramped two-bedroom and drank wine and passed a joint around while talking about Malcolm X and Che Guevara and Frantz Fanon. Louie couldn't join in these conversations, and he didn't like to get high.

My mother's deception went as planned, and after her time with Ron, she insisted on walking home by herself. She couldn't risk being seen alone with him, and anyway, it was only a few blocks. Her attacker had come up behind her on the sidewalk outside her own apartment building. She felt the blade of his knife against her neck before she saw him, and then he was dragging her behind the dumpster by the back lot, telling her not to scream because she was too beautiful to kill.

She didn't scream but she bucked and kicked and twisted and thrashed. As a result, he was only able to jab himself inside her a few times before she managed to dislodge him, and he ended up mostly spraying her. The worst part of the whole thing wasn't even that, it was the knife at her throat and the damp cold metal of the dumpster at her back and the rotten sewage smell all around her. And the way Louie slapped her, hard across the face, once she reached their apartment and told him what happened. Afterward he said it was because she had been hysterical. But she knew it was really because he was ashamed of her—angry with her—for being raped.

But back to this March afternoon: a blustery day in the Bronx. The date marking the official start of spring had come and gone, but the temperature still hovered just below freezing and the wind was howling around my mother's fifth-story window. My mother spent a long time at that window throughout that morning. She saw a drunk passed out on the curb, with one foot sticking out into the street. At one point a cab ran over that foot and still he didn't stir.

She was thinking that she should never have married Louie. At the time he had been her ticket out of a tricky situation, but still, she should not have married him. They really had nothing at all in common. He was in California right now so he could make her dream come true, but it wasn't because he himself felt the pull. If left to his own preferences, he'd have been happy to turn gray and die in the Bronx without so much as seeing California. Happy just to drink five or six bottles of Corona on hot summer evenings and play dominoes with the other men on their block. Happy with day trips to Orchard Beach or Far Rockaway or Coney Island. And the music she loved so much, it didn't speak to him at all.

She was lonely with him. But this loneliness would not last forever. When it was a bird's time to fly, it flew.

Meanwhile, there was still the pregnancy to deal with. Ron had a friend who was a nurse, and she had pledged to help. Ron was probably paying her, but my mother was never told any details of this arrangement, if there was one. That was all right; she preferred not to know.

They came by just a little after noon, during the children's naptime. The nurse was blonde and prim-faced with an air of martyrdom. My mother had pictured a white uniform and starched nurse's cap but she was in regular clothes: green corduroy bell-bottoms and a gingham shirt. She did have a white smock that she put on after washing her hands at the kitchen sink. She also had a medical bag and a gallon jar with a black rubber seal.

There were no introductions. Ron had warned ahead of time that there wouldn't be. The nurse would lose her license if anyone found out; she could even go to jail. She did not want my mother to know her name.

Ron was wet-eyed and resigned. He felt bad about what she was planning to do, but he shared her fear that the baby might be his and her belief that ending the pregnancy was for the best. He stood holding her hand while the nurse put a pot of water on to boil, so she could sterilize her equipment. Then they watched in silence as she draped several towels across the kitchen table and set out an array of gleaming metal rods.

Something about the towels and the jar and the rods made my mother shiver. She found herself suddenly cold and breathless, overcome by what they were about to do. The nurse's implements looked sinister, and violent, and *unnatural*. Just then, she felt the baby flutter in her belly and she knew she couldn't do it. Or at least she could not do it this way. There had to be a better way, a gentler way. She began backing away from the table. She backed away until she found herself against the wall and then she slid down to the floor and started to cry.

Ron came over and sat down beside her and took her hand. He stroked her hair and whispered encouragement in her ear. My mother rested her head on her knees and just shook her head *no* over and over. *No, no, no.*

The nurse packed up her equipment. She told my mother to drink quinine—a bottle or two of tonic water might do the trick—and then spend the afternoon moving her furniture around.

Ron went out and got her the tonic water. There wasn't much furniture in the apartment besides the nubby orange and brown tweed sofa and Louie's matching La-Z-Boy recliner. She threw herself into tugging them around in circles. The kitchen table and folding chairs were way too light to bother with.

By evening, there wasn't so much as a spot of blood. She didn't even have a cramp.

All across the nation
Such a strange vibration
People in motion
There's a whole generation…
If you come to San Francisco
Summertime will be a love-in there…

MY MOTHER WOULD attempt to end her pregnancy in other ways. She would try to starve the baby by eating nothing at all for days on end. On other days, if she felt light-headed or dizzy or faint with hunger, she would nibble a package or two of Saltine crackers. Every time she felt the baby move, she would imagine it was in its death throes.

For good measure, she would try every psychedelic she was offered during the weeks and months leading up to her due date. She had heard of people losing pregnancies to LSD. Maybe if she were lucky enough the same thing would happen to her. Acid made everything better anyway. It brightened the long days at home with her kids. It made the Bronx bearable.

By May she would go west as she had dreamed of doing for so long. She would settle with the kids in the apartment that Louie had secured for them in the Haight-Ashbury district of the city, and not long thereafter she would leave him for a grifter named Rick.

In the meantime, she would be in the audience at the Monterey Pop Festival. She would listen live to The Mamas and The Papas and The Grateful Dead and Ravi Shankar and Otis Redding and Jefferson Airplane. She would watch Jimi Hendrix set his guitar on fire and she would hear Janis Joplin keen and croon and growl and caterwaul her way through "Ball and Chain." She would festoon police officers with flowers as they tried to break up the tripping, half-naked, and ecstatic crowds.

And on a July evening in 1967, after all of it—after the nurse showed up in her Bronx apartment and then left again; after the bottles of tonic water and the hours and hours spent hauling her sofa around; after the fifty-calorie days and the nothing-but-air-and-water days and the peyote and angel dust and acid days—my mother burst through the emergency room doors of the San Francisco General Hospital, clutching her swollen belly and gasping that her baby was coming; it was coming *now*.

The ambulance driver who just happened to be standing there swiftly assisted the intake nurse with guiding her onto the nearest gurney and then, true to her word, she gave birth within the next ten minutes. The baby was a girl, pinched-looking and underweight, shriveled and tiny, purplish and nervous, startling at the slightest noise or unexpected touch from the very first moments of life.

As for the birth itself, there was no difficulty at all. There was no striving; there was no pain. As my mother tells it, she didn't even have to push. She knew then that nature had taken its own course from the start, and she had never been anything but powerless to stop it.

Because each earthly being must obey a certain pull. Every living creature has to answer its own call. As migrant birds are pulled south by the sun, as my mother was pulled west by the summer of love, I was pulled headlong and headfirst into this world; I answered the call to survive.

Chapter 2

THE WOMAN ON the other side of my desk was making me uneasy.

"I had a brilliant career in graphic design," she was saying. "We're talking dozens of layouts in national magazines, and a lot of high-level awards."

Karen was applying for admission to the college I own and run, the Heritage School of Interior Design. At first glance, she didn't come across as the typical candidate. She wore a shapeless black dress with no accent pieces or jewelry. Her graying hair hung over her eyes and she kept brushing it back.

So far, I'd heard a lot about how successful she'd been until a sea change in her industry had stripped her of her prospects and optimism. To give herself a lift, she'd remodeled her kitchen—and the result was so stunning, she wondered if she'd stumbled on her next move.

"I've worked with world-famous photographers," she went on. "I've done multimillion-dollar ad campaigns."

"That's very impressive," I told her, hoping I didn't sound as impatient as I was starting to feel. "With a portfolio like that, are you sure you want to walk away from graphic design?"

"It's not that I *want* to," she said. "And I wouldn't say I'm walking away. I'm getting bounced out on my butt!"

"I'm sorry," I said, a little bewildered. "How so?"

"Overnight it's like I've become a dinosaur. You have to understand, I spent *decades* building my reputation in print media. Honing my skills in darkrooms and type houses. My God, when I think of the hours I put in . . . and now? Just like that," Karen snapped her fingers, "it's all about web design."

I was quiet for a moment. Karen was angry, and I didn't blame her. She was afraid, too, as anyone in her place would be. I could understand her bitterness.

But it still wouldn't serve her. In fact, it would hurt her. It would make others want to steer clear of her.

I said none of this. If she ended up a student at Heritage, she would leave a different person than she was today.

For now, I said only, "The good news is that all those skills will enhance your interior design work. Every creative practice you've ever undertaken will end up informing your work in some way. So with that in mind, let me ask you: Are there any other art forms you've pursued, even as a hobby?"

"Well . . ." she said. "I guess so, if you count my quilts."

"You've done quilting? Of course that counts. In fact, sewing skills are prized in the design world."

Suddenly, she was fumbling in her purse and withdrawing an iPad.

"Wait," she said. "I created a website gallery of the quilts I've done. Just give me a second to pull it up . . . here."

She thrust the tablet at me, and what I saw was so startling that at first, I could hardly form a response.

Her quilts were a revelation. They were playful and poignant and piquant and uplifting. They revealed an extraordinary sense of color and composition. You could see Karen's love of life in each one, her appreciation of nature's beauty and bounty.

Many of them had an unassuming simplicity. Several featured childish flowers: tulips, poppies, and snapdragons. They were intensely hopeful and open. It was nearly impossible to reconcile the undefended hope and openness of those images with Karen herself at this moment in my office.

The spirit emanating from those quilts was irresistible. It had come from within the woman in front of me. Where was it?

"Karen," I said. "These quilts are breathtaking."

And with these words, Karen's face transformed before my eyes. The relief of being seen etched itself into her features.

"You have an incredible sense of design," I went on. "One of the very best I've seen. Learning to apply it to interior spaces should be a very natural step for you."

That much was true. I wasn't worried about her technical ability.

"But I imagine you have some questions about the school," I said. "Is there anything you'd like to ask?"

She hesitated. "Well," she said after a moment, "I've always thought of interior designers as very chic people. And as you can probably tell, I'm not much interested in fashion or makeup. Is that going to be a handicap for me in this business?"

I was quiet for another moment. I wanted to tell her no. That the industry's obsession with aesthetics did not extend to a designer's appearance.

But it wouldn't have been true. Most of us expect other designers to show some personal flair. The way we present ourselves is itself a statement. That's true for everyone, of course, but it's especially true for us. A designer needn't be a classic beauty, but her personal presentation should be intentional, self-possessed, and visually interesting.

"I wish I could tell you it doesn't matter," I finally said. "I can't. But I can tell you that you'll have the opportunity to explore that side of yourself here. You just made over your kitchen. You knew just how to highlight the natural and unique beauty of that space. Can you imagine making yourself over?"

This question is really at the heart of every interview I conduct with prospective students. *Can you imagine making yourself over? Can you imagine making your life over?*

It's hard to put into words just how much I love my school. I love everything about it. The wide windows overlooking Mississippi Avenue. The coziness of the classrooms, the wooden beams, and the tables of live-edge cherry. The full wall of fabric swatches—thousands of them, in baskets, in books, on racks—that showrooms send over. Sometimes when I'm having a hard day, I'll flip through a new fabric book and feel restored by the velvets and silks and brocades and damasks. Above all, I love the atmosphere itself, charged with passion and purpose and industry.

I get a lift from seeing my students. Every single one of them is lit with a sense of their own possibilities. Every one of them found the grit to invest in themselves, to take a risk. Some of them have been obsessed with design since early childhood. Many are making this investment well into middle age.

Before Heritage expanded to serve design students in other cities, I met individually with each student when they began the program. I sat with them for as long as they needed and asked questions about their hopes, their goals, and their concerns.

These conversations became intimate very quickly. The students on the other side of my desk were usually in a vulnerable place. For them, this tended to be a time of transition and uncertainty. They were leaving a way of life that no longer felt right. Some of them told me they felt unfulfilled as stay-at-home mothers now that their children were of school age. Others wanted to leave a career that no longer inspired them or—like Karen—an industry that had imploded. For those who were switching careers, starting over could feel perilous. The ones who hadn't worked outside the home for a long time were often afraid to take themselves seriously.

Usually these discussions stayed focused on the students. But once in a while, over the years, I found the spotlight turned back on myself. "Where did you grow up?" someone might ask, or, "What do your parents do? Are you close with them? Do you have any brothers or sisters?"

Very early, I became adept at sidestepping these questions, not only with students but with everyone: "Oh, I grew up in different places, what about you? Are you from here?"

Or: "My mom and I actually aren't all that close, how about you? Do you have a good relationship with your parents? Are they proud of all the amazing things you've done?"

I wasn't about to tell them my mother was criminally insane, that I'd grown up mostly in a series of ghastly foster homes, that the man

I'd believed was my father had killed himself and I had no idea who my real father was. I wasn't going to say that two of my siblings were convicted felons, one was on disability for mental illness, one was a depressive recluse, and one was dead.

Instead I asked admiring and leading questions meant to draw them out, make them forget about me. And usually it worked. Once in a while, though, someone would persist, and whenever that happened, I felt myself breaking into a sweat of alarm beneath the cover of my clothing.

When no other form of deflection was at hand, I'd find an excuse to bolt. I went for almost fifty years without telling anyone about my past—not my trusted staff, not my closest friends, not even my own children.

My husband, Jim, knew. Eventually I had a therapist who knew. But no one else.

This deception, this omission, began to leave me depleted, strung out. Day after day, in an attempt to soothe myself, I would take stock of how far I'd come and how much I'd built. This list included a happy marriage of more than twenty-five years. A stable, close-knit family, with two sons who had come to us in the usual way and a daughter we'd adopted from Guatemala. A cherished career as an interior designer, ownership of my own design schools, a cabinet full of tennis trophies. A devoted staff and beloved friends. A beautiful house in a tranquil neighborhood. Security and achievement against the most staggering odds.

From the outside, it all looked good—very good.

But what no one knew was the fact that I would come home from my days, go straight to the bedroom, lock the door, and pull all the shades. I'd sink down onto the edge of the bed and weep.

Once I released the tears I'd held back for hours, I often couldn't stop. Sometimes these crying jags lasted the whole weekend. I wouldn't get out of bed between Friday evening and Monday morning. I cried into my pillow. I cried in the shower. I cried until I couldn't draw a breath without shuddering.

Sometimes I had panic attacks, episodes that left me clutching my chest, fighting for air, afraid I was dying.

My husband had stopped asking questions. The first time I was overtaken by this nameless grief, he pressed me for a reason, and all I could say was: *I'm sad.* It was as if an invisible wave had broken over me, broken something inside me.

Jim tried to help. He cooked for me, brought me gifts, wrote me cards, told me jokes. When nothing else worked, he simply stayed with me. Holding my hand. Stroking my hair. Lying beside me in bed with his chest pressed against my back.

If I could have given words to what weighed on me, what was breaking me, I would have talked about the unbearable burden of secrecy, of feeling like a fraud. I needed to come out of hiding and come clean with others—even with myself—about my life. I needed to finally face my past.

And the day of my interview with Karen, that process was irreversibly set in motion when my cell phone rang and my mother's name appeared on the screen.

My heart pounded at the sight of it. It had been years since we'd spoken. Her call now, if indeed it was her, was in violation of her stalking order, the one I'd filed against her after she threatened to burn my house down.

Since that stalking order had been set, I'd seen her just once while picking up a furniture shipment for a client's renovation. I pulled into the warehouse parking lot, which was next to a local Motel 6, and there she was. Sitting on the curb in front of room #107 and smoking a cigarette. She looked wild, and her eyes were drawn into slits behind her tangled hair.

I didn't get out of the car for a long time. I sat in the driver's seat and watched her, holding myself very still. More than once, I had to close my eyes against the agony of being within fifty yards of her but not able to approach or speak to her. I longed for her.

After a while, she got up and went into her room—and what was going on behind that closed door, I couldn't guess. How long had she been there? How long would she stay? Who—if anyone—was she with? She might be staying for a night or two or twenty, alone or with the last man to score her some drugs.

I never knew what to expect when I saw her name on my phone. So often it was someone else calling from her number. Like Bart, the manager of her apartment complex, getting in touch to report an emergency. Or maybe the police, to let me know she was under arrest. Or it could be the intake personnel at the state psych ward, informing me that she'd been committed again.

Even when it was her, there was no telling which persona would be on the other side of the line. If she identified herself as my mother, or by her given name of Florence, then we might have something resembling a regular conversation. But if it were Flow, the persona she identified as an "Indian," I could expect psychotic rambling, hostility, curses, threats, and abuse. And if it were Agnes, I would inevitably spend time trying to console her. Agnes was an eleven-year-old girl: fragile, broken-hearted, and inconsolable. When my mother was Agnes, she played with dolls, or lay on the floor and crayoned, or crouched in the corner and sobbed. She bit her cuticles until they bled and slept with a teddy bear.

Seeing her name on the screen sent a violent tremor down my legs. The peaceful evening I'd hoped for at home was undone in that moment. No interaction with her came without high anxiety and lingering distress.

I wish I could say I wavered over whether to pick up the phone, but I didn't. I snatched it up the moment it began to ring. I missed her.

"Hello?"

"Stephanie? It's Mom."

"I know," I said. A sharp ache rose in my throat as I asked, "How are you, Mom?"

"Well, I'm not so good, to tell you the truth."

"What's going on?" I asked, afraid to know.

"The doctors say I have lung cancer," she said.

"Lung cancer?"

I felt tears come into my eyes. Wasn't that the worst kind? I'd never heard of anyone surviving lung cancer.

"I'm so sorry, Mom," I said. "Do they know how far it's progressed?"

"It's stage four," she told me. "I have two tumors, and it's already spread to my spine. They told me I have about six months left."

My throat closed over. I managed to choke out that I would call her back soon. And that I would come see her.

As painful and crazy-making and difficult as my relationship with my mother had always been, it was even more difficult to imagine it ending forever. I wasn't ready. There was too much I still didn't understand, too many questions left unanswered.

But one thing was clear. I couldn't put off the asking, or knowing, anymore. Time was suddenly much too scarce for that. I had to confront our shared past and all its mysteries before she was gone for good.

I could no longer tell myself I'd get to it someday. I had to do it now.

Chapter 3

THE QUESTION I'M asked most often is *How?*

I've heard it from therapists, social workers, case managers, and cops. The people well acquainted with my mother tend to do a double take when they meet me.

"You're Florence's daughter? *You?*"

It's been asked with respect and with disdain.

"You sure got some messed-up genes," one of my in-laws remarked not long ago. "I don't know how you overcame all that."

"Your mom is trash," a former neighbor of hers told me recently. "How'd you turn out so different from her?"

And then there was the judge who recently granted me legal guardianship of my mother after her terminal diagnosis. She looked at the long, long list of her psychiatric hospitalizations, arrests, felonies, misdemeanors, and mental illnesses. Then she looked into my eyes with a gentle regard that brought a knot to my throat. "If you don't mind my asking," she said, "how did you rise above . . . all this?"

The answer I give depends on the day.

Sometimes I say it's the decision I made when I was still a child, to be the opposite of my mother in every way I could and in everything I did. My college friends dabbled in recreational drugs; I didn't dare. They flitted from lover to lover; I was already married.

Sometimes I say that being the kind of mother I never had is what saved me.

Sometimes I say that my passion for design carried me through: the drive to create sanctuary, shelter, and beauty for my own family and for others.

But the real answer, the answer threaded through everything, lying beneath and rising above everything—the truest answer to *How?*

Is Jim.

I WAS ONLY fifteen when I met my husband. I was standing on the sidewalk outside school with my brother Allan when he coasted up to us on a skateboard. He was tall and lean with blue-green eyes and longish blond hair. He and Allan had met at a party the weekend before, and as they spent a moment in banter, I felt his gaze on me. It was strong and warm, and even in that brief wordless instant I had the urge to turn all of myself toward it as some flowers turn toward the sun.

"Who was that?" I asked Allan afterward. He hadn't thought to introduce us.

"Oh, that was Jim. He's cool," Allan said.

Allan was my favorite sibling, really the only friend I ever had within the family. I trusted his judgment. He was someone I'd confide in. But I remember dropping my eyes, jamming my hands into the pockets of my sweater, turning inward. *Premonition* would be too strong a word for what I felt. It was more like a faint rustling, some secret and speculative tendril that unfurled inside me, a conviction that something important had just happened.

And I wasn't wrong. The next day during P.E., when I finished the 200-meter race, Jim was lingering near the finish line.

"You're Allan's sister, right?" he said. "My name is Jim."

I know, I almost said, but didn't. "I'm Stephanie," I said instead.

"Hi, Stephanie."

"Hi."

I could barely look at him. I was disheveled from running, winded, and sweating. Jim looked athletic and handsome. He carried himself with the confidence of someone who sat down with his family and said grace.

But he kept showing up. It seemed that every time I turned around, he was there, or nearby. I saw him in the halls, in the cafeteria, on the front steps after school let out. He always sought my eyes, always said hello.

I returned his greeting every time, but then I dropped my gaze. Afraid to believe this was real, that he could really be interested in me. I didn't belong with someone like him. I was marked. I was damaged. Couldn't he see that? Couldn't everyone?

And then, on Friday of that week, as I sat apart from the other kids in the auditorium waiting for an assembly to begin, he materialized beside me and took the empty seat next to mine.

"Hey, Stephanie. How's it going?"

"Hey," I said.

I don't remember what else we said as others filled in the seats around us. And I don't remember what the slide show presentation was about. All I know is that as the principal stepped up to the podium and the lights were lowered, Jim reached out and took my hand.

I WAS NEVER alone again. Jim walked me to my classes. He walked me to my bus after school. Later when I took a waitressing job in town, he was there to pick me up each evening at the end of my shift and walk me the two miles to my house, after which he would walk another three miles back to his own house. He did this many times a week.

When I was sick, he came to sit with me. He brought me aspirin and ginger ale and sat by my bed stroking my hair.

He was at my side at every possible moment, but beyond that, he insisted on knowing me. All my life I'd kept others at a safe distance, lest they get too close and learn too much. Occasionally I went to other kids' homes to play, but I could never have them over in return. Who knew what they might see?

With Jim, I could no longer hide. I didn't want to. He made me feel safe and let me step out from beneath the crushing yoke of secrecy. It happened early, just a week or two into our fledgling romance. We were at the house of one of his friends, alone in a borrowed bedroom.

I'll never forget that room. There was a red lava lamp on the bedside table, an overflowing laundry hamper in one corner, a set of weights beside it, clothing strewn all over the floor. There were posters on the wall: a Seattle Seahawk tackling another player, Christie Brinkley in a bikini.

Jim and I were lying on the twin bed with all our clothes on. We were kissing, touching lightly, pressed together. Outside it was raining. I loved the sound of it on the roof. I loved the feeling of lying next to Jim with my head against his shoulder and both of his arms around me. Being held was such an unfamiliar sensation. Love was happening; it was happening to me. Every single thing about it was a shock, and I was living in a state of continual disbelief.

"What time does your mom want you home?" Jim asked. It was such an innocent question. He had no idea what it was about to unleash.

"I don't live with my mom," I heard myself tell him.

"Oh," he said. He was startled. "Are your parents split up? Do you live with your dad?"

"No, I'm in a foster home right now."

Consternation creased his face.

"Wow," he said. "I . . . I didn't know. Is that rough?"

I choked back a laugh. Was it rough? Compared to the other homes I'd lived in, it was a dream. Bonnie left me alone. She didn't demand that I turn over most of my earnings to her for rent, as my mother did the moment I got a job. True, she took no interest in me at all, never showed any warmth or asked how things were going, but at her house, there was safety and order. There was food in the refrigerator every day and dinner on the table every night. I could concentrate on my homework. There was no drama, no violence, and no abuse. There was no terror. I could close my eyes and fall asleep at the end of each day without the dread of someone coming into my room, into my bed, in the deep of night. All these things added up to the sweetest relief I'd ever known, and every waking hour I was grateful for them.

"No, it's good," I said. "I like it there."

"Why don't you live with your mom or dad?"

For fourteen years, I'd shied away from personal questions, responding with vague answers or other evasions. But on that bed with Jim, for the first time ever, I felt I could loosen the lid I kept on my life story.

"My father's dead," I told him. Then seeing his stricken expression, I added: "I don't really remember him. He died when I was three."

"How?"

"He committed suicide in a motel."

Jim let this reply hang in the air for a moment before asking, "What about your mom?"

"My mother is . . . well, to be honest, she's clinically psychotic," I said. This was a phrase a social worker had used to describe her, and I liked the air of distance it seemed to lend me now. As if the conundrum of my mother could be contained in a label, filed away with professional detachment. "I've been in and out of foster homes all my life, whenever she's in jail or in a psych ward."

I could hardly believe I was telling him these things. Telling felt perilous and electric and suddenly as destined as a fate foretold in a legend. As if it had been written that Jim, and only Jim, was to be the keeper of my secrets.

"Is she in jail right now?" he asked. "Or in a psych ward?"

"Actually, right now she's not in either one."

"Then why are you in a foster home now?"

I wondered how to tell him about the incident that had driven me from my mother's home this time around. It had happened on a Sunday morning. I'd slept at a friend's the night before because some man was passed out on our couch. He showed up at our door that morning, saying he was a friend of Rick—my stepfather—and that he needed a place to crash. My mother let him in even though we hadn't seen Rick in months, but then she went out, leaving us alone with him. I didn't like the way he looked at me, so when Leigh-Ann, a friend in the same apartment complex, invited me to sleep over, I was glad to go.

Even now, my memories of the next morning aren't more than a series of snapshots, lacking clarity or continuity.

Snapshot one: I'm easing myself through the front door of our apartment. From the moment I step inside, I know something is very wrong. The air is eerily silent and still, rank with stale alcohol and cigarette smoke and body odor and something else. A heavy and suffocating musk hangs in the air, an atmosphere of terror.

Snapshot two: The kitchen is a mess. Crushed beer cans and empty liquor bottles and overflowing ashtrays and BB guns are lying on the counters, the table, the floor. Dirty dishes are piled in the sink. Flies are crawling on every surface and dotting the air; their buzzing is the only sound. A set of stairs just off the kitchen leads to the bedrooms, where I'd meant to go in search of my bathing suit, but for some reason I'm afraid to venture up there. My heart is beating hard as I tentatively call, "Hello?"

Snapshot three: Isabella is peering around the wall at the top of the stairs, as if to confirm that it's really me, that no one else is with me and it's safe to emerge. Her eyes are wild with fear; I can see it from fifty feet away. Then she is flying down to the kitchen like a hunted deer might burst from the brush into a clearing. She is in a tank top and shorts and even in the blur of her descent I can see that something unspeakable has been done to her. From the hem of her shorts to the middle of her calves, her legs are purple with bruises. Her inner thighs are a deep black and blue, with raw bloodied punctures here and there as if she has been shot with a pellet gun.

Snapshot four: I'm gasping, crying. *Isabella! Isabella, what happened? What happened to you?* But she won't answer. She won't even look at me.

Snapshot five: The police are at the door, responding to a report of an assault. They drape a dark blanket around my sister's shoulders and take her away in their car.

FOR THE FIRST time in my life, I told this story to another person. I told it to Jim. I told him a lot of other things too.

I told him about the stepfather who drifted in and out of our lives between prison stints, other lovers, and criminal enterprises of all kinds. About the parade of drug-addled, lawless, and marginal men my mother brought home in relentless succession. About the cast of characters that inhabited my mother and never knowing which of them I'd be dealing with on any given day. About living in our car and the long aimless days of wandering the beach and eating nothing but seaweed.

I told him about living in the dependent unit of the state of California, with all my belongings in a trash bag. Not knowing where my brothers were or whether I would see them again or where the screams were coming from in the night. I told him about the foster homes where I was violated on a nightly basis. About the vision issues I had as a child that were never addressed by an adult, therefore never treated by a doctor, and ultimately led to blindness in one of my eyes. I told him about the hunger and the cold and the homelessness and the loneliness and the chaos and the drugs and the confusion and the abuse.

I told him everything, and with each word I spoke I felt the weight of isolation being lifted from me, almost as if a heavy animal hide were being tugged from my shoulders. It felt as if I could draw a deep breath for the first time.

"I feel funny telling you these things," I said after we'd been talking for a long time.

"Why?"

"I've never told anyone before," I said. "About any of it."

"I'm glad you told me, Stephanie," he said. "I want to be here for you. I don't want you to feel alone."

AND I NEVER WAS. That autumn was dazzling: The trees were ablaze with color, the light was golden, and the days were crisp and clear. The scent of wood smoke hung in the air and I wasn't alone anymore. *I wasn't alone anymore.*

Then we turned back the clocks, and the golden light waned, and the leaves fell off the trees and evening set in at four thirty in the afternoon, but none of that mattered because I still wasn't alone anymore. The darkness could not engulf me. The chill in the air couldn't touch me.

And then suddenly it was Christmas.

Throughout the holiday season, there had been parties and visits hosted by Bonnie's friends. And in each of these homes, amid the joyful greetings at the door, I was aware of an undercurrent of alarm on the part of the hostess, a whispered flurry of instructions to the nearest family member.

Oh . . . she's here . . . I forgot Bonnie's fostering some friend of Leigh-Ann's . . . quick, get one of the spare gifts in the hall closet . . .

And out would come a generic present kept on hand for emergencies like this, carefully chosen to work for any age or gender. Like a knitted red scarf. Or a reindeer mug with a package of cocoa mix and marshmallows tucked inside. Or a desk calendar of inspirational quotes.

But on the Christmas Eve of my fifteenth year, a car pulled up to the curb outside Bonnie's house and Jim got out. He wasn't yet old enough to drive. His mother had brought him over and she didn't get out of the car. From the window I watched him open the trunk, and a minute later he was at the door, holding a box in both gloved hands.

How can I describe the wonder of that moment? Since then, Jim has given me much more extravagant gifts, and each one has brought me joy, but none of them ever made me happier than I was that cold, clear starry night when he came through the door with *a present he had chosen for me*, in a shining red-and-gold-striped box.

In my entire life, I had never celebrated a holiday or birthday with my family. Neither my siblings nor I had ever gotten a single gift for Christmas. The holiday-standard and impersonal items from strangers here and there—plainly wrapped and waiting in supply closets for spare guests—were the only ones I'd ever received.

So when Jim held out the box for me to take, I was too stunned to speak or move.

"Steph?" he said. "What's wrong?"

"That's for me?" I asked.

He laughed. "Of course it is. Open it."

When I still didn't react, he said, "Want me to bring it up to your room?"

I nodded and followed him upstairs to the room I slept in. He set the box down on the rug beside my bed. I sank onto the floor beside it, put both my arms around it, and began to cry.

Did it matter that a stereo was inside the box? One that likely cost him an entire paycheck? *Yes*, it mattered beyond measure. It was the kind of gift a grown man would buy. It cast an impossibly sophisticated sheen over the inherent miracle of a gift expressly for me. *A stereo*. A stereo!

And no. It didn't matter at all. He had me at the box, whatever was inside.

MANY OF MY friends marvel at the fact that I married my first love, a boy I met at the age of fifteen. Some people see our story as a kind of fairy tale. A young man came along and fell in love with me, and his love was steadfast and true, and his devotion never wavered, and that's what saved me.

It's the truth, but there's another truth just alongside it: Our love was not just something that came along, something that happened to me. It was something I reached for with both hands and held as tightly as I could. I made a decision to receive his love, to return it, to love him and all of him and only him, forever. I insisted on purity.

Purity is a fraught word, a standard that religious zealots brandish at one another. It reeks of sanctimony; it implies judgment. But when I say I wanted purity, I don't mean it in that way at all.

I mean only that I wanted, always, to be the polar opposite of my mother. That I watched her give herself to one man after another from as far back as I could remember. And growing up with the fallout of her promiscuity raining down around me left me with a fervent wish to give myself to only one man. Nothing else felt safe to me.

Here is a final snapshot from that era of my life:

Jim and I are studying in his bedroom. I graduated high school just a few months ago and am now enrolled at the local community college. Jim is in his second year at Portland State University. I'm still a waitress at Elmer's, a local diner, and Jim works for UPS.

I love being at Jim's house. He describes his own family as dysfunctional, but for the life of me, I can't imagine what he means by that. From my perspective, his family is a model of structure and stability. Right this minute, his mother is making hamburgers for dinner. She'll serve them with real sesame seed buns and all the fixings—tomato slices, pickle chips, and sautéed onions—arranged on a platter.

"We should get our own place," he tells me between calculus problems. "Now that you're done with high school, it's time. With both of us working, we should be able to rent a decent apartment somewhere."

My last foster mother has recently kicked me out of her house because I was one day late renewing my registration tags at the DMV. I'm still reeling from that blow. I've known too many homes, too many broken attachments, and too many betrayals to enter another makeshift arrangement.

I long for the kind of commitment that's formalized, certified, official. I need a stamp of permanence. I yearn for a family of my own.

"I want that too," I tell Jim. "But we have to get married. I'm not going to just shack up with you somewhere unless we're married."

Jim looks up from his calculus book. His eyes meet mine. His expression is vague, as if he needs a moment to process what I just said. Then he nods briefly, as if I've suggested we see a movie later that evening.

"Okay," he says, and turns back to his book.

"Steph? Are you sure you want to do this?"

Jim was standing at the foot of our bed in black thermals. It was barely daybreak. He and the kids were heading out to Timberline Lodge for a day of skiing at Mount Hood.

No, I wanted to tell him. *I'm not at all sure I want to do this. In fact, I know I don't want to do this.* I hated that he would be so far away while I was at my mother's. I didn't want him to go.

I was still curled beneath the comforter. If it were a regular Saturday, Jim would still be in bed with me. We would have coffee and then walk our dog together. We'd go to our favorite local hole-in-the-wall for brunch.

But it wasn't a regular Saturday. Instead of joining my family on the mountain, I would go see my mother. And I was afraid.

Jim was afraid too. I could see it in his eyes. My mother was unpredictable. Sometimes she was violent.

Jim's way was always to be there for me. He had been at my side for every hardship of the last three decades, but I knew if he were at my side today, I wouldn't be able to have the conversation with my mother that I needed to have. My mother didn't like him. She never had. As she saw it, I'd fully belonged to her before he came along. I'd been a model of compliance. In her version of things, Jim was to blame for the loss of her perfect servant, and I knew I'd have no hope of drawing her out and getting the information I needed if he was there. I would have to go alone.

Two hours later I pulled into the parking area of my mother's apartment complex and saw her right away. She was in a little sheltered area, a kind of gazebo next to the lot. She was standing there, it seemed, so her cigarette would be safe from the rain.

I took one look at her and went cold with alarm. She was Flow today—I could see that from the car.

She wore a long green washed-out dress, faux suede knee-high moccasin boots, a white headband, and black shades. A blood-smeared surgical mask was dangling from her neck. The bones of her face stood out in sharp relief, and deep grooves were etched around her downturned mouth. As Flow, she held herself stiffly, and from long experience I knew that behind the shades her eyes were glittering with rage.

I hoped the coffee in its tall take-out cup had cooled somewhat by now. I didn't put it past her to hurl its hot contents at me. I eased the car into a parking space in the section reserved for guests, cut the engine, and just sat there a moment with my eyes closed and tried to slow my breathing.

And then I was standing in front of her, trying to smile.

"Mom," I said. "Hi."

She glared at me without answering.

"It's good to see you," I tried.

She took a deep drag on her cigarette and held her silence.

"I brought you coffee from Starbucks," I said, holding it out. "It's mocha."

At this, her jaw unclenched. The lines on her face seemed to soften. She took the coffee and ground her cigarette out underfoot.

"Can we go inside?" I asked.

"All right," she said.

I trailed her to a ground-floor apartment just across the lot. As Flow, my mother moved with what I can only describe as a prowl—the slinking stealthy gait of a cat on the hunt. At her door I waited while she fished the key from the deep pocket of her dress. Then I followed her over the threshold into a small living room, furnished simply with an old sofa, two chairs, and a coffee table. The room was littered with prescription bottles, a full ashtray of cigarette butts, and a pipe she used for her herbs.

She sank down onto the sofa and took a sip of the coffee. "It's good," she told me.

It was unnerving not to see her eyes. "Mom, why are you wearing shades?" I asked. "It's raining out there and we're inside now anyway."

"I need them," she said fretfully. "There's a glare in here."

"And why do you have a mask around your neck?"

"In case I get a nosebleed," she said. "That keeps happening. I don't want to ruin this dress."

I took the opposite corner of her sofa and positioned my cell phone beside me, in the shadow of my jacket. I'd already pressed the button that would record our conversation. Now that I knew she was dying, I felt compelled to preserve whatever account of the past she might offer me.

"How are you feeling, Mom?"

"I'm in pain," she told me. "I've had a lot of pain."

"I'm so sorry," I said. I felt a rush of pity for her. "Is there anything I can do?"

"Maybe you can get me some of that medical marijuana."

Marijuana was legal now in Oregon, so she didn't need a prescription, but I knew the real issue was the expense. "I'll try," I told her. "I'll see what I can do."

Now she did take the shades off. Her blue eyes were blazing but tired. "Are you sleeping all right, Mom?"

"Not since they switched my pain meds," she said. "These new pills aren't working."

"Do you want me to talk to your doctor?"

"If you think it might help," she said.

"I'd be glad to try. I'm sorry the meds aren't better. Where are you having pain?"

"The worst of it is in my back. The doctor said the cancer already spread to my spine."

An ache rose in my throat. Flow seemed to have departed. It was just my mother in front of me, and she suddenly looked girlish and fragile.

"We'll figure out the meds," I told her. "I won't let you suffer."

She regarded me for a long moment and then she smiled. "You love me," she said. There was a note of wonder in her voice. "You really love me."

"I do. I love you, Mom."

She sat back against the sofa, satisfied.

"Mom," I said. "I have so many questions. There's so much about our past that I don't understand. I don't want to wear you out when you're sick, but you're the only one who can give me the answers."

She eyed me from her corner of the couch. "What do you want to know?"

Under the cover of my jacket, I angled the phone in her direction and glanced down to make sure it was recording.

"Let's start at the beginning," I said.

Chapter 4

IN SOME WAYS my visit with my mother was better than I expected. She didn't attack me or curse me out. She was forthcoming and matter-of-fact in her account of my birth: all the ways she had tried to rid herself of the pregnancy and my arrival despite her best efforts.

I left her apartment on the verge of tears. As soon as I was inside my car, I began to cry. I hadn't known about her attempts to terminate her pregnancy. She'd never told me. Given everything else she'd said and done, I didn't even know why it mattered, but it did. The sorrow of it lodged like so much silt in my throat.

She didn't want me. My own mother didn't want me. She tried to get rid of me.

There it was—irreducible, undeniable. Final.

Driving home, I felt so tired I was afraid I might fall asleep at the wheel. It was the deep of winter, dark before five o'clock, and for once I felt grateful that night was here so early. At home I went straight to the room I shared with Jim and got into our bed. I knew my husband and daughter would have dinner at the lodge and be home late. That was for the best, since I didn't think I could deal with talking to anyone just yet.

Jim was asleep beside me when I woke up the next morning, and I almost wept with the relief of seeing him. I lay there aching and dazed, feeling the old orphan loneliness, overcome by the urge to draw my own family close around me. Within the hour, I'd wrangled my two sons—Josh and Jeremy, both in their twenties—into coming to dinner that night.

For the rest of the day as I prepared for their visit, I was spurred by the same frenetic intensity that had driven my domestic efforts a thousand times before. I wanted a fire in the hearth and every light and candle in the house ablaze. I wanted a laden table and the warmth of both ovens on at once. I wanted delicious cooking aromas to fill the air. There was something almost manic about the way I tied up the blade roast, scrubbed the potatoes, and chopped the vegetables. After searing the meat, I simmered it for hours in a concoction of beef broth and red wine, root vegetables and bay leaves. A rich fragrance filled the kitchen as I turned to setting the table.

I loved our dining room table. I loved the rustic wood, its length and heft, its weight and majesty. It could seat twelve people. It was *solid*. It was *permanent*. It was the table of a woman who had put down roots.

I brought out my embroidered linen tablecloth and favorite set of gold and white dishes. I'd have just enough time to go out for flowers. All these details seemed very important.

I felt compelled, as I so often did, to conjure a feeling of bounty, abundance, comfort and well-being. Seeing my mother brought back this ancient hunger. Literal hunger: the emptiness of a child who hasn't been fed and won't be fed. Hunger that twists in the gut like an eel on a hook. Seeing her brought back the chill of my childhood. The cold, damp car that was our home.

I would beat it all back yet again with a feast on my dining room table, smiling faces around it, classical music and candlelight, warmth and laughter.

Finally, by five o'clock, Jim and all three of our children were beneath our roof.

There was Andrea, still at home with us. The daughter we'd adopted from Guatemala, who seemed to have the world on a string. Athletic, lovely, filled with such dazzling self-assurance she barely seemed to notice or appreciate her own popularity.

There was Josh, who quickly and easily found his way in the world.

His boyish, bearish good looks and ready smile lent him a social ease that I envied. Josh loved life and it showed. He was a sales executive at a national software company, and his rollicking good nature made him a favorite with customers.

There was Jeremy, my sweet, easy-going younger son who'd built his own business selling shoes. These days he was keeping his dark hair buzzed short and sporting a sparse goatee.

Josh was the first to put his arms around me. "Hey, mom," he said. "Is everything okay? You look a little worn out." Josh was always the one who could read me, the most intuitive about how I was feeling.

"I'm fine," I said into his shoulder. "Everything's fine."

All their lives I'd wanted above all to protect them in the ways my mother had never protected me. Often that meant protecting them from her. I made sure their contact with her was sharply limited. Years had sometimes gone by between visits. They didn't yet know that she had cancer or that I'd been to see her. At the moment, there was no reason to tell them. I wanted to keep her, even the mention of her, far away from us tonight.

At dinner, I barely ate. I had no appetite at all. It was enough to watch my family eat. Everything was just as I wanted it.

My friends often told me I made it all look easy. None of them knew the desperation lying beneath it all. The way I did these things as if my next breath depended on it.

It wasn't until Jim and all the kids were on the sofa, watching the Mariners game, that I let myself remember the rest of my conversation with my mother.

"Wow, Mom," I'd managed to say, after hearing my birth story.

"I guess I never told you any of this before," she said.

"No," I said. "You never did."

"Well, there it is. For some reason, I decided to save you."

That was how she saw it, how she'd spun it to herself. She hadn't tried to kill me; *she'd decided to save me.*

The sorrow and grief, it would surface after I left. I couldn't let it overwhelm me then, not before I'd gotten more of what I'd come for.

I looked down to confirm that my phone was still recording. Then I made myself meet her gaze.

"I'm glad you decided to save me, Mom," I said. "So then what?"

ON A TUESDAY in late summer, a young woman on Haight Street—passing out fliers for her temple—invited my mother to her first Buddhist meeting. My mother liked the look of her. She had light blonde hair falling nearly to her waist, wide green cat eyes, and a lovely vibe: peaceful, centered, and serene.

My mother was lonely. She loved San Francisco but she didn't like living with Louie. She wanted a spiritual partnership. She wanted to live on a higher astral plane. She wanted to be a vegetarian. She took the light green paper the woman held out to her. It was the address of a Buddhist temple, where there would be a meeting at eight that evening.

Later that same day, in Buena Vista Park, someone left a local newspaper laid open on the bench my mother was sitting on. Right there on that page, staring up at her, was a description of Buddhism by members of the very same temple. This was an unmistakable instance of synchronicity. My mother picked it up and read this statement of purpose:

This project is an ecstatic exercise in action. Our purpose is to turn people on. The results of our actions, money, vibration, influences will be dedicated and used for the good of all sentient beings. Out of the heart-glow of the red Buddha come the vibrations that unite us to act.

After that she could have no doubt that Buddhism was for her. That evening she walked to the address printed on the paper. The meeting room was long and plain with an altar at the front. Hanging on the wall just above it was a framed scroll bearing Japanese calligraphy. Lamps made of bamboo and rice paper stood on either side and hung from the ceiling, and the dusty scent of cypress incense hovered in the air. The floors were made of polished hardwood, and they gleamed beneath the bare feet of all who were gathered in the room.

On the altar were various objects that she would learn about in the days and weeks to come and eventually bring into her own home. She didn't have a chance to look at them closely that first evening because a man standing near them drew her gaze away. *Beautiful* was not a word my mother tended to use when referring to a man. But it was the word she used when she talked about Rick.

Rick Haskell had more power over my mother than any other man ever had. From the moment she saw him, she was under his sway. He was tall and lean with shoulder-length light brown hair and blue eyes like a rogue Jesus. He was also a con man, an alcoholic, a heroin addict, and a convicted felon, just out of prison for armed robbery.

Rick was beside her when they received the mantra that was the key to life itself, the culmination of the Buddha's teachings:

Nam Myoho Renge Kyo
I devote myself to the mystic law of the Lotus Sutra.

It was a wedding vow of sorts, a pledge to be faithful to the Buddha nature deep within her. Secretly, in her own mind, it was a wedding vow for her and Rick as well, enclosing the two of them in its petals of protection.

My mother loved everything about her Buddhist practice. She loved her *mala* with its varicolored *juzu* beads of jasper, amethyst, white jade, and Jerusalem stone. She loved the altar she and Rick set up together in a corner of their bedroom, with its candles, incense, water cup and bell. She loved the branches of *shikimi* flanking these items. Later a photograph of Dominic, my youngest brother, would be added to this display.

She loved the meditative state she could access so easily by chanting. The chanting itself was magic. She experienced that magic firsthand too many times to discount it, and never more so than on the day of the crash.

The car accident happened on her impromptu trip to Mexico with Rick and all of her children. By that time, she'd asked Louie to move out so Rick could move in.

Louie did not go gently. He punched a hole in the cheap wall of their apartment when she told him it was over. There were terrible scenes:

tears, shouted recriminations, bitter words to describe her. She was a *puta*, a whore; she had ruined his life. Just how did she think she was going to pay the bills with him gone?

My mother shrugged. There were her waitressing tips; there was welfare. Rick had a few ideas of his own. My mother urged Louie to buck up and go back to the Bronx. He said he would never go so far away from his own children.

Poor Louie. He'd come three thousand miles west for the sake of her happiness, and now he was trapped here if he wanted to live close to his kids. There was nothing he could do about it. She had never really loved Louie, but what she felt for Rick left her nothing to decide.

Louie moved into the cheapest local motel he could find, where he proceeded to soothe his broken heart with Spanish rum and various street drugs. Rick moved in, and my mother was never happier than she was then.

Meanwhile, as she'd noted, Rick really did have an idea of his own. He'd heard her say that her mother—a resident of Mexico for the last several years—had some money. He thought they should pay her a visit in her adopted town of Guadalajara and see if she couldn't be persuaded to part with some of it.

My mother had a mysterious grudge where her own mother was concerned and preferred not to be within a hundred miles of her. But then and forever, she was helpless to deny Rick whatever he said he wanted. Like a snake charmer, he drew her beyond her boundary lines; she emerged from the vessel of her own heedless whims and undulated in front of him. Rick wanted to go to Mexico? To Mexico they would go, then.

My mother was easy but not naïve. She knew Rick was just after money. When it came to that man, she was like a junkie who would lie down in traffic and let a truck roll over her if it meant she could get her next fix. She didn't care what she had to do to make him stay. If he was at her side and in her bed because of her own mother's money, she would lead him to it and help him get it.

The day they were married at the Ananda church was the happiest day of her life. My mother wore a dress that a neighbor helped her make. It had a gathered purple bodice and a pink-and-purple flowered skirt. Rick wore a white shirt.

At the altar they exchanged roses, a white one for her and a red one for him. Neither of them had a single family member in attendance, but two friends showed up, and one of them served as their official witness.

Not long afterward, Rick got a job at the local Salvation Army. He held it just long enough to steal a retired and donated mail truck, and we all set out for Mexico in this. My mother sat holding six-month-old Dominic in the front seat, and the rest of us rode in the back, along with an unsecured vanity table that had been in the back of the truck when Rick took it. My mother liked it so they decided to keep it.

She and Rick were chanting together—*nam myoho renge kyo, nam myoho renge kyo*—when they plowed straight into an oncoming battered and brown Chevrolet.

"THE CHANTING PROTECTED US," my mother told me as I faced her on the sofa in her living room, my phone, set on audio record, beside me on the seat.

"How so?"

"Well, it was an awful crash, a head-on collision. That car smashed right into us. The driver had been drinking. Well, we had been drinking too, to tell you the truth, but the accident was his fault."

"A full-on car crash while chanting is proof of protection?"

"Well, none of you kids were hurt. Dominic was just a baby, and he hit the dashboard but he was fine. Allan bumped his knee on the dresser but that was it. You didn't have so much as a scratch. Rick got the worst of it. He was almost impaled by the steering wheel. And I smacked into the dashboard hard. But none of us broke any bones or needed to go to the hospital or anything like that. Not like the other driver."

"What happened to the other driver?"

"His windshield was shattered. His face—I'll never forget it. That poor man's face was slashed to ribbons."

"Good God," I said.

"Like I told you, it was his fault just as much as ours. He was as drunk as Rick was. He didn't want to involve the police any more than we did."

"So what happened then?"

"Well, the truck was finished in the crash," my mother recalled. "We were stranded in Tecate, so we called your Aunt Beth," her brother's wife, "and she drove down from San Diego and picked us all up in her car."

"That was nice of her."

"Oh, that woman was a bitch," my mother snapped. "Just a bitch to the core."

"Why do you say that?"

"Once we were back at her place and we unpacked our things, she would not stop carrying on about some of the stuff we had with us. She said we put her life at risk, smuggling drugs across the border in her car without letting her know. She kept saying if we'd been caught, she could have been sent to prison for years. She was just so uptight. And she was *ungrateful.*"

"Ungrateful for what?"

"Well, I did the dishes for her one time during the weeks that we stayed with her, and she didn't show any appreciation at all. And she made us get rid of our entire stash before she would let us back in her car. I mean, we used it up at her place anyway, but she insisted on looking through all our bags before she drove the six of us back to Mexico."

"The six of us? Don't you mean seven?"

"No. She offered to keep your brother Allan until we got back to California, and I agreed," she said. "Why not? It was one less kid to worry about."

"Why did she want to keep Allan?"

"I really don't know. She seemed to think all you kids were going to die, and she said they had room in their house for one child, so they decided to save him. Maybe they picked him because he was the oldest, and he was white like them."

"As opposed to Puerto Rican like the rest of us?"

"Well, you're white too," my mother said. "Your father was the man who raped me, and he was white."

My mother had told me this all my life and it was like an ice pick in my heart every time. But I didn't believe her. I looked Puerto Rican too, and by all accounts Louie had treated me as his own.

"I hate when you say that," I told her.

"Well, it's true. Louie wasn't your father."

I resolved not to have this conversation with her again. There was no point.

"What was Grandma's house in Mexico like?" I asked instead.

"It was very nice. She had a lot of space, especially compared to the neighbors around her. She had an outhouse for a bathroom, who knows why? She had the money for a proper bathroom, but I guess she didn't mind going outside every time.

"Her house was all white inside. No decoration at all. No pictures hanging up anywhere, not even her own artwork. She kept all her paintings stacked against the wall.

"She had a good life in Mexico. She sketched and painted all day. She had a maid, and a lover named Roberto. I think he was her driver. He couldn't have been much older than I was back then.

"Oh, what a time that was. All four of you kids were sick with stomach parasites. Dysentery. Probably from the water. I thought you'd die of dehydration. I thought Beth was going to be right, you were all going to die!

"And Stephanie, that was when you stopped talking. After the accident, you didn't say a word for the next six months. You were a little chatterbox right up until the crash, the noisiest little thing I ever knew, but after that you went silent. Even sick as a dog, you didn't make a sound."

SOMETIMES I TRY to imagine why Rick would have been at that Buddhist temple. I can only guess that he was hoping for what actually happened: that some crazy flower child woman would be his next mark and give him shelter.

My mother had never offered my siblings or me any structure or safety, but with Rick's entry into our lives, things devolved into total mayhem. With Louie in the home, there was relative stability. There was order and sanity and solvency.

When he moved out and Rick moved in, the fabric of our lives began to unravel. Our family had no real income, and soon we were homeless. Rick dragged us to Mexico, hoping for some of his new mother-in-law's money. When my grandmother wanted nothing more than to keep us in her home and take care of us, he was the one who dragged us back to California.

On our return trip from Mexico, we visited the home of Rick's estranged mother, not far across the border. He hadn't spoken to her in years, but all of us kids stood waiting in the front yard while he rang her bell. When a white-haired woman in a print dress opened the door, he begged her to let us in, pleaded for a hot meal.

At long last she said yes, but—after looking over my siblings and me, and noting that most of us were brown—she added: "Those little niggers better not touch my furniture."

She allowed us to sit at the kitchen table, where we ate plates of warm and filling Rice-a-Roni. Sticky and flavorful.

TIMES WITH RICK were overwhelmingly dark.

I stepped into our garage to try out a bicycle that arrived one day when Rick walked it home. He was sitting on the concrete floor against the far wall, a bandana tied around his head. There was a bandage wrapped around his upper arm and just below, a needle stuck in his skin. I was eleven or twelve years old. His head was thrown back, resting against the wall. His eyes were closed. He must have sensed someone. He opened his eyes and looked straight at me. The emptiness of his gray gaze that day will always be with me. I was scared. He was like a spirit in a story, there and not there at the same time. We didn't speak. I took the bike by the handlebars and hurried past him.

He beat my mother. Often. Throwing her on the kitchen floor and kicking her. Dragging her by the hair. Neighbors called the police in response to the bedlam they heard: the crash of overturned furniture and thrown objects and her screams rising above it all. They came and arrested Rick, and he didn't come back for months.

There were times he was so drunk behind the wheel of our car that he would use the sidewalk to pass people.

He made me steal food from the grocery store when we needed it. Sometimes I was sent to buy drugs for him and my mother. "The pigs won't hassle a little girl," he'd said, and my mother would agree.

Their dealer lived in a corner house a few blocks away from our apartment in the worst part of Hillsboro, a town just west of Portland. Two of its front windows were covered with plywood, and the rusted shell of a car took up most of the front lawn. I would walk to the front door with a five-dollar bill and knock. The same hefty and long-haired, dead-eyed man came to the door, emerging from the darkness of the dimly lit house. He never spoke. He just took my money and handed me a baggie, pungent with "herbs." I would push it to the bottom of my sock before running home.

Yet there were glimmers of goodness here and there. Sometimes Rick smiled at me. He called me his Ragamuffin. He and I would talk about things that mattered to me and when I told him about my day, he made eye contact and listened. He showed me some semblance of tenderness that I never got from my mother, and I loved him for that.

One day he came home from his job as a sheet rocker with a vintage emerald sofa. He had done some work in a rich lady's house, and she offered the crew extra money to drop it off at Goodwill. Rick brought it to our apartment instead. It was weathered and threadbare in places, and it bore the faint claw marks of the woman's pet poodle, but it was so much fancier than anything else in our place that it was like a remnant of some fabled kingdom, glinting improbably against the grayish wall of our living room.

I loved that sofa. I loved to caress the jewel-toned velvet and run my fingertips over its intricately carved back. I regarded Rick with awe when he and his buddy carried it into our midst and set it down with fanfare. It was as if he'd strolled in with a treasure chest recovered from a shipwreck.

Life was worse in many ways—volatile, frightening, and unpredictable—when Rick was around, and yet in some ways it was better. My mother remained in his thrall for my entire childhood. She fell apart when he disappeared, as he often did, and it was like a holiday in our home every time he came back. I was sorry whenever he went away, and happy to see him when he showed back up.

It HURTS TO know my grandmother wanted to shelter us kids from all of this but my mother wouldn't let her. Our stay in her Guadalajara home was the first and last time I would ever see her.

I have one of her sketches on my desk at home: a dour Mexican troubadour walking along a dusty road. He has long hair and a drawn face, a downturned mouth, a guitar slung over his shoulder. He is wearing a thin jacket, and a pendant dangles from his neck. It looks as if it were rendered in seconds with a stick of charcoal, then passed over lightly with a wet brush so that the edges blur dreamily against the background. The paper turned sepia.

My grandmother was an eccentric. A survivor of breast cancer, she did nothing to augment the half of her chest left flat by the mastectomy, nor did she try to hide its asymmetry. She lived alone with at least a dozen Chihuahuas. She sat by her window for hours each day and sketched the people passing by, a can of Budweiser within easy reach. She was happy to see my mother and happy to see us kids.

Her warm welcome did not extend to Rick. She saw through him from the start. She wanted my mother to stay in Guadalajara so she could help raise us kids. She got us our own apartment and a maid but refused to hand my mother the wholesale transfer of cash she was hoping for.

When Rick realized that no money was forthcoming and never would be, it was time to go.

My mother rounded us up and took us away willingly. She never went back, no matter how harrowing things became. She would sooner be homeless and live in a car on the beach than return to her own mother's safe and spacious house.

Therein lay the mystery, the one she would never explain: the mystery of why my mother was always on the run. She had fled from her family of origin before; she'd gone to New York the moment she was old enough. And now, at her lover's bidding, it was time to run again.

Chapter 5

"STEPH, I KNOW you were hoping to go to the gorge this weekend, but I need to work," Jim said. It was the morning after my mother told me about Mexico.

"Oh, Jim, come on. You promised."

It was a rote response; my heart wasn't really in it. This was a timeworn argument I'd given up on winning. Jim almost never had a weekend to spend with the family. His ski trip with Andrea a few weekends before had been a hard-won concession, and I knew better than to expect another so soon.

"Steph?"

Gradually I became aware that Jim had said something else and I hadn't caught it.

"I'm sorry, what?"

"Stephanie, are you even listening? It's like you're somewhere else."

"I'm sorry," I said again. It was true; I was somewhere else. I was learning that I'd always feel deeply disoriented after these conversations with my mother. The next day, I'd be in a kind of trance, replaying her words, arguing with her in my mind, grappling with the pieces of the past she'd laid before me.

The images she conjured were hard to look at. They were like a series of yellowed photographs unearthed from a dark drawer: the drunken man at the wheel of the mail truck, the drugged-out woman beside him, the defenseless baby in her arms, their zombie chant lulling them into oblivion. The five children in the back along with an unsecured vanity table, rattling around like dice in a cup.

And the woman who was certain we would die but who only had room for one of us. The shadowy grandmother who'd wanted to shelter us but couldn't persuade my mother to stay. The four small children ridden with dysentery, one of them newly mute.

I always had the same pressing need after these conversations to gather my own family around me.

"Okay, forget the gorge," I told Jim. "Just be home for dinner. The kids are coming, and I want us all to be together."

"MOM," JOSH ANNOUNCED at the table that evening. "We're going to Quail Creek Ranch next weekend to get a Christmas tree."

"Oh no," I said. "Honey, please. The one in the garage did just fine for us last year. Why bother getting another one?"

"It's fake, Mom. We let you try it but we agreed ourselves that it wasn't as nice. We decided we'd go back to the real thing this Christmas, and didn't say anything at the time because we didn't want to upset you during the holiday."

I looked around the table at my family. Jim and all three of our children were clearly aligned against me.

"Oh, come on. Seriously?" I asked. "It's just not worth the hassle. It's almost an hour's drive, the farm is *always* mobbed, we stand around in the cold forever and then we have to haul it through the snow and tie it to the roof of the car and—"

"Mom, you don't have to do a thing. Just stay home and relax. We'll take care of everything."

"No, I have to come," I said.

Our children turned to their father. "Dad, tell her it'll be fine," Josh begged.

Jim put his hand on mine. "Let go for once, Steph. You have enough to do with the holidays coming. We've got this."

"No, I *have* to come," I said again. "It *has* to be the right tree."

———

LOOKING BACK ON that winter, I can see this insistence in everything I did. I see my obsession with appearances. My need for control over every aspect of them. Jim might have been keeping his distance, but I can see how tempting I made it to stay away.

Just a few days later, for instance, I opened a shipment of holiday tapers and cried out in distress.

"Steph! What is it?" Jim appeared in the doorway of the kitchen.

"These candles!" I said.

"Good lord, Stephanie, this is about candles? You scared me. I thought something bad happened."

"This *is* bad."

"What's wrong?"

"These candles are *white*. They're supposed to be ivory."

Jim's brow creased in confusion. "Ivory is white," he said after a moment. "Isn't it?"

"Not *bone* white. Ivory's more like cream. Like almond. It's off-white."

"All right . . . is that . . . important?" my husband asked carefully.

"It's very important!" I exclaimed. "Ivory is soft, and subtle, and comforting. This shade is sterile and soulless and awful."

Jim looked at the candles again and then back at me.

"I'm going for a soft rustic effect," I went on. "These are like candles for a freaking séance. I mean, they hurt my eyes."

"Honey?" Jim said finally. "This is a first-world problem if I ever heard one. Do you think anyone besides you could possibly care?"

"Jim, you don't get it," I told him. "Design is a subliminal experience. People might not be aware of how a color affects them, but that's beside the point. I know the experience I'm trying to create in my own space. We have to send these candles back, because there's no way I can use them."

My husband gave up and retreated to his home office.

The month of December was like this. It was like no other time of the year. Seven days a week, I set my alarm for four thirty a.m., ninety minutes earlier than usual, and I went to bed later than usual, after midnight on most nights. I spent these extra hours decorating the tree, making wreathes, baking and freezing five or six kinds of cookies, wrapping dozens of gifts to put beneath the tree. The rest of my week was as usual: designing homes, competing in tennis matches, and managing Heritage School.

Each night I fell into bed exhausted, depleted, and anxious. Back aching, feet hurting, head swimming with ideas, worries, tasks. *None of this is worth it*, I told myself. *I will never do this to myself again.*

Yet when the night of our party was finally upon us, I felt the usual rush of triumph. Our house looked enchanted. Garlands of holly and pine were twined along the mantel and the staircases. There were candles in every window—a bright and cheery crimson since I hadn't been able to find the right shade of ivory—and poinsettias adorned every surface.

The tree was beautiful, trimmed in gold and white and ablaze with hundreds of tiny, twinkling lights. I had trays of canapes out on the island: jewel-colored caviar piled on rounds of toast, walnuts and blue cheese nestled into split figs, smoked salmon and chives on squares of rye. There were little hot dogs wrapped in phyllo dough and tiny mincemeat pies. There were rich cheeses and assorted olives and marcona almonds and roasted chestnuts. There were cut-glass bowls of punch and eggnog set out on the sidebar, where guests could spike their drinks with anything they wanted. In the ovens were roasting Cornish hens and a maple-glazed ham, scalloped potatoes, bacon-wrapped asparagus.

I took in the scene around me in the lull before the first guests arrived and felt a tug of pride. All the kids who sneered at me as I was growing up, for being poor and dirty and illiterate: Wouldn't they be surprised if they could see me now?

Jim's family was the first to arrive. His older sister, Joyce, came through the front door along with a blast of wind. Snowflakes were clinging to her hair and coat. Her cheeks were rosy, but her face was drawn and mournful.

"The roads are a mess," she fretted. "I'm surprised we made it here in one piece. I honestly thought the wind was going to blow us off the bridge."

"Merry Christmas, Joyce!" I said, with a cheer so forced it bordered on aggression. "May I take your coat?"

Crystal, his younger sister, arrived next, wearing mittens and clutching a glass pan.

"Merry Christmas, Stephanie," Crystal said. "Do you have a nice serving plate I could use? I don't own any dishes in Christmas colors, but I don't think my casserole looks very nice in the baking pan."

"It looks lovely to me!" I told her. "But I'm sure we can find another holiday platter."

Jim's parents then came in. They greeted me with warmth, but their faces lit up at the sight of their son and three grandchildren. Or so at least it seemed to me.

Joyce glanced around the room. "You sure went all out for this party," she said. "Look how you've done the place up—everything's so fancy."

Fancy? Was that a compliment? I waited for her to go on, to say that it was beautiful, magical. But it seemed that no other commentary was forthcoming, and I was suddenly grateful for Crystal's request for a holiday casserole dish. It gave me a reason to turn my back and rummage in my cupboards.

"Here we are," I announced as brightly as I could, pulling a red oval platter from my holiday serving set.

"Oh, look, honey, this should be perfect," Jim's mother said as she and Crystal moved to the kitchen island. "I'll help you transfer the casserole. I'm amazed you found time to make it. I know how busy you've been."

I watched as Jim's mother helped Crystal arrange her candied yams just so, my throat aching with the childish howl it held: *What about me? What about everything I've done and how busy I've been?*

Joyce seemed to share my angst. "I wanted to bring something," she told her mother. "I was planning to make my cranberry Christmas cake. I ran out of time, and with all the holiday expenses, there's just nothing left over for extras. Nothing at all!"

She burst into tears and covered her face with both hands.

Jim's mother looked aghast. "Joyce sweetheart, I wasn't criticizing you! We know you always bring something when you can." She put a consoling hand on her daughter's arm, but Joyce shook it off and ran out of the room.

We all stood in silence for a moment, and then Crystal handed her mother the spatula. "Could you finish this, Mom?" she said. "I'll go talk to her."

Jim's mother turned to scraping the last of the casserole from the pan onto the plate.

"I hope you can understand, Stephanie," she said, her voice low and pained. "Joyce is going through a challenging time, what with her divorce and financial upheaval and such. So naturally the holidays are a hard time for her."

THE NEXT MORNING, I lay in bed, drugged with exhaustion and resentment, barely able to imagine getting up and facing the day. All that work, all that loving effort, and for what? Jim's mother would never love me like she loved her own daughters. They would always come first in her heart.

That was only natural. I knew that. And yet.

I'd turned off the ringer, but I heard my phone vibrate on the night-stand, and a notification that I had a voicemail appeared on the screen. The message was from my favorite client.

"Stephanie, my sweet girl, it's Mama Mae. Can you fit another client into your schedule? My son just bought a new home and, well, you know how men are. He has no idea what to do with it. Do you have time to meet next month? I'd love to take you to lunch and then send you over to his house."

The last few weeks had been fraught with so much tension and sorrow that Mae's message in my inbox made me feel weak with relief. I listened to it several times, drinking in the warmth of her voice and the love for me that was always in it.

I didn't really have time for lunch during my workweek, let alone space for a new client, but the thought of saying no to Mae never occurred to me. For her, I would make time. I loved Mae, loved being in her presence and basking in the tenderness she lavished on me. And after the holidays with Jim's family, I was starved for it.

"Of course I'd love to help your son," I said when I called her back. "And I could meet next Friday, if that can work."

"Oh, thank goodness," she said. "Owen saw what you did with his sister's beach house, and of course he's seen what you did with mine, and he's ready to give you full creative control. His girlfriend is no help at all. She just doesn't have the eye."

Mae had a homespun beauty. There was a light within her and around her, and she was wonderfully real. There were crinkles at the corners of her eyes, laugh lines around her mouth.

Mae had been a secretary before meeting her second husband, a local real estate magnate, and though she was very wealthy, there was nothing intimidating about her. She had the wholesome look of a small-town librarian, with her tidy brunette hair, her sweater sets, the reading glasses that hung around her neck on a beaded chain. Her eyes were gentle and her smile was kind.

Her daughter Kim was the first in her family to become a client of mine. I'd designed her beach house on the Oregon coast. Several months later, she called to say there was an emergency. The designer working with her mother was turning out to be a disaster.

"My mom's calling the whole thing off," Kim reported. "She's literally returning one hundred thousand dollars' worth of furniture and fixtures. We're scrambling here for someone to step in and save this renovation. Please, Stephanie, she loves the beach house so much, she thinks you're just brilliant, can you help?"

Mae lived in the upscale neighborhood of Lake Oswego, on the Willamette River. I loved everything about her house. The intricately carved red front door. The great room with the double-sided fireplace and the authentic Ming Dynasty panels on the walls. I loved the infinity fountain in her courtyard, the koi pond in her backyard and the stone bridge across it.

Her children and grandchildren were always over, and I envied them for having her love all their lives.

Mae took in any stray or injured animal that was lucky enough to cross her path. She had a pair of rabbits, three or four dogs, and half a dozen birds. Sometimes I felt like another wounded creature slinking around her doorstep.

"What a lovely woman you are," she said a week or so into our acquaintance. We'd spent hours poring over paint chips, flooring options, and swatches of upholstery, and now we were having lemonade on her patio. "Is your mother as proud of you as I would be?"

"Well," I said. There was an awkward pause while I wondered how to answer her. The quick deflections and evasions that I'd practiced so long on everyone else, I couldn't bring myself to draw on them now. "Well, no, she isn't," I said finally.

"Oh dear," said Mae. "She hasn't passed on, has she? Is your mother still with us?"

"You mean, is she alive?" I asked. "Yes, she is."

"I apologize if I said the wrong thing," Mae said. "I take it she's not very supportive of you. Or perhaps she's not in your life at all?"

"Well, right now she's in jail," I said.

I don't know who was more surprised by this disclosure, Mae or me. It had been more than three decades since I'd told Jim about my mother, and I'd told no one outside of our family since. But I couldn't bear the idea of lying to Mae. I wanted to confide in her, wanted to surrender to the safety of her gentle gaze.

It was easy to be honest with her. She was stricken; she was sympathetic. It wasn't long before I'd told her much more. With every detail I disclosed, it felt as if heavy boards were being pried away from some self-imposed prison and sunlight was slanting in. It felt as if—just as in a fairy tale—I'd found my real mother at last, and the one I'd grown up with was just a jealous stepmother, an evil stand-in.

Mae made it easy to indulge in this pretense. She told me I was like a daughter to her. She even asked me to call her "Mama Mae" as the rest of her family did. She said I was like a lotus flower, blooming above the darkest mud. She was always cooing over me, sending me loving notes, making me lunch. She had a yacht docked on the river beyond her house, and she invited me along whenever she and her daughters were taking it out.

"Kim and Lara want to go out on the boat this weekend," she'd tell me, "and please, Stephanie, I hope you'll join us. I'd love to have *all* my girls with me on the river."

I loved Kim. She was easy-going, down-to-earth, and fun to be with. And her sister Lara was lovely too. So why did I always feel like an outsider on the yacht?

It was because it drove home the hard truth that Mama Mae was not, in fact, my mother after all. She was theirs, and that was manifest in her every gesture around them, her every glance at them. She loved me, I knew that, but I was not her blood and never would be.

When we gathered in her house before going down to the boat, her kids were rummaging through her purse in search of a pen, they were eating out of her refrigerator, disappearing into her bedroom to take a phone call. It was their house too, and they felt a freedom and license there that I never would, no matter how many times she made me lunch.

I loved spending time with Kim and loved to be around Mae, but I didn't feel good when I was around both of them at the same time.

It was startling, though, to realize now that as close as we were, I had never met Mae's son.

"Owen will love you," she promised on that bleak post-holiday Friday. "I told him you'd be over at the end of your work day. He knows how busy you are and he's just grateful that you're finding a way to fit him in. Here, I'll text you his address right now."

THE MAN WHO came to the door toward five o'clock that afternoon had cropped dark hair, blue eyes, and a strong build. He wore blue jeans and a dark gray t-shirt. He looked like he knew his way around a loading dock or construction site. I hadn't expected Mae's son to be so good-looking.

"I'm Owen," he said, extending a hand and ushering me inside. "I've heard a whole lot about you. And I've seen your work. You're great at what you do."

I felt myself flushing. "Your mom is very special to me," I told him.

"Well, it's mutual. She raves about you too. And you did an amazing job on her house."

"Thank you," I said. "That means a lot to me. And I intend to do an amazing job on yours too, so why don't we talk about your vision for your home?"

"If I had a vision, I wouldn't need you. Listen, I trust you with this space," he said. "Just tell me what you have in mind and I'm sure I'll sign off on it."

I let him provide a tour of the place. It was a typical builder's special. It was as dark and drab and artless as a college dorm and looked as if it had last been remodeled in the late eighties. He showed me the still-empty bedrooms, the spare room, the living room and the basement, and finally we ended up in his bistro-style kitchen.

On the island was an open bottle of Cobos Malbec and a glass, half-full.

"That's a fantastic wine," I said without thinking.

Immediately he whisked a second glass from the nearest cabinet. "Join me?"

"Oh no," I said. "I mean, thank you, ordinarily I'd love to, but I shouldn't."

"Why not?"

"I'm working," I said, and cringed inwardly as soon as I'd said it. I sounded prim and uptight even to myself. "It would be unprofessional," I added lamely.

"It's Friday," he said. "It's five o'clock."

"That's true," I conceded.

He poured a generous portion into a glass and held it out to me. "I'm not a man who likes to drink alone," he said. "Hey, every true professional will tell you the customer is always right."

I took the glass, swirled the wine a few times and breathed in the aroma. It was potent and lovely.

"To guilty pleasures," he said, and touched my glass with his. The wine warmed me through, and I found myself laughing.

"Are you always so charming?" I asked. "Your mother should have warned me."

"And me as well," he said, smiling. "She never told me you were so beautiful."

As we laughed and bantered and flirted and drank, I was overcome by a feeling of well-being, the kind I hadn't felt in a very long time. When was the last time a man had told me I was beautiful? Had any man besides Jim ever dared? I'd married so young, and my wedding ring tended to deflect such remarks.

Is this what life was like for young single people? I'd missed it all: the chance to meet exciting strangers, to feel this romantic tension.

What I liked was the sense of safety, the sense of irony, beneath our playful repartee. None of this was serious and we both knew it. I was married; he had a girlfriend. He was Mae's son and I was her adopted daughter. All this innuendo was a mutual joke; we could enjoy it while knowing full well it would never cross a certain line.

Or so I told myself.

Chapter 6

ON MAY 13, 1972, my mother was summoned by the police to a motel two miles away, where she was asked if she could identify the dead man on the bed.

She confirmed that it was her former husband, Louie Madera. It was his birthday. He was forty-two.

On both nightstands, the rickety dresser, atop the television, and along the windowsill were dozens of photographs of his children. Of us.

In the bathroom, hanging on the shower rod, were two red dresses: the larger one in Isabella's size and the smaller one in mine.

The stale motel air reeked of cigarette smoke and liquor. Empty bottles were everywhere, as well as a nearly drained liter of tequila. There were a few pills scattered on a side table as well. Later they were identified as secobarbital sodium, a barbiturate that people were then calling "reds" or "red devils."

Once my mother had made this identification, the police did not keep her long. But she would encounter them again, later that day, when they were called in response to a naked woman running through the streets. She was holding an infant in her arms, and she was screaming. Over and over, at the top of her voice, she shrieked: *You can't kill me because I'm already dead!*

The baby was Dominic, born earlier that year. He was Louie's son. His father had never laid eyes on him.

It took two cops and a burly paramedic to wrestle my naked mother into a straitjacket while a second medic held the baby. As they secured the straps that would hold her immobile with her crossed arms pinned against her chest, she screeched at them, eyes wild, neck cords straining.

How dare you put your hands on me? I am a direct descendant of George Washington! I come from aristocracy! My ancestors founded this country, and my family built it from the ground up!

That evening, she was committed to the psychiatric ward of the San Francisco General Hospital, and my siblings and I were consigned to the dependent unit of the state of California. Isabella and I were sent to the girls' unit and our brothers to the boys'. We would remain there for the next several months.

It was autumn before my mother was released and another few weeks before she was allowed to resume custody of us. When we were finally reunited as a family, all of us in the same apartment again, Dominic was gone.

Where's Baby Dominic? We asked her this question again and again. *What happened to Dominic? When is Dominic coming back?*

"He's gone," my mother told us. "He isn't coming back."

Our voices rose in a desolate clamor. *Where did he go? What happened to him?*

And all our mother would say was: "He was kidnapped."

"Jim, I can't stop thinking about the day my mother identified Louie's body," I told my husband. It was late at night and I couldn't sleep.

I'd been to see my mother that morning. We'd talked about Louie's death and its aftermath. Some of it she told me, and some I recalled myself. I remembered her psychotic break and arrest as well as the shame of seeing her outside with no clothes on, screaming as she disappeared into the frightening white cocoon of the straitjacket.

"You know what my mom was yelling, about being a direct descendant of George Washington, about coming from the aristocracy?" I went on. "That's what she always reverts to, when she's in the midst of a break."

"Yeah, you've mentioned that."

"Well, don't you think it's bizarre? Why would she say that stuff?"

"Because she's crazy?"

"Well, sure. But still."

Jim took a moment to consider this. "Don't grandiose delusions come along with bipolar disorder? I mean, she *has* been diagnosed as bipolar. Among other things."

"Yes," I said, "but manic people usually claim they're Christ, or the messiah, or Joan of Arc or someone like that. A martyr or a savior."

"Okay. And?"

"Well, I mean, you know my mom. She's a hippie and a Buddhist. What does she care about George Washington, or the *aristocracy*—why is that her version of grandiosity? Why isn't she claiming that she's, like, achieved perfect enlightenment, or she's some goddess of love or something?"

"Yeah, I see your point," my husband said. "I don't know. My guess is she's sensitive to people thinking she's white trash. Maybe that's her way of saying she's better than they think."

It came to me then that I'd never asked myself this question before. I'd been too busy surviving my mother to worry about understanding her. I was an adult now, and she was dying, and I was intrigued by her response to Louie's suicide.

His death affected my mother. This was surprising but undeniable. It flipped a switch in her that I'd thought was broken. She displayed what I'd never seen her reveal in any other situation: guilt. I didn't think she was capable of guilt.

I was a good mother, she would say. *You had everything you needed. I home-schooled all of you.*

You never starved, she would tell me. *Seaweed is one of the healthiest things you can eat; it's full of protein and minerals. People in the city paid top dollar for it!*

I protected you, she said. *My chanting protected you. After that head-on collision, you walked away without a scratch. All of you did.*

But when she was faced with the lifeless body of her estranged husband? It's the only time I can recall when the harm she did was revealed to her, made real to her: irreparable, irreversible. She couldn't write her own version of it. She could not rationalize or revise it. For once, the truth was immutable: as cold and rigid as the dead man on the motel bed.

Even recalling it must have affected her, because soon afterward my phone rang, and the voice on the line was that of her most inconsolable persona.

"Hello?"

"Stephanie? It's Agnes."

It had been years since I'd heard from Agnes, and that was a relief. I didn't know which persona I dreaded more: Agnes or Flow. As Flow, my mother was hostile, implacable, violent, and dangerous. But as Agnes, she was pathetic, and in a way that was even worse. Agnes always spoke in the whiny, fretful tones of a very young girl, and even a few seconds of this felt like more than I could bear.

"Stephanie?" she said again, a sob in her voice.

"What's the matter, Mom?" I asked.

She started to cry. "I don't know if I want to live," she wept. "I took a bunch of pills but they didn't work. They didn't do anything at all!"

"Mom?" I said, alarmed. "When did you take a bunch of pills? Was this today?"

"No, not today."

"When?"

"Before."

I closed my eyes and exhaled sharply. "You scared me, Mom."

"I need you to come over," she begged.

"Right now? Why?"

"I'm all alone and I'm scared."

I looked at the clock. It was nine thirty in the evening and I was tired. Jim was home for once, and leaving the house was the last thing I wanted to do.

"I have a lot going on tomorrow, Mom. I wanted to go to bed early tonight."

She began to shriek. "Stephanie, you have to come! I need you right now! I'm all alone!"

I STOOD FOR a moment just outside my mother's apartment and peered through the window of her front door. I could see her lying on the living room floor. She was wearing a yellow t-shirt and pink shorts, and she was coloring with crayons. It was almost a minute before I could make myself ring the doorbell.

"Where were you?" she demanded as she opened the door.

"Mom, what do you mean? I came right over after we talked on the phone!"

"I mean, where have you *been*? Why did you leave me all alone?" She sank down onto her sofa and put both hands on her belly.

"Mom," I said. "You're acting like a child."

"I think I'm pregnant," she whimpered.

"You're not pregnant, Mom. You're seventy-six."

"Stop calling me Mom," she whined. "My name is Agnes."

I sat down beside her. She grabbed my hand and clutched it with all her strength. I felt pity in spite of my irritation.

As gently as I could, I said, "Your name is Florence. Why are you saying it's Agnes?"

"Agnes means *pure one of God*."

I choked back a laugh.

She glared at me. "You don't believe me, do you? That's how much you know. I was baptized in the highest Episcopalian church in this country!"

"Okay, Mom. I mean Agnes. It's okay, take it easy."

She eyed me fearfully. Without quite planning to, I found myself reaching out and stroking her hair. "I mean it. I'm sorry. It's okay. You're safe now."

She seemed to relax. "Do you want to see my drawing?" she asked.

"Sure."

She went to the spot on the floor where she'd been lying a few moments ago and retrieved her picture: A smiling blue-eyed girl with sunny yellow hair, standing beneath a rainbow. "Do you like it?" she asked anxiously. "I made it for you."

IT WAS HOURS before I could make my escape. First I had to brew her a cup of tea with milk and honey, and rub her back while she drank it, and then coax her into bed. I had to sit beside her as she drifted off, murmuring to her in the low, gentle tones I used with my own children whenever they were sick, or after they'd woken from a nightmare.

By the time she was asleep, it was past two in the morning and I was exhausted, depleted. For just a moment I wavered over whether to crash on her sofa rather than begin the half-hour drive to my own house. But no. The moment the idea occurred to me, I dismissed it. I would rather drive all night than wake up beneath her roof.

How was I going to get through the next day? It wasn't until I was finally in my own bed again beside Jim, setting my alarm for just three hours later, that I let myself consider the schedule ahead of me. I had meetings all morning, several student presentations to attend in the afternoon, and an interview with a prospective student at three.

But then at four—at four I would see Owen again. We were meeting to design the bar area in his living room.

The thought of Owen was like a life raft. I reached for it with something like desperation and held on for all I was worth, and in spite of everything, I fell asleep smiling.

Chapter 7

IT WAS TWO full weeks before I could make myself return to my mother's apartment, and when I finally felt able to face her again, I had to deal with Jim's resistance along with my own.

"The last time you went to see your mom, she kept you there half the night," my husband reminded me. "Why are you going back there again?"

"Because I still have so many questions."

It was six in the morning. Jim was shaving at the bathroom sink, and I was sitting up in bed, holding a cup of coffee and trying to steel myself for the hours ahead.

"It's been a very peaceful couple of weeks since then," Jim said, rinsing his razor and splashing aftershave on his face. "No crying jags, no misery, no rage. Taking a break from her was a great idea. Are you sure you don't want just a little more time away?"

"She has lung cancer, Jim. That's the problem. We don't have time."

"Hey," Jim said suddenly. He had moved to the doorway of the bathroom and now stood leaning against the jamb. "*Hey*. Did you cut your hair?"

"Two days ago, yeah." It was a pretty dramatic cut, in fact. I'd had at least six inches taken off. It now came to just above my shoulders, whereas before it had touched the top of my back.

"It's nice," he said. "It's great. I can't believe I didn't notice."

I can, I thought.

"I won't stay more than an hour or two this time," I said, returning to the topic of my mother. "I swear. She's not going to be needy this time anyway, I can tell. There was no trace of Agnes when we talked last night."

"What are you going to ask her about?"

"I've been having such vivid memories of this family I lived with when I was really little. The best memories of my entire childhood took place in their house, but I don't even remember their last name."

OUR FAMILY WAS reunited, minus Dominic, after my mother was released from the psych hospital in 1972. But we weren't together for long before my mother was arrested for welfare fraud. Because of a clerical error, she had been receiving each check in duplicate for many months. It didn't occur to her to report this oversight, just as it didn't occur to her that eventually it would be discovered and she would be guilty of a felony.

In the meantime, she used the surplus income for breast enhancement surgery. Overnight she went from a nearly flat chest to a double-D endowment. But whenever people asked what the procedure had been like, she pretended not to understand the question.

"I never had anything done!" she would say. "The hormones are so different with each pregnancy. My breasts got so swollen when I had Dominic and they just never went back to their old size."

She said it so often that I half-believed her, right up until the day I saw one of her medical reports, which listed—among literally dozens of other ailments—*breast-implant-associated capsular contracture*. In any event, she was sentenced to six months in the county jail, and my siblings and I were left with Rick.

I imagine Rick trying to make sense of the idea that he suddenly had sole custody of four kids. Did he ever try to feed us or put us to bed? The answer is almost certainly no. My mother never did those things, so he would have no reason to do them in her absence. Moreover, his every waking hour was focused on scoring whatever drugs he could get. He was wasted on alcohol, heroin, and whatever else was within reach twenty-four hours a day.

I remember being in our car, though, with him at the wheel. I recall being upright one moment and tipped into pandemonium the next. He had tried to take a corner while going seventy miles an hour. The car went onto its side and then upside down and onto its other side and just kept rolling.

It was loud, *so* loud, as metal met concrete and the windows shattered. But somehow, within that violent tumult, I barely moved. For the second time in my life I was inside a vehicle as it was totaled, and I walked away without a scratch.

When the police showed up in response to the accident, Rick reeked of alcohol and couldn't talk without slurring his words. He was arrested and had no way to make bail, which left us with no adult in our home.

Isabella was taken in by her second grade teacher. Social workers showed up at my brothers' school and brought them back to the dependent unit. But the police put me in the back of their squad car and initially drove straight to our home to search it for drugs, which is how I somehow ended up—for a brief and beautiful interlude of my life—in the most wonderful place I had ever been.

My mother was watching *Jeopardy!* and she didn't even look up as I let myself into her apartment. I stood for a moment beside the front door, adjusting to the dim interior, and let my own gaze be drawn to the television.

"I'll take World Capitals for three hundred, Alex," said a player who looked like a college professor.

The clue appeared on the screen as Alex read it out loud. "The name of this Ethiopian capital means 'New Flower' in Amharic, the country's official language."

"What is Addis Ababa?" my mother said, just ahead of the contestant.

I turned my head and stared at her.

"That's correct!" said Alex as the studio audience applauded.

"World capitals for four hundred, please," the man said next.

"When this city became the capital of the new Mongolian People's Republic in 1924, its name was changed to honor the 'Father of Mongolia's Revolution.'"

"What is Ulan Bator?" said my mother.

I felt my jaw slacken in stupefaction.

"Mom," I said. "How . . .?"

"What's the matter?"

"How do you know these capitals?"

"Doesn't everyone?"

"Uh . . . no. No, everyone does not. Most people wouldn't know *any* of them. I don't know any of them."

"Well, why don't you? Oh, never mind," she said dismissively, without waiting for my answer. "You were never anywhere near as smart as me."

I stood there for a moment absorbing this. It hurt, like almost everything else my mother ever said to me, but then again it wasn't much to her credit even if it was accurate.

I sat down beside her on the sofa and took her hand. It was skeletal, the blue veins standing out in sharp relief against her translucent skin. Her face looked even gaunter than the last time I'd been here, her cheeks hollowed out like a famine victim.

"Mom," I said. "How are you feeling? You look so thin."

She shot me a sidelong malevolent glance. "I can't say the same about you," she said. "And why did you cut your hair?"

I touched the feathery ends that now came to just below my ears. "I wanted a change," I told her. "I haven't done anything different for a long time."

"Well, it looks terrible."

"That's your opinion," I said, stung again. "Several people have told me it looks great." Including Owen, who'd said so more than once.

"They just didn't want to hurt your feelings. You took way too many inches off. I've told you so many times: A woman's hair is her glory. It's her mystique. Her *power*."

"My God, Mom," I said. "Jim was right. I don't know why I come here."

"It's too bad you can't appreciate my honesty," she said. "I'm telling you the truth for your own good, so you'll never make such a terrible mistake again. If your own mother won't tell you, then who will?"

Another time, I might have walked out. Today I wanted answers about the people I had lived with after the crash.

"Mom, listen," I said. "I keep thinking of this family I lived with for a while, when I was around five years old. I must have been with them for several months, because I remember it being summer and then winter. I called the mother Mama Bee."

"Oh, you mean the Bertolinis," she said. "They were our next door neighbors on Dutton Avenue, in Santa Rosa. When Rick and I were both in the slammer, they offered to take you in. Then they didn't want to give you back!"

"Just me? I know Isabella was at her teacher's house, but not the boys?"

"Just you."

"Why only me, do you think?"

"Who knows? Their house was small. There was no way they could take you all. They probably thought you were shy and sweet and wouldn't be much trouble."

THE BERTOLINIS' HOUSE was cozy and quaint. It was the prettiest house I'd ever seen, though, as my mother said, the family was not wealthy and its dimensions were modest. The kitchen was a sun-splashed yellow and filled with light. There was a cookie jar on the counter that was shaped like an owl. There were colored potholders her children had woven from a loom, hanging on the oven door. Mama Bee kept a blue bowl of lemons on the kitchen table, and she used them for everything.

She made fresh-squeezed lemonade, which she served in a glass pitcher with lemon slices floating on top. She made lemon popsicles and lemon custard and lemon meringue pie. She used lemons for cooking and baking and cleaning and shining the silverware. The sight of lemons has lifted my heart ever since, and I keep a bowl of them on my own kitchen counter for this reason.

When I stepped out of the bathtub at their house, the warm fluffy bath mat beneath my feet felt like a miracle. Mama Bee cooked dinner every night, and this too felt like a miracle. Her simple dinners were by far the most wholesome and delicious food I had ever eaten. Spaghetti and meatballs. Macaroni and cheese, baked in the oven with buttery bread crumbs on the top. Fried chicken and mashed potatoes with gravy. Mama Bee's food was *warm* and nourishing and it filled me up.

In the backyard was a little garden plot where they grew their own vegetables. Every day I went out and sprinkled the plants with water from a light green watering can, and I gathered every cherry tomato that was red on the vine.

Each of their daughters had a lunch box with a red plaid pattern, and they gave me one as well. I loved to spring it open and then press it shut with a satisfying click. In our shared bedroom there were pink gingham curtains on the windows. There was a braided rug and a rocking chair and a magical night light with a clown and a dog and a bouquet of colored balloons. The balloons were the part that lit up, from within. That night light filled my heart with happiness.

Every night, Mama Bee tucked me under covers of lavender flannel. She smoothed my hair back from my face and kissed my forehead. Papa Bee knelt beside my bed to pray, as he did with each of his children in turn.

He said words I didn't fully understand but I loved the sound of them anyway.

Lord, thank you for delivering this precious child into our care. Her young life hasn't been easy so far, Lord. As You know, she has been at the mercy of some very dark forces. But she is thriving here with us, and we hope to keep her with us. If you see fit, Lord, please continue to grant us the privilege of sheltering her and watching over her. Let us fill her innocent heart with the knowledge of Your grace and Your everlasting love. Amen.

No one had ever prayed for me or with me before. No one had ever told me about God, who had created the earth and everything in it. But the Bertolinis said He was everywhere at once and I could talk to Him directly, anytime I wanted.

I could feel God in that house. He lived in every one of those warm and cheerful rooms. He was holding us in His hands all the time, like the song we sang in the children's service at their church while Sister Paula rattled a tambourine:

He's got you and me, brother, in His hands
He's got you and me, sister, in His hands
He's got the itty bitty babies in His hands
He's got the whole world in His hands.

In bed one night, after learning that song in church, I thought about our car, turning over and over on the concrete, and how I'd stayed in one place within it, like a sock in the very center of a dryer full of clothes. This made perfect sense now. All the while the car was rolling like a tumbleweed across the road, I was tucked inside the cup of His mighty palm like an egg in a nest.

THE FIRST MORNING we saw frost on the ground was the morning my mother showed up on their doorstep, and the dread of that moment will never leave me. All these decades later, I can feel it burning a hole in my stomach. At the sound of her voice from inside that house, a splotch of urine blossomed suddenly on the front of my green corduroy pants, and a moment later I felt it flowing down my legs and pooling on the floor.

And then I was snatching my shoes from under my bed and pushing them beneath my pillow. It was winter. Every day Mama Bee said I couldn't leave the house without my shoes on. If my shoes were nowhere to be found, then surely I would not be able to go with my mother.

From my own hiding place behind my bedroom door, then, I listened to the voices floating up from the floor below.

"I'm here to take Stephanie home," I heard my mother say.

"She *is* home," Mama Bee said sharply, her voice scaling up like mine did whenever I was about to cry. "She's very much at home here. She eats three meals a day, she has a regular bedtime, she's been to the dentist, and she just learned the alphabet. None of those things were happening on your watch. Five years old and she didn't even know the alphabet when she came here! But she does now."

"Well, thank you for looking after her," my mother said, as if I'd merely been there for an afternoon.

"Why don't you let her stay here with us?" Mr. Bee broke in. "You can visit any time you want, but she'd be one less child for you to keep track of and feed and whatnot. You have your hands full with so many."

"Nothing doing," said my mother. "She's mine. Of all the nerve! Stephanie!" she called out.

"Florence," Mama Bee tried again. "Think of the child. Don't you want what's best for her?"

"*I'm* what's best for her!" my mother said hotly. "Children belong with their mother!"

"You," said Mr. Bee, in a voice like spitting. "You're not fit to take care of a cat."

My mother's tone was more venomous still, though shot through with the strange formality she resorted to whenever she felt defensive. "How dare you address me in that manner? Get my daughter down here this instant or I'll call the police!"

Through the crack along the edge of the door, I saw Mama Bee stagger a few steps backward and then crash to her knees on the floor.

"Mickey!" her husband cried, rushing to help her.

Mama Bee brought her apron up to her face and wailed. It was the kind of sound you might hear from someone wild with grief at a funeral.

My mother stepped past her with perfect composure. As she mounted the stairs, I suddenly sensed the inadequacy of my hiding place and bolted to the other side of the room. The closet—I would hide in the closet. She reached me before I could even wrestle its folding doors apart. When she grabbed my arm, I went as still as an insect paralyzed by a spider.

The best part of my childhood was over in that moment. As soon as she touched me, I was hers again, and I felt the futility of resistance in my bone marrow. I had always been hers. I would always be hers. That was the way it was, and fighting it would only make it worse.

I was mute and compliant and already dead-eyed as she tugged me down the stairs and out the door. Away from the lemon-scented kitchen and the cookie jar and the garden and the balloon man night light and the lunchbox and God.

BACK IN MY car after our visit, in the parking lot of her apartment complex, I rested my head on the steering wheel. Jim was right. I should have let more time go by. Once a month was enough, even if that meant only a handful of interviews before she was gone.

As I took the car keys from my coat pocket, a text notification appeared on the screen of my phone.

Stephanie, my love, it's Mama Mae. Will you come out with us on the boat this Saturday? For once I'm going to have all my children with me on the river: Kim, Lara, and even Owen! His girlfriend is away and he's at loose ends this weekend. And Kim and Lara are coming as usual. So I just need my last daughter to feel complete. I'm talking about you, sweet girl!

I hesitated before typing a reply, remembering that I always felt out of place on the yacht. As if I didn't belong. Painfully aware that, underneath her lavish affection for me, I was not truly her daughter, as Kim and Lara were. But I felt a flutter inside at the mention of Owen. And it didn't hurt to know that his girlfriend would be elsewhere. I wondered if he was hoping I'd come. I even wondered whether he'd asked Mae to invite me.

I found myself calling her back instead of typing a reply. I felt a sudden longing to hear her voice.

"Tell me you're coming," she said as soon as she answered.

I laughed. Why not? Andrea would be with her friends at the mall. I didn't even have to ask Jim if he'd be around; I knew the answer. Why shouldn't I spend a beautiful afternoon on the river? No one would even know I was gone.

"I'm very tempted," I told her. "Actually, I just might."

"Oh, you *must*," Mae said. "Owen told me you got the most beautiful haircut. I can't wait to see it!"

Chapter 8

THE FOLLOWING WEDNESDAY, I woke excited. A tennis match was on my morning schedule. Tennis was the one interruption I allowed in the course of a workweek. It was my passion and a cherished form of catharsis.

Before every match, I would see Andrea off to school and then go out to the garage and hit balls for an hour. It didn't matter how well I hit: how hard, how fast, or how relentlessly. The wall always returned the ball. There was something calming about that.

Tennis was an escape for me. When I was playing, everything else went away: the teacher I was probably going to have to fire, Jim's perpetual absence from home, my mother's withering criticism and her cancer and her insanity. Even my opponent disappeared, or at least seemed incidental. There was nothing but the next ball and my will to reach and return it.

I went to meet it wherever it went. I did whatever it took to get to it and send it back over the net. I lunged, I stretched, I dove, I jumped. There was at once a desperation and a strange sort of serenity in this. It was a relief to be empty of everything but a mindless drive.

Tennis represented the unlikely life I had made for myself. The missed opportunities I chased down and claimed. We'd joined a sports club as a young family, and soon afterward I found myself gazing at the couples on the tennis courts.

That looks fun, I thought. *I want to try it.*

Even this kind of speculation was new to me back then: the idea that I could cross the invisible line that had been there all my life, the line between me and people with normal lives, people with money. Who was I to try tennis? Tennis was for *them*. It wasn't for someone like me.

But in the private introductory lesson that I scheduled soon afterward, I surprised both my instructor and myself with what was either beginner's luck or considerable natural ability. The racket felt natural in my hand. Hitting the ball felt natural too. I could do it right away and I could do it pretty well. That introductory session turned into a series of lessons, and a kind of fever took hold of me. Before long, I was on the tennis court every spare hour of my week.

When the club first paired me with a practice partner, I felt afraid to show up, certain that I wouldn't be able to hold my own. After a few weeks, the club had to find me someone more advanced. Within the year—the same year I picked up a racket for the first time—I was invited to join the club's competitive team.

When I tried on the team tennis outfit, the one I'd need to wear in official matches, I could not stop staring at my reflection in the shop mirror. Who was this pony-tailed woman in a white skirt and white visor, little white anklets for socks and pale gray sweatbands on her wrists? I gazed and gazed at this vision of privilege and could not reconcile it with myself.

It was still a marvel to me: the apparent fact that I could simply buy these clothes and stride onto a court with my racket. That there were no border police at the club, and nobody who would demand special papers or a secret password.

I could barely eat anything before a match. The first time I was slated to face a formal opponent, I was so sick with anxiety I could eat nothing but Wheat Thins. I won that match 6–2, 6–2, and, as superstitious as the next athlete, I ate Wheat Thins before every match for the next fifteen years.

Today, as always, I took a special pleasure in preparing my tennis bag. I packed two rackets, grip tape, bottled water, Gatorade, those lucky Wheat Thins, and two extra tennis outfits. And inwardly it was still a thrill to walk onto the court with my bag and my teammates, all of us wearing matching tennis colors. Those colors said I belonged, even if I knew in my heart that I did not, even if I was sure they would find a reason to throw me out of the league if they knew my background: that I was white trash passing as one of them, and blind in one eye to boot.

When I reached the court, I shook hands with my opponent, a blonde and muscular woman from another Portland club. I noticed that her daughter had come along to cheer her on. I was alone, as I always was. No one in my family ever watched me play. I forbade them to set foot inside the club when I was competing. I could not risk letting them see me lose.

But I almost never lost. I hadn't lost in nearly a year. And I didn't lose this time either. The final score was 6–4, 6–1.

I'D SCHEDULED A design session with Owen for just after the match. The timing was deliberate. I wanted to show up in my tennis dress, still rosy-cheeked from exertion and victory.

Today we were planning his young daughter's bedroom. There was something bittersweet for me about designing the perfect room for someone's sheltered little princess, just as I had done for my own daughter. It was both a deep pang and a strange consolation to create for other little girls what I'd never had.

"Hey," Owen said as we climbed the stairs together with all of my materials. "Are you coming out on my mom's boat this Saturday?"

"That's the tentative plan," I told him.

"You don't strike me as a tentative woman," he said. "What would it take to get an upgrade?"

"An upgrade? To what?"

"To a hard yes."

"To a . . . *hard* yes?"

Here we were again, laughing at our own cartoonish flirtation. Making fun of ourselves and each other. It was ridiculous. It was delicious.

"Well, with your powers of persuasion, I'm sure you'll think of something," I said. "You don't strike me as a tentative man."

"What if I brought your favorite wine?" he asked. "You gotta be there. My mom really wants you along."

"Well, I wouldn't want to disappoint Mama Mae."

"No, ma'am," Owen said. "We wouldn't want that."

I couldn't help smiling.

"Okay!" I said, turning to the materials I'd brought. "Let's focus on this bedroom! I have some paint samples for you to choose from."

His daughter's favorite color was pink. Owen had already picked out an area rug shaped like a pink rose. He'd chosen a vanity table and softly lit mirror, an overhead chandelier dripping with pink crystals, and a canopy bed. Now I set out the paint swatches I'd brought with me.

I dipped a paintbrush in Persian Rose and left a broad swath of it on the wall. Doing this always made me feel gleefully transgressive, even though it would soon be painted over.

"Nice," Owen said, standing back to appraise it. He shot me a meaningful glance. "Warm."

I added swaths of Valentine Candy and Pastel Fantasy. "So what do you think?" I asked. "Do you have a preference so far?"

"You're asking a very straight man to pick a shade of pink?" he said. "Come on, you're the girl. Which shade would you choose?"

"Actually," I said, opening the last sample I'd brought and adding it to the display, "I would go with Sunrise on the Beach."

I dipped in the paintbrush and drew it across the wall again, leaving a color like a pink mango in its wake.

"Wow," Owen said. "You're good. I think that's the one."

"It is, isn't it?"

"The name fits," he said. "Have you ever seen a sunrise on the beach?"

I choked back a laugh.

When I was his daughter's age, I'd watched the sun rise on the beach every morning. Maybe that was why it called to me when I'd scanned the colors for her room. It was in fact the most hopeful color I could imagine: the pink of promise, of a new day. It meant dawn; it meant renewal. It meant the darkness had lifted.

———

DURING THE BRIEF period between my mother's arrest and Rick's own, he managed to sell most of her possessions. Once he too had gone to jail and there was no one to pay rent, the owners of our house obtained an order of eviction and disposed of the rest.

As a result, six months later when my mother was released, she had nothing left to her name but the clothes she was wearing and the car that was still parked on our old street. Everything else was gone: our home, clothes, linens, toys, photos. Everything.

When she'd recovered all her children—Isabella from the home of her second-grade teacher, my older brothers from the state dependent unit, her newest baby Walter from his foster home, and me from the Bertolinis' house—she spent the remaining gas in her tank on the drive to Mendocino Headlands State Park.

So began our months of living in the car and on the beach. Months of frigid ocean air and bran cereal and seaweed. Months of homelessness, aimlessness, truancy. Long days wandering the shoreline and the outskirts of the village with no adult supervision, no schedule, no structure. Dinners taken in the parking lot of the nearest convenience store, eaten while sitting on the curb. It was winter in Mendocino, and our only shelter was a station wagon.

I imagine my mother shooing us out of the car and onto the beach upon our arrival, leaving the older kids in charge, so she could drive back alone to a local motel where letters spelling out Help Wanted had been added to the vacancy billboard. I see her sitting in their parking lot, combing her waist-length hair with her fingers. I picture her walking into the motel office and turning on her charm. And then I imagine her returning to us, flushed with triumph and employed.

Her hourly rate was low—minimum wage around that time was $1.60 an hour—but they paid weekly and in cash. I picture her with her first week's pay and the competing needs it had to cover. Which felt the most pressing? What did she spend it on? First something to eat, I would think, but after that?

Diapers for the baby? A hairbrush, laundry detergent, aspirin, tampons? Her first fix in forever? She doesn't remember these details.

Harder for me to imagine is how she made it until her first payday. But then, hippies were everywhere: all along the highway and all over the village. And hippies were all about sharing. Did people help her out with some food, a cigarette, or a little cash? I try to imagine having five children and no home, no possessions, and no money. What would it be like to be an adult woman without a change of underwear, without toothpaste, without a pillow?

If any of this was hard for my mother, or frightening, or demoralizing, she never showed it. I can't recall a single moment of reflection or introspection on my mother's part, not one in all the years I spent with her. She didn't cry in the car at night. She didn't seem horrified to be homeless. She simply went along. She rose before dawn, returned in the evenings, took us to the public showers, did whatever she could to score her acid and her herbs. She took her life in stride, wherever she found herself.

I've never met anyone else of whom this could be said. All the homeless women I've encountered while doing volunteer work speak the language of therapy and recovery. They will mention their bad choices, their addictions, and their codependency. They talk about hitting rock bottom. They attend AA and NA meetings, support groups, counseling, and anger management classes. They are earnestly trying to salvage themselves, their relationships with their children, and their employment prospects.

My mother did none of these things. She did not take stock of how far she had fallen. She did not seek to make amends to anyone. She didn't try to get clean. She never recognized the harm she inflicted on her children. She never despaired and she never apologized.

A few days before, during our most recent visit, I'd asked why she hadn't let me stay with the Bertolini family while we were homeless. She'd left Allan with her brother and his wife when we went to Mexico. She reported that Dominic had been kidnapped without ever seeming to grieve his disappearance. Why didn't she let them keep me just a little longer? Such an arrangement would have left her with one less child to feed and more room in the car.

"They taught you to be ashamed of me," my mother said. "When they brought you to visit me, I could see it."

With a sudden shock, I flashed onto a memory of the visit she was referring to, one I hadn't thought about in decades: the visiting area of the jail, with the plexiglass divider and the telephones on either side. It was true, I didn't want to be there at all. I didn't want to talk to my mother or even look at her. All I wanted was to go back to my new home.

Mama Bee had to gently prod me into my chair and coax me into picking up the phone. My mother sat down across from me and picked up her own phone. I don't recall our conversation, but I remember that she had something for me—something she'd made herself. She slid it through the hole at the bottom of the glass and I took it.

It was a doll made out of a brown paper bag. It had long black yarn for hair, a ribbon headband glued across the forehead, and a feather sticking up from beneath the ribbon. It had button eyes and she had colored an elaborate pattern on its dress. Zig-zagging stripes of red and blue alternated with rows of different shapes: circles and spirals and stars and moons.

I was happy to have something from my mom. I brought it home and put it in my drawer. But I also felt the first stirrings of shame in response to my mother, a dawning awareness that I did not want to be like her.

"I only felt shame because we were in a jail," I told her. "I didn't really understand why you were there, but I knew that jail was a bad place."

This was the truth. The Bertolinis didn't plant the seed of shame. It had flowered on its own.

"Well, you never looked at me that way before."

SEVERAL MONTHS INTO her housekeeping job, my mother got a lucky break. The largest unit in the motel became available for long-term rental, and her employers allowed her to move into it for a vastly reduced rate.

The motel was a long, low-slung tan building. It was modest but clean and well-kept, and it even had little touches of charm. The door to each room was red with a tan trim, and each one opened onto a low brick doorstep. Cultivated flowers grew along the edge of the building: lilies and poppies and agave. Between these little bordered flower beds and the doors of each unit were walnut-stained Adirondack chairs.

I loved every single thing about living in this motel. Our rental unit, which was essentially one big room, felt palatial to me after living in the car. At the far end, on the other side of a wooden divider, was a little kitchenette with a refrigerator, a couple of cabinets, and a few feet of counter space. There was a small kitchen table—not much bigger than a card table—made of pale plywood, along with four wooden chairs. In the main room were two queen-sized beds draped with burgundy sateen.

I loved helping my mother with her housekeeping tasks: replacing the towels in each guest bathroom, setting out the tiny bottles of lotion and shampoo, stripping the beds and making them again. I loved pushing the tall laden cart from room to room, puffed up with the importance of my role.

I loved to make her coffee just the way she liked it. Every morning I put two heaping teaspoons of instant Swiss mocha into a mug, heated water in a shallow pan, poured it in when it was boiling, and stirred in a spoonful of honey.

The motel felt impossibly luxurious after living in the car. It was heavenly to sleep in a bed, warm beneath clean blankets. It seemed the height of good fortune to have running water and electric lights, a range with two burners, a shelter spacious enough to walk around in. It was like a miracle to have functional plumbing and toilet paper and privacy, and to be able to go to the bathroom without stepping outside.

The motel had a pool, and this too was a pure joy: a rectangle of shimmering aqua cut into the concrete. On those hot and arid summer days, relief was just a moment away.

My siblings and I were splashing in the shallow end one day when my mother, who was sitting off to the side and watching us, suddenly rose and dove in at the deep side. She had never joined us in the pool before, and we all stared in wonder as she surfaced several yards away.

Then we watched her body arc out of the water like a dolphin and plunge back in, again and again, as her flashing arms swept the air. Back and forth she went with a swift efficient flip-turn on either side, her strokes powerful and practiced and rhythmic. It was an astonishing sight: the sudden transformation of a wraithlike junkie into a self-assured Olympian.

THE FOLLOWING SATURDAY was warm and clear, a perfect day to go out on Mae's yacht. I crossed her backyard that morning in a new red sundress. I felt pretty and youthful and playful as I made my way down the gangplank to where Mae was waiting for me.

"Oh, my sweet girl!" she exclaimed, gathering me into a hug. "Don't you look beautiful! Your haircut is stunning! You look younger than ever."

Owen extended his hand to steady me as I stepped onto the boat. He hovered nearby while Kim and Lara greeted me as warmly as Mae had. Then with the slightest touch at the small of my back, he guided me to the bar.

"Let's get you a drink," he said. "What would be your pleasure, lovely one?"

"Have a mimosa, Steph," Kim called. "His mimosas are killer!"

"Killer," Owen affirmed, reaching for a silver shaker. "May I?"

I watched him create my drink with fresh-squeezed blood orange juice, Dom Perignon, and Grand Marnier. His motions were deft and sure. The weather was balmy and the pine-tinged Pacific Northwest air was like a caress.

The boat moved away from the dock. The sun was shining and the river was sparkling. I watched a flying fish trace an arc in the air and recalled my mother in the motel pool. For the first time it occurred to me to wonder, *Where and when and how did she ever learn to swim like that?*

Then I pushed the thought of her away. I wasn't going to dwell on her today. As promised, my drink was delicious: crisp and sweet and strong, the color of a sunset. The wind lifted my hair as I stood at the railing.

I feel good, I thought for the first time since I'd last seen Owen. *I feel really, really good.*

So often I'd ached to be a part of Mae's family. And now, a little buzzed already from my mimosa, I felt as if I really were.

I felt as if I belonged, truly belonged. It was as if I'd stepped into an alternate world in which I was her daughter-in-law: someone with the true right to call her *Mama*.

I didn't belong in the family I'd been born into, and I had never felt truly taken in by Jim's. But Mae's—I fit so naturally into Mae's. And it felt at that moment as if stepping into it would be as simple as stepping onto a boat.

Chapter 9

I WAS MAKING a guest room bed with my mother when our time at the motel came to an abrupt end. I thought about that a lot afterward: how swiftly and suddenly everything went dark. How rich life had seemed to me at the motel! Six people in a single room for several months on end might not sound blissful to most people, but it was so much better than living in a car that it felt like a dream to me.

Shelter, blessed shelter. Electricity and heat. And space, so much space compared to a car. Water on tap, hot food we could cook ourselves, a television and a refrigerator and a bathtub. The pool, too—an oasis from the heat, but one that was calm and placid, nothing like the pounding ocean.

And then there was the cleanliness, the order. Fresh clean towels every day, and fresh clean sheets on our bed. A ready supply of soap and shampoo, and even little luxuries like body lotion.

Finally, there was my role as my mother's helper. I'd been too young before to really help her with much, but at the motel, we were a housekeeping team. I loved fluffing the pillows, folding the bedspread just so, arranging the little bottles in the bathrooms, making each modest room as pristine and welcoming as I could. Though I couldn't articulate it yet, even to myself, I was already deeply interested, deeply invested, in learning how to make a space into a sanctuary and tending to the comfort of displaced people.

My mother was glad to have my help. I could sense that too, though she never said so. And I loved being of service to her. If I were of use to her, if she needed me even a little, then my place in the world was more secure.

I loved being of service. My siblings all survived our childhood in different ways. Some of them became hard and reckless and lawless. Some withdrew into chronic solitude or addiction or mental illness. The desire to serve, to be of assistance to other people, is one of the traits that saved me.

I was folding the bottom edge of a flat sheet into hospital corners when the slow whirl of red and blue lights lit the room. A police car was in the parking lot.

My mother was on her knees folding the opposite corner of the bed. She understood in an instant that they were here for her. I could see that knowledge in her face as her gaze met mine. She looked for a moment like a trapped and wild-eyed animal.

Then the blue-uniformed figure of a cop filled the doorframe. He had sandy hair and a handlebar mustache. "Florence Haskell?" he said.

The couple who owned the motel stood just behind him. "That's her," the wife said mournfully.

"Ma'am, I'm going to need you to come with me," he said.

My mother rose and faced him. Her eyes narrowed and her stance was defiant. "What for?" she wanted to know.

"For aggravated assault and battery," he said. "It's my understanding that you attacked one of the motel guests."

I believe the owners of the motel had already grown wary of my mother. They'd begun to ask questions about us. Why were we unsupervised at the pool all day? Why weren't we in school?

Even I could see that my mother's behavior was ever more erratic. She went around with a deep scowl, muttering and cursing under her breath. She lit joints in the laundry room, and there were complaints from guests about the smoke-scented linens.

The owners of the motel, an aging Asian couple, had always struck me as good and decent people. They worked hard to keep the motel tidy and respectable. It's easy to imagine that my mother posed an ever-deepening dilemma to them. She was moody and unpredictable. She was clearly an irresponsible parent, but what would happen to us if they fired her? They likely understood that we'd been homeless before. If they ended her employment, would we be homeless again?

But when she assaulted a guest, there was nothing left to decide. They could not keep her on, and of course they were obligated to report violence inflicted on a customer.

As always, it took several men to subdue my mother, to drag her out to the waiting patrol car and fling her face down across the hood. Another cop ushered Isabella and me into the back of a second car, and through the windshield I could see them wrestling her arms behind her and cuffing her wrists. She was thrashing and kicking, and by now her howl of indignation was familiar to me.

Don't you know who I am . . . ?

The motel owners must have mentioned a slew of truant children in their call to the cops because a social worker materialized on the scene: a sweet young woman with long dark hair and glasses. She wore a navy skirt and a blouse with a bow at the throat. In the back seat of the police car, she kept one arm around my shoulders. With her other hand, she smoothed my hair and spoke in a soothing murmur.

"My name is Adele," she told me. "I know you're scared, but everything is going to be all right. Your mother needs help, and the policemen are going to take her to a place where people will help her. And we're going to find help for you too. You're going to be okay."

I liked Adele. I liked her sweet face and her gentle voice. I felt lulled by her reassuring words. I wanted to stay in the police car, cuddled close to her in the back seat, breathing in her flowery perfume.

"Where are we going?" Isabella asked her.

"We're going to get you help," she repeated.

Maybe we could go home with her. I felt safe with her.

All my possessions—two outfits and a doll—were in a black trash bag in the back seat with me. Isabella was holding her own black bag. Our brothers were on the beach, and I wondered whether anyone would help them too.

The police car pulled out of the motel lot and began the long drive to our unspecified destination. I studied the men in the front seat, the way they said code words into their radios, their almost identical close-cropped hair. I leaned into Adele, loving the feeling of her arm around my shoulders, nestling into her warmth as we drove away from Mendocino, out of the town and into the hills, up winding roads and into the dark immensity of the redwood forests.

As an adult, I can appreciate the majesty of those beautiful ancient trees, but as a child in the back of that police car, they filled me with wild foreboding. They were a canopy overhead, blocking out the light. The temperature of the air dropped, and the little bit of sky we could see was the dark blue of a bruise.

At long last we came to a vast building with a circular driveway. Adele helped Isabella and me out of the car and, still murmuring reassurances, brought us inside to a small waiting room. Two women sat at a table near the entrance. Without pleasantries, one of them spoke directly to her.

"Their bags," she said in a tone of command.

Adele knelt in front of us. "Girls, they need your things for now. You'll get them back, I promise. Okay?"

"Can I have my doll?" I asked.

Adele looked up at the woman behind the desk.

"Can she have her doll?" she asked.

"No."

"Not right now, sweetheart," Adele told me, as if she were an interpreter bringing a gentle translation to a harsh foreign language. "But like I said, you *will* get it back. Honest, you will."

Mutely I surrendered my bag to Adele, who placed it on the table. A moment later, Isabella did the same. The angry-sounding woman at the table told Adele: "It's time for you to leave now."

Isabella and I weren't close. My sister probably suffered more deeply during her formative years than I did. She was angry and she was violent and she'd never had any use for me. Throughout our childhood years, she was as likely to cut or claw me as look at me. But we clung to each other then. I held onto her with all my might in the waiting room of the dependent unit and she put her arms around me and held me too. I could feel her trembling.

———

WHAT FOLLOWED WAS the darkest era of my childhood, easily the most painful period of my life. But there was a brief, bright reprieve before it began. I have a single memory of the dependent unit that doesn't feel like choking sadness and abandonment, like something crushed on the side of the road. Before Isabella and I were taken to the girls' dormitory, we were sent to the clothing room. Inside were what seemed like endless racks of donated clothing sorted by gender and size. We were allowed to choose six items of clothing and two pairs of shoes.

I had never chosen clothing for myself, and in that moment, I felt only excitement: the brief falling away of sorrow and terror as I focused on treasures all around me. I pranced up and down the aisles, a little half-gallop of pleasure at the sight of all the floral prints, velvets, satins, and silks. (That rush in response to a bounty of fabrics has never left me. My heart still pounds when I step into a showroom and I'm surrounded by lush panels of variety and possibility.)

I chose a drawstring peasant blouse with a delicate pattern of pink flowers embroidered around the neckline, then a cheerful red corduroy jumper. There were a few Christmas dresses in jewel tones with white lace collars, and I selected one of these next, in emerald.

I took a light blue sweater, the color of a robin's egg and so soft. Its blue pearl buttons were iridescent, and I loved the feel of them beneath my fingertips. I found a pair of denim pants with little patches on it: a mushroom, a flower and a butterfly. Finally, there was a light green dress with strawberries stitched onto the deep front pockets.

For shoes, I chose penny loafers and patent leather Mary Janes. I was also given a new package of knee socks and a five-pack of panties.

Then the fun ended. It was almost time for lights-out.

The children's residence was divided into two blocks, the girls' and the boys'. One of the matrons brought us to a long room where dozens of children slept, and though we were each assigned our own bed, I crawled with Isabella into hers that first evening. I wrapped both arms around her and clung for dear life as, all around us, sobs and shrieks and screams tore the black air all night long.

Nobody ever responded to these screams. No adult came to investigate, or to quiet or comfort anyone.

My brothers would arrive within the next day or two, but I would never see them. After a couple of weeks, Isabella too would disappear. A family had selected her.

I slept alone after she was taken away.

"STEPH? THESE AMEX bills are out of control," Jim said. "Can you explain these charges to me? $2,700 to Kravet?"

"That was to reupholster the sofa."

"What sofa?"

"The living room sofa. Did you actually not notice that it used to be blue and gold brocade and now it's Belgian linen?"

"I did not notice that, no."

I pretended incredulity but I wasn't really surprised. Jim was never home. He hadn't looked at *me* in months, so why would he notice the sofa?

"Was there some reason to reupholster it?" he asked. "I wasn't aware there was anything wrong with it."

"Well, the room is a much warmer taupe now that I had it repainted, and the sofa clashed with the new shade," I told him. "You know I had the walls repainted last month."

"Yes, that I do know. To the tune of several thousand dollars as well. And I don't know why you needed to do that either."

"They were too yellowish!" I protested. "I started to feel like there was something sickly about them."

"You are killing me, Steph. Do you know how many unnecessary things you've had done to the house in the last six months?"

I knew very well, but I stood listening as Jim ticked them off. In addition to repainting the living room, dining room and entry—and reupholstering the sofa—I had changed all the drapes and accent pillows in those rooms. I had pulled out the bathroom vanity and installed a copper sink along with imported travertine tile. I had all the oak cupboards in the kitchen painted white and then inlaid with leaded glass. I'd ripped out the Formica countertops and replaced them with quartz. I put in recessed lighting. I made the surface of the kitchen island one vast wooden butcher block.

"Well, you're right, that is a lot," I conceded. "but I really needed a change, and I'm almost done."

"What do you mean, *almost*?"

"I've had my eye on a chandelier at Porteco and a couple of rugs in the Pearl District. And there's a vintage tapestry from—"

"Stop," Jim said. "Just—time out for a minute. Listen to me: You need to put a freeze on the spending, at least for a little while."

"Why?"

"What do you mean *why*? Because I can't keep up with you! Honestly, it's out of control. It's starting to seem like a compulsion on your part, this need to keep redesigning and overhauling every aspect of the house."

"I'm a designer, Jim," I said haughtily. "It's my art form. It's what I do."

"I thought the point was to do it to other people's houses."

"The best showcase for my work is my own house! Do you know how many jobs I've gotten because people want me to do their houses the way I've done ours? Why don't you worry about your own work and let me worry about mine?"

"I am worried about my own work," Jim said. "That's what you don't seem to get. You seem to think NexPractice is a done deal, that it's already a success story, but that's not the case."

NexPractice was the start-up that currently consumed all of Jim's waking hours. To say I resented it would be an understatement—by now I hated even the sound of its name. I was tired of competing with it for my husband's presence and attention, and I was tired of losing every time.

My husband had always been what I considered excessively driven. The very long hours he put in at work had been our deepest source of tension for well over a decade. He was a serial entrepreneur, but

NexPractice demanded a level of commitment that made all his other ventures seem family-friendly in comparison.

By now it seemed that Jim was married to the company rather than to me. It was as if NexPractice were the wife and I the mistress, settling for scant and stolen hours. With something of a shock, I realized that my spending had been spurred by this resentment. If I was going to be the kept woman in Jim's life, then by God, I was going to be kept in style.

"Well, you've always talked like it's a done deal," I said. "The big payoff is just around the corner. Isn't that what you've been saying forever?"

"I wouldn't have put in this kind of time if I didn't believe that. I've killed myself trying to make this company work, but I no longer know when or even if that will happen."

"What are you talking about?"

"Which part don't you understand?"

"You're suddenly saying you don't know if you can make NexPractice work?" I heard panic edge into my voice. "I have essentially been a single mother for all the years you've put into that venture. Now you're telling me it might all be for nothing?"

Jim was silent. I saw his jaw twitch.

"Well?" I demanded.

"Stephanie, I have done everything in my power to build this company. I have given it my whole life. Do you think I want to tell you it might not work?"

"Jim!" I heard myself becoming shrill with anxiety. "Failure is not an option after all this. It has to work."

My husband jammed his fists into the front pockets of his jeans and turned away. I followed him into the next room.

"Jim? Do you hear me? You have to make it work. Our family has sacrificed too much."

"Sacrificed? Isn't that a little over the top? Has this family wanted for a single thing?"

"Oh, just a husband and a father."

"Don't give me that," Jim said. "Don't I detail your car, don't I de-ice your windshield in the morning, don't I make you coffee before I leave and do a hundred other loving things despite the *very* long hours I work? Frankly, comparing yourself to a single mother is obscene."

"Those things are nice, Jim. But they aren't enough. I'm sorry, but you are *gone*. You just aren't in our lives anymore."

We stood there for a moment with this accusation hanging in the air between us. When I spoke again, I was fighting tears.

"You said you would never leave me," I said. "But you have. You've abandoned me in all the ways that matter. I feel completely alone."

Chapter 10

JIM AND I had breakfast in near-silence the next morning. We were at an impasse: I could not abide his working hours any longer, and he was in too deep to ease back. There was nothing left to say. While he sat at the kitchen table, I busied myself at the counter, pouring coffee, hovering over the toaster, not wanting to take the seat across from him.

The sky outside was still dark. It matched the color of my mood. I'd just locked the house behind me and was walking out to my car when I felt the buzz of my cell phone from within my purse. It was my mother.

"When are you coming to see me, Stephanie?" she asked fretfully. "My pain meds aren't working. I can barely get around the apartment, and I need Starbucks and cigarettes and herbs." By *herbs* I knew she meant marijuana. Nothing else ever seemed to bring her pain relief.

"I don't know when I can come, Mom," I said. "I'm not feeling well myself today."

"*Stephanie*," she said, in a tone of pure command. "Don't let me suffer like this! It's *cruel*. I need you."

"I'll get there when I can," I told her. "I just don't know if it'll be today."

But we both knew it would. She had said the magic words. She needed me.

—

IN MY CAR, going up and down the dial of its satellite radio stations, I stumbled across a channel titled *Broadway*, caught by the opening of a song I knew. I froze, remembering the last time I had heard the tune.

Years ago, I was sitting with my young sons in a children's theater in Portland, watching a local production of *Annie*. Listening to the opening lyrics of "Maybe," I was suddenly so awash in tears that I had to step out into the lobby.

To my boys, and probably to everyone else in the theater, the dream of being adopted by a loving family described in that song was pure entertainment, and hit no closer to home than Cinderella's desire to attend the ball. But to me, the orphans' longing for parents to love them and bring them home was achingly familiar and real.

My time in the Bertolini house had planted that seed—the seed of How Things Could Be, How Things *Should* Be. The dream of a small, cheerful, well-kept house. A sun-splashed kitchen and garden, bookshelves and rocking chairs and rag rugs, kindness and coziness and bedtime prayers. A mother and a father. Home.

IN THE DEPENDENT unit of Santa Rosa, the dream of a real home was impossibly distant, and yet occasionally it glimmered into view, like the North Star. Children disappeared from the place every week. They simply vanished, as Isabella had. There one day and gone the next.

Taken. Chosen. Plucked from the rabble, the rubble. When I tried to imagine where they had gone, I pictured a house like Mama and Papa Bee's, and I wished with all my might to be selected next.

Then one day it happened, just like that. I was in the yard, which wasn't a yard at all but a cement enclosure between two buildings, bordered on the other two sides by wire fencing. A wild game of dodgeball was underway, and I was cringing on the fringes of it, trying mostly to stay apart from the action, when there was a tap on my shoulder.

"Come with me," said one of the matrons who staffed the unit.

Mutely, I trailed her into the nearest building and down the hall to an office. My file was on the desk, along with the black trash bag I'd had to surrender upon my arrival. As promised that day, my doll was still inside. The matron sat down and stamped a release form.

"Stephanie Madera," she said, squinting at the top page. It was startling to hear my name from an employee after so many months. To remember I had a name at all. Then she pushed the black trash bag across the desk to me.

"You're out of here," she told me. "Somebody picked you."

Those shimmering words—*somebody picked you*—seemed to tamper with the air and sunlight as I followed the matron across the parking lot to where a social worker was waiting. *My* social worker, Adele, the soft-spoken and gentle one who had been in the police car with Isabella and me. She knelt down and put her arms around me, and I clung to her with all my strength.

"I'm so happy to see you again, Stephanie," she said into my hair. "I was so happy to hear the good news. A family wants you to come and live with them! A very nice family with other children for you to play with. Would you like that?"

I nodded, my face pressed against her neck, too pleased to speak, and too shy.

She opened the back door of her car, ushered me in, and fastened a seatbelt around me. Then we drove down the winding road, away from the dependent unit and onto the avenues of Santa Rosa, the matron's words still echoing in my ears. *Somebody picked you.* Oh, the joy of it!

I'd been chosen. I was wanted. I was going to a real home.

MY NEW FAMILY lived on Creekside Drive. I was enchanted by the sound of it. To me it sounded like something from a fairy tale. I pictured a mighty creek winding through a village, with charming houses along either side of it. I had never seen the residential canals of Venice or Amsterdam, or even pictures of them, but a similar image took hold in my imagination.

My hopes were high and yet, when the car pulled into their circular drive, the splendor of their house and yard left me breathless. There was an above-ground swimming pool—*a swimming pool*—and a lush garden filled with all kinds of vegetables: tidy rows of cherry tomato plants and purplish asparagus and mustard greens and rainbow chard. There were snap peas and kirby cucumbers. There were lavender cabbages that looked like roses. The herbs were clustered at the far end: cilantro and basil and dill and mint. Looking at it, I remembered helping Mama Bee in her garden and felt a surge of hope.

The whole family, it seemed, was standing in the yard, awaiting our arrival as if it were a special event. The woman was dark-haired and slender with a wholesome beauty. She wore a fitted white shirt and held a toddler in her arms. Next to her was a blond, blue-eyed boy who looked a little younger than me, as well as a dark-eyed girl about my age. The girl had blunt black bangs and wore a red dress.

"Hello, Stephanie," the woman said, her smile wide and warm. "We're so glad to have you with us. My name is Lorraine."

Adele squeezed my hand and gave me a little nudge toward her. I was too shy to speak but I smiled back at her, filled with an eager pleasure. Chosen.

"And this is Ted, your foster father," she said next, touching the arm of the tall man beside her.

Ted was sunburned and muscular, with curly blond hair, a chevron mustache, and deep crow's feet radiating from the corner of his eyes. "Hi there, honey," he said. He leaned down to me in a half-crouch, like a football player about to hike the ball. "Aren't you just the sweetest little thing."

I smiled at him in turn, unable to think of anything to say.

"Michael and Steven here are our own children," Lorraine continued. "And this," she touched the shoulder of the girl, "is Paige. Can you say hello to Stephanie, Paige?"

The girl tilted her head and regarded me without speaking.

"Paige came to us from the dependent unit, just like you," Lorraine told me.

Paige and I looked at each other. There was something unsettling about her eyes, huge and sunken and dark in her very pale face, that I didn't like. They didn't really focus but slid past me while these introductions were made. Her knees were scabbed and dirty, and her lips were fixed in a strange half-smile.

Adele suggested we go inside. "So Stephanie can see the house," she told Lorraine, "and we can take care of the paperwork."

Their living room was high-ceilinged and warm. The couch was upholstered in a floral-patterned fabric of orange and yellow and tan. An intricately carved wooden clock, shaped like a house, hung on one wall, and as we entered, a little wooden door swung open beneath its pitched roof. A tiny yellow bird emerged before my startled eyes, cooed twice, and went back into its hole before the door swung shut again.

Adele glanced down at me and smiled. "Have you ever seen a cuckoo clock before, Stephanie?"

I never had.

"Michael and Steven share a bedroom," Lorraine told me. "Stephanie, you and Paige will be sharing a bedroom too. Paige, do you want to show Stephanie your room?"

Paige grabbed my arm and tugged me toward the stairs.

The bedroom I would share with Paige was as plain as could be. There were two twin beds and a lamp and a dresser. That was it. No curtains or rug or art on the walls. No other furnishing or decoration of any kind.

The family cat wandered in. It was a beautiful animal, silvery gray with blue eyes like two cloudy marbles. With no warning, Paige yanked up her dress, ripped off her panties, and sat on the floor with her legs spread. "Here, kitty," she called.

The cat approached cautiously and spent several moments sniffing at the place between her legs while Paige squirmed and giggled.

"It tickles," she said. "The whiskers tickle."

I watched, cringing and transfixed, alarmed and faintly queasy at the sight.

"Want him to do it to you?" Paige asked.

I shook my head and backed away. She tilted her head up at me from the floor but again, her eyes slid past mine, darting back and forth without coming to rest on anything.

"It feels good," she urged. "Try it and you'll see."

I found my voice. "I don't want to."

She flipped her dress back down and straightened up, her panties still wadded in one white-knuckled fist.

The cat came over to me and I reached down to stroke its back. I wanted to pick it up and run with it, far away from Paige.

"Stephanie!" I heard Adele call. "Come give me a hug before I go."

With relief, I fled the room. Adele was standing at the bottom of the stairs. I went to her and she lifted me into her arms, holding me close for a precious fleeting instant.

Then she was gone, and the moment the door closed behind her, it was as if a chill blew through the house.

"All right, you two, clear out of here," Lorraine said to Paige and me. Her voice was flat and cold, her tone so different than it had been just a moment before. "I don't need you underfoot while I'm getting dinner. Go play outside."

SO BEGAN MY time in the house on Creekside Drive.

Lorraine was gentle and loving with her real children, Michael and Steven. She was harsh and impatient with Paige and me. Sometimes the two of us were allowed to eat with the family, but often we ate by ourselves in the kitchen while the family sat together in the dining room. The boys' room was decorated with a sports motif and filled with toys and games and bean bag chairs. Lorraine drenched them with affection. Very soon it was clear she had no use for us.

We were there for Ted.

On my second day in their house, he led me into the room he shared with Lorraine, stripped off his pants and boxer shorts, and lay back on the bed. The sight of his privates was dreadful and grotesque, like the fleshy red wattle dangling from a turkey's throat. There was an odor emanating from his crotch. He smelled unwashed and musty and pungent.

He put my hand on it—a live tensile thing, like an eel—and I jerked it away. With something like a growl, his fist closed hard around mine and he brought it back.

"Be a good girl," he said, his tone like a warning. "It's time you learned how to please a man."

He pried my fingers open, clamped my hand around the shaft of his penis, and forced it up and down. I gave up on resistance and did as he told me. "That's it," he said, letting his head fall back and closing his eyes. "Don't stop."

I moved my hand the way he wanted for what seemed like forever. After a while he pried my palm away again and spat on it—*spat on my hand*—before returning it to its task. This went on until his face screwed up and he emitted a terrifying moan. Then, shockingly, white stuff shot out of him in all directions, like a faucet gone haywire.

THIS ORDEAL AND countless variations on it happened over and over for the next eighteen months. Sometimes he brought Paige and me into his bed together and made us take turns while the other one watched. He made me use my hands and eventually my mouth.

Sometimes he came into our bedroom, into my bed, in the middle of the night. Eased open the door like an intruder. Stealthy. Silent. He didn't speak at these times, just put his hands all over my body, hands that eventually guided mine to the place between his legs. Always his rank and terrible breath was in my face, reeking of beer and tobacco chaw.

Once when Paige and I were with him in his bed, doing his bidding, the door opened without warning and Lorraine came in. She didn't seem shocked or even surprised. She looked exasperated, as if she were finding a mess in a room she had just cleaned. "Get the hell out of here, you little pissants," she said to Paige and me, as if we were to blame.

Sometimes at night, Ted would get me out of bed and bring me outside to his green Jeep. He lifted me into the back, not bothering with a seat belt, not bothering to speak. I lay across the seat and trembled as he drove way too fast up and down the hills of Santa Rosa, drinking Cutty Sark whiskey straight from the bottle, tilting his head back even as the car careened down the dark streets. After a while, I kept my eyes closed tight, haplessly sliding across the vinyl or tumbling onto the floor whenever he turned a corner.

I WAS EIGHT years old, but I started wetting the bed again that year, which enraged Lorraine.

"You little pissant, what's the matter with you? Even Steven doesn't wet the bed anymore and he's only three!" She slammed the pots and pans around in the sink. "The whole bedroom stinks like piss now. We paid a pretty penny for that mattress too, just a few months ago, and now it's ruined."

I stood staring at the linoleum. I was trying hard not to cry—Lorraine hated crying—but I couldn't stop my lower lip from quivering with shame.

Later that day, I heard one of the neighbors declare across the back fence, "You are an angel on this earth, Lorraine."

"Oh, I don't know about that," she murmured with a little laugh.

"Caring for these poor wards of the state like you do. It takes a special kind of person, that's all."

"Well, I don't know about special," Lorraine said in that low and honeyed tone. "But we have the room, Ted and I. In our house and in our hearts."

Her voice so soft and flowery, like a caress.

MY FAVORITE PLACE to be each afternoon was in the backyard with the animals. Every day I cleaned the chicken coop and scattered corn in the yard for them. I brushed Lorraine's horse and mucked out his stall and brought him fresh hay. I played with the cat, and the rabbits in their hutch.

I felt safe with the animals. The horse was old and gentle. He nuzzled me when I brushed him. The chickens rushed over when I came into the yard with their feed. The speckled one even liked to be snuggled. I stayed with them as long as I could, until Lorraine called everyone in to dinner.

The clock in the living room sounded every hour on the hour. It went off at breakfast and in the evening. It went off in the middle of the night. It never became less frightening to hear its urgent clanging and cooing in the darkness. That sound—mocking, mechanized, relentless—was the sound of savage misery.

For years afterward, I tried to fathom the mystery of Lorraine. Sleek, attractive, an accomplished gardener and equestrienne, a woman who appeared so workaday and reasonable, who had beloved children of her own. She knew just what her husband was doing, and she was fully complicit in bringing him the most vulnerable children, throwaway children, to sodomize. I eventually gleaned that Paige and I were not the first children they fostered. They returned to the dependent unit again and again over the course of many years, looking for children—children who were already broken, children with no recourse and no one to tell— to use.

I do all I can to forget Creekside Drive, but the memories still surface without warning. Not long ago, I was at the home of a friend who kept a flock of chickens in her backyard. We were sitting out on her patio, sharing a bottle of wine, when a speckled hen darted over. Without even thinking, I startled both my friend and myself by drawing the bird to me and snuggling it on my lap.

Once I had to leave a dinner party because the hosts had a cuckoo clock. I didn't notice it at first but during the cocktail hour I was standing with my husband and two other guests, a drink in my hand, when from a shelf high above I heard that lunatic sound, saw the little wooden door open and the bird pop out like a flasher revealing himself.

"Stephanie! What is it?" Jim asked. I turned to him with a stunned expression, wondering how he knew.

You went so pale, he told me later. *You know that saying "white as a ghost?" I didn't think people really turned pale like that. I never saw it happen before.*

I met his eyes, unable to answer, nausea breaking over me like a wave.

"Excuse us," my husband said swiftly, putting a hand on my back and ushering me through the throng of people. In the foyer he gently took my face in his hands.

"Are you all right?" he asked.

"I need to leave," I whispered.

Jim asked no questions, just retrieved my coat from the front closet and put it around my shoulders.

"I'm sorry to have to cut out so suddenly," I heard him saying to his associate. "I'm afraid my wife is ill."

AND NOW, on the way to my mother's apartment, I drove past an old-fashioned diner and suddenly another memory from that era came to me: the one of seeing my mother from Ted's Jeep. She was in the parking lot of a local Sambo's restaurant, wearing a waitress' uniform, a little white dress with an orange apron. There she was, casually at large, out of jail and apparently on her way to work. I had gasped but was borne past her before I even had time to cry out.

A year before, I'd have given anything to get away from her. But by the time I saw her from the window of that Jeep, I would have given anything to go back to her.

Seeing her left me feeling gutted. She was so near. She was free and on the streets. *Why didn't she come for me?*

I BARRELED INTO the parking lot of my mother's complex at high speed, turning the heads of all the tenants smoking inside the nearby gazebo. I threw the car into park, leaped out as if the vehicle were on fire, and burst through the front door of her apartment in a frenzy.

"*How could you?*" I howled.

My mother, who was lying on the sofa, bolted upright, a look of confusion and fright on her face. I'd woken her, perhaps from a deep sleep, the kind she rarely got these days.

"What? Stephanie? What happened?"

"*How could you leave me in that terrible place?*"

She blinked at me in bewilderment, but beneath her incomprehension, I thought I could see a certain caginess.

"What are you talking about?"

I dropped onto the sofa. It was all I could do not to take her bony shoulders in both my hands and shake her. "I saw you from the window of Ted's Jeep. In that Sambo's parking lot. You were going in to start your shift. You were right in Santa Rosa, not five miles away, and you had your own car. Why didn't you come and get me?"

"Oh, that." My mother sighed and looked away. "Listen, Stephanie, I wanted to. I tried. There were things I had to do to get you kids back, and I was doing all those things. I had to hold a steady job for six months. I had to test clean for drugs for six months. I had to get an apartment. If I didn't follow their rules, they just would have taken you again."

I turned away from her and my gaze fell on the prescription bottles littering her coffee table, the kitchen counter, and nearly every other available surface. Then I looked back at her wasted face: her hollow cheeks, the jutting prominence of her facial bones, her skull itself seeming to rise into relief before my eyes. My mother was going to die, she would die very soon, and all that was unresolved between us would be unresolved forever.

"You have no idea what it was like," I said more quietly now. Finally confronting her about the abuse had taken the rage out of me. "To be trapped in that house. To be violated, day after day."

"That's what you think," she said.

"What does *that* mean?"

"You think I don't know what it's like. What do you know about me, Miss High and Mighty? You have no idea who I am. I am a *direct descendant—*"

"Of George Washington," I said, cutting her off. "I've heard it all before, Mom. And there's a term for that. It's called *delusions of grandeur.*"

"You see?" she answered. "You don't believe me."

"No one believes you, Mom. You're always playing the George Washington card, every time you were arrested, whenever the chips are down. You never seem to get that no one's impressed. No one cares. Because it's bullshit."

"That's what you think," she said again. "But what do you know?"

"I know you aren't related to George Washington," I told her. "And I know you haven't been through half of what I have. I know you were never held captive in hell, trapped with sexual predators, used as a plaything by sick people, when you were just a little girl."

Abruptly it was very quiet in her apartment. There was a charged and wild hush, as when a storm is gathering and the air is electric and still.

My mother's eyes met mine. The expression on her face was like none I'd ever seen before. There was no trace of Agnes, no trace of Flow. There was no one but her. She looked at me steadily, without a trace of crazy, her eyes as clear and penetrating as a prophet's.

"You're mistaken," she said.

Chapter 11

I FELT SUDDENLY cold, there on my mother's sofa. The skin prickled on the back of my neck, and I crossed my arms against the chill.

"What are you talking about, Mom?"

"I never told you what happened to me."

I waited. When she said nothing further, I asked, "Well? What happened?"

"I was raped."

"You did tell me, Mom. It was by the dumpster outside the apartment you shared with Louie. You told me that story a lot. You even told me the rapist was my father."

"That's not the time I'm talking about."

Again I waited. Again she was silent.

"Were you raped another time?" I finally asked.

"Yes."

"When?"

The same electric storm warning was in the air. The space between us was almost vibrating with portent. My mother's lips were quivering. I saw a tremor in her hands and knees.

"I was just eleven. Just a little girl on roller skates. It was a beautiful summer day. I was skating outside with my cousin when some men grabbed us and threw us into their car."

I sat there as stunned as if she had bashed me in the face with a rock.

"Really?" I managed after a long moment.

"Yes," she said. "They took us to a building, and I didn't see her again after that. They brought me up the stairs to a room with no windows.

There were so many of them. Fifteen of them. They kept me there a long time."

I stared at her. She looked straight back at me, as clear-eyed and lucid as she'd ever been.

"How long?" I asked after a moment.

"Ten days."

"*Ten days?*" I heard my voice scale up an octave.

"They took turns. They did terrible things to me. Things I never wanted to think about again. Look what you're doing, you're forcing me to think about them. It's so *cruel*."

"Mom! I'm not forcing—"

"The mayor's son was there," she said, cutting me off.

I choked back an incredulous laugh. "The mayor's *son*? Really?"

"They were powerful men, society men. They had ties to the mob."

The mention of the mob, the mayor, and these so-called powerful men brought a moment of relief. This was—this *had* to be—another one of her delusions.

"Mom," I said shakily. "This sounds pretty crazy to me."

"I didn't think you would believe me," she said.

And you were right, I thought.

"Well, how did you get free?" I asked, trying to keep the skepticism from my tone. "I mean, what ended this ordeal?"

"An Indian was there. He saved me."

"An Indian? Do you mean a man from India, or a Native American?"

"An American Indian. He kept me alive the whole time, in fact."

"How?"

"It was the way he looked at me. His face was so full of compassion. And he tended to me whenever he could. He was my angel in that pit of hell."

This settled it: another delusion.

"Mom, this sounds like a bad acid trip. I think it must have been a very vivid hallucination."

"I knew you wouldn't believe me," she said again. "Well, go look it up then. You'll see. It was all over the news. It was a huge scandal."

"What news? Where?"

"In Baltimore. When I was eleven. It was in all the papers."

She put her head back against the armrest of the couch and closed her eyes.

WHEN I GOT back into my car, I sat there for at least five minutes with my head against the steering wheel. There was no way my mother's story was true. The terrible images she had conjured left me sick and shaken anyway. My own daughter was eleven.

Why did I keep coming to see her, every time she summoned me? Sometimes it took days to recover. With something like desperation, I reached for my phone to text my "good mother," my Mama Mae, the one who loved me.

I know this is short notice, I typed to her. *But is there any chance you're around this afternoon? I'm going through a rough time right now and it always helps to talk with you.*

Come right over, my sweet girl, she wrote back immediately. *I'll make you lunch and we'll eat on the back deck. It's been too long since I've seen your beautiful face.*

My eyes welled with gratitude as I put the key in the ignition.

"I'M SO GLAD you're here," Mae said, leaning across the table to push a strand of hair back behind my ear. As promised, we were on the deck overlooking her lovely backyard. It was so tranquil here, so serene. "I couldn't believe it when you texted. Owen and I were talking about you not one hour before! He says you're almost done with his house and, well, maybe I shouldn't repeat this, but he told me he'll miss you when you're done."

"It's been great for me too," I said. I found it hard to meet Mae's eyes just then and looked away instead.

"Oh, I shouldn't say this, I know I shouldn't," she continued. "But

Steph, honey, I can't help wishing for a daughter-in-law just like you. Even though I know I'm pining for the impossible. You're happily married, after all."

"Not so happily lately," I heard myself say.

"Will you tell me what's going on? You look positively haunted."

I looked away again, afraid I was going to cry uncontrollably. Mae's love affected me that way.

"Is it your mother?"

I brought my gaze back to Mae and nodded.

"I just don't know how she can torment you so," she said softly. "I would be so proud to have a daughter like you. She doesn't know how lucky she is."

"I wish I had never let her rope me back in," I told her. "The most peaceful years of my life were after the court issued a stalking order against her. She wasn't allowed to contact me. I never should have let her violate it."

"I didn't know you had a stalking order against her," Mac said. "Oh my goodness. When was this? What brought it about?"

It began with a call from my son's high school office.

"Mrs. Plymale?" the secretary said. "A woman who says her name is Flo is here to pick up Jeremy."

In the background, I could hear my mother's strident voice. "I'm taking him to the dermatologist because his mother won't do it!" she was ranting. "She's nothing but a selfish bitch, content to let her own son walk around with hideous red craters all over his face."

She was referring to Jeremy's case of mild acne, no more than was typical for any teen.

"That poor boy was so handsome and his good looks are ruined!" I heard her yelling. "All because of her!"

"Do not, under any circumstances, let him leave with her," I said, alarmed. "She is mentally unstable and dangerous. Please call the police."

I had already risen from my desk at work. I was reaching for my keys. "I will pick him up," I told the school secretary. "Do *not* let her anywhere near him."

The school day had just ended when I arrived on the street flanking the right side of the building. Kids were still streaming out the door. Jeremy was standing out front, next to the assistant principal. I hurried over to them.

"We called the police," she told me. "They came and told Jeremy's grandmother that she couldn't be on school grounds. She's across the street right now." And she pointed to the opposite sidewalk, where my mother was sitting cross-legged on the ground. Even from this distance I could see that her mouth was drawn down in a deep scowl and feathers were sticking out of her hair.

Jeremy looked at me with tears in his eyes. "The freaking cops were here because of her," he said hoarsely. "A couple of the other kids were in the office when she was here, and now they'll probably tell the whole school. Why would she do this to me, Mom? This is the worst day of my life."

"I'm so sorry, honey," I said, tears pricking at the corners of my own eyes. This was my fault somehow. I had failed to protect my son from her.

I put my arm around his shoulders and ushered him off to the side of the building, where my car was waiting at the curb. I did not look in my mother's direction. She was still sitting on the sidewalk as I put my car in gear and drove away.

Soon afterward the phone calls began. They came at all hours. In the afternoon, in the evening, in the middle of the night. I don't have words for the terror of those phone calls. Even now, recalling them, my mouth goes dry, and I can feel my blood pressure spiking.

How dare you ignore me at Jeremy's school? I was just trying to help him. I was there to take him to the doctor since you're too selfish to take him yourself. And you treated me like I was nothing, like I'm nobody, like I wasn't even there!

The voice was Flow's. Low and venomous. Almost purring with malice. On, as she would say, the warpath.

You've always thought you were better than me. I don't know what happened to you, Stephanie. You used to be such a sweet little girl. But now you're ruined. Money ruined you. Jim ruined you. He turned you against me and now you've turned my grandson against me.

Whenever I saw her name on the caller I.D., I would feel myself quivering like a rabbit in a trap. I had an urge to hide, even inside my own house. Sometimes, like a child, I would put my hands over my ears. I always let these calls go to voicemail. The messages just piled up, each one more unhinged than the last.

You think you can get away from me so easily? Think you can just discard me like I'm trash? You'd best think again, you traitorous little bitch. I'm coming for you and I'm going to kill you. You'll be thankful to go to hell to get away from me. I'll burn your house down while everyone in it is asleep, and I'll haunt you even after I'm dead!

After this last dispatch, Jim called the police, and they came to the house. They listened to my mother's messages and drove directly across town to arrest her.

"Good God," murmured Mae. "I can't fathom this insanity. My poor baby girl. What happened after that?"

"She was charged with criminal threats and with stalking me. Both are felonies in the state of Oregon. The police advised me to take out a stalking order against her, and the judge set a court date to hear that request. In the meantime, she was in jail for a month."

"That must have been a relief," Mae said. "And then what happened?"

"The judge granted us a stalking order right away. Another witness had come forward by then. My mother tried to get a pawn shop owner to sell her a gun, and she left crazy messages on his machine too. He played them in court."

I need to kill my daughter, she had told the man. *She's possessed by an evil spirit and killing her is the only way to get rid of it.*

The judge finalized the stalking order on the spot, and on my way out of the courtroom, the bailiff stopped me. With tears in his eyes, he begged me to never let it lapse.

"But you did," Mae said gently.

"She called me after being locked up for six months, pleading for forgiveness. She said, *I'm sorry, I don't know what happened. I was hearing voices and they were telling me crazy things.* She had never—and I mean *never*—apologized to me before, not once in my entire life."

"And you forgave her."

"I did. I couldn't help myself. I wanted to believe her," I said. And then I added what to me was the saddest, most shameful revelation of all— proof, I was sure, of a pathology even deeper than hers. "You see, even then, I still loved her. All my life, I've always loved her. No matter what."

Chapter 12

I FELT A little better after seeing Mae, as I always did. But I was still shaken by my mother's story, and suddenly I longed above all to talk about it with Jim.

The truth is that by then, Jim and I hadn't really talked in months. But he was still the only one I could see myself telling. He knew my mother. He knew my history. I was anxious to hear what he'd make of her story. However, Jim was at a trade show in Florida, and he would be gone all week. I could call, of course, but it wasn't the kind of thing I wanted to tell him over the phone.

Feeling forlorn, I wandered into his home office and snapped on the light. Suddenly I was struck by the gloom of the space. The hunter-green walls. The black leather chair. The photos he liked but hadn't gotten around to framing, piling up and gathering dust on his desk. The plain tan settee against one wall, unadorned with any accent pieces.

If nothing else, I thought, *I should repaint the walls.* That would brighten the room at least a little, even if it still retained the low-lit ambience of an opium den. I'd get rid of this dreary green and replace it with some warm and uplifting color.

And his desk. I'd never liked that desk: modern and black and expansive, its width almost spanning the room. Jeremy could have it. I'd bring in something rustic—walnut maybe. The tan settee would still work, but I'd find some pillows or a throw to add a splash of color, make it more inviting. And I'd find nice frames for some of those photos.

I worked in a fever all week, as if something essential were at stake. It made me feel good after all these months of resentment to do something loving for Jim. It hurt my heart to suddenly notice that his space was so devoid of warmth or cheer. I brought so much love and attention to other people's spaces. Why not to my own husband's?

By Thursday, it was done. The somber green of the walls was gone, replaced by a shade called "Tuscan Sunset." The monolith of a black desk was gone, and a new one of hewn walnut was in its place. I'd taken seven or eight of the best photographs—Jim with the kids, Jim and I by the Seine, Jim with his softball team—and found the right frame for each one. Several of them were grouped on his desk, a few stood on the shelves, and I'd hung the rest in a gallery on his walls. There was a new hand-knotted Persian rug in deep red and caramel, and several textured throw pillows were now scattered along the settee.

When the room was finished, I stood in the doorway, filled with anticipation. I did this kind of thing for clients all the time, of course, but the gratification went deeper when it was for Jim. It seemed to me that I should have done this long before I did. Maybe it would renew the sense of closeness between us that had been gone for so long.

My husband came home just after nine that Friday night, looking as tired as I'd ever seen him. He dropped his bags just beside the front door and sank onto the living room sofa.

"Hey, stranger," I said, coming over to him. "Welcome home."

"Thank you," he said. He kissed me briefly, a kiss very unlike the hungry and lingering ones I used to get after he'd been gone awhile.

"Is everything okay?" I asked. "You seem down."

"I'm so beat after this week," he told me. "I'm ready to just crash, honestly. I'll unpack in the morning."

"That's fine," I said. "But first I have a surprise for you."

"A surprise?"

"Come," I beckoned, motioning for him to follow me.

Gamely, he trailed me to the door of his office, where I had him close his eyes. Then, I led him to the center of the room and told him he could look. He opened his eyes and just stood there. I laughed at his stunned expression.

"Well?" I asked. "What do you think?"

"Seriously?" he asked.

I laughed again. "Won't it be so much nicer to work in here now?"

He ran his hand through his hair, rubbed his eyes. "I mean . . . are you kidding me, Steph?"

"Do you like it?" I asked eagerly. "I made it my project for the week."

He continued to look around, dumbfounded.

"You know what, Jim?" I asked. "We've been so distant. I wanted to do something nice for you. Something loving."

"Is that the story you're telling yourself?" Jim asked. "That you did all this for *me*?"

Abruptly the breath left my body. It was my turn to be stunned.

"Jim?" I ventured after a long moment. "Are you saying you don't like it?"

"It's not that I don't like the new look," he said. "It's okay, I guess. What I don't like is your unilateral decision to spend thousands of dollars —because I'm sure that's what all this cost—on yet *another* unnecessary renovation that I didn't ask for and had no need of. I mean, you can't tell me all this wasn't a ton of money."

I felt my throat close over.

"I feel like this is an ambush," he said. "You do this yet again, but this time it's *for me*, so if I fail to be happy about it then I'm just an ingrate and a bastard. It makes me furious, to be honest. I'm sorry, but that's the truth."

My eyes filled and spilled over. I felt so crushed I couldn't speak.

"This is a compulsion on your part," he went on. "You just can't stop, you're never done, and the bills just stack up higher and higher. It's like you think you can fix every problem with a new coat of paint and a bunch of different furniture, and an endless influx of freaking *pillows*. I hate to break it to you, but that's not the way it works."

I heard myself start to sob. After a moment, I sank down along the doorframe and sat crying on the floor. No matter how angry Jim ever became with me, he would always soften when I cried. But not this time.

He just stood there looking at me. His expression was cold, detached and implacable.

I drew my knees up to my chest and covered my face with my hands. Jim stood a moment before leaving the room without another word. I heard him return to the sofa and sink back down into the spot where he'd been before.

WHEN I WOKE up the next morning, my whole body hurt. The ache in my throat felt permanent, as if it would never be dislodged. The room was cold and I was cold. I huddled beneath the covers. Jim was already gone. He'd left without a word to me, without even kissing my forehead as he always did.

Only the thought of Owen pulled me out of bed. Today we would be doing the last few rooms in his house. After today, my time with him would be over.

As I drove to his home, I brooded over the evening before, easily the worst night in my three decades of marriage.

JIM HAD NOT spoken to me again. Despite his stated intention of going to bed early, he remained on the sofa for at least another hour, eyes fixed on the television. He stared at a news segment, then the tail end of a baseball game, and finally the middle of a murder mystery. I could tell he was taking none of it in. It was just a way to avoid me.

Before she went to bed, our daughter Andrea came down from her bedroom and hugged him. He hugged her back without really looking at her. "Hi, sweetheart," he said. "I've had a tough week and I just want to sit here for a little while. I'll see you in the morning, okay?"

"No worries," Andrea said. I waited until I heard the door of her room close behind her and then positioned myself directly in front of the TV, my face still stained with tears.

"Look at you," I flung at him. "Look at the way you've totally checked out of being a husband and father. There's always a good reason. You're exhausted. Wiped out from a trip or back-to-back all-nighters at the office or your third-quarter push or whatever it is on any given week. You have nothing left for us. You can't even receive a loving gesture with any grace or engage with your daughter after a whole week away from her."

Jim didn't even meet my eyes. He rose from the sofa and, once again, left the room.

I stayed downstairs, crying, pacing the floor, and finally going to our liquor cabinet in search of comfort. Just one glass. Just to take the edge off. Just so I had some hope of sleeping that night.

It turned out to be no help at all.

THE MOMENT I pulled my truck to the curb outside Owen's house, he appeared on the front walk. "Hey!" he called, a grin lighting his face. "Am I glad to see you. It feels like it's been forever."

It had only been a week. The same amount of time Jim had been gone on his trip.

Owen was clad in denim pants that fit him very well. His immaculate white t-shirt emphasized the natural tan he somehow had in midwinter. He smelled so clean, like shaving soap and sunlight.

He helped me unload all that I'd brought from the truck, handling everything with ease in his usual offhand, competent way. I couldn't help smiling to myself whenever his back was turned. No matter how bleak things were at home, Owen always managed to make me feel good. He was like a happy, rollicking circus bear.

A light snow was falling as we brought everything inside. I'd set aside the entire day for this, and the thought of the next eight or nine hours was a lovely flutter inside me. The sight of the snow filled me with joy as well. Nothing was more romantic to me than a deep snowfall.

That I was allowing Owen to be here at all was highly unusual. Usually, I never wanted a client around while I was overhauling a space.

The work was loud and often messy, the process could be unpredictable, and it was pointless and stressful to have them on the premises. It also ruined the reveal at the end, my favorite moment of a renovation: when all the elements were in place, when everything was pristine and perfect, and I finally had the chance to dazzle my client.

Owen was different. It was like we were a team, and a seamless one. With him to help, I didn't even need a contractor. He was a highly skilled jack-of-all-trades, and together we tackled each room in turn, measuring, cutting, laying down carpet, hanging up artwork, and assembling furniture. We found a rhythm early in the day, and the hours flew by as we worked and bantered and jousted and flirted.

Spanish guitar was playing on his sound system, and the flamenco strains were like yearning itself. As the afternoon waned, the sky went periwinkle, and the sparse snow took on heft and intensity. The bare branches of the trees outside were dusted and then lined and then laden with snow. The flakes seemed to blossom into something like white flowers—clustered together and slapdash and voluptuous. Snow filled the air and covered the ground.

"Man, is this beautiful or what?" Owen asked.

I stared out the window. It was impossibly beautiful. I felt a deep pang at the beauty and impossibility in front of me.

"This makes me want to break out the wine," he said. "Let's see if I still have a bottle of your favorite somewhere."

"You don't mean the Cobos?" I asked.

"That's the one."

I raised an eyebrow at him. "You just happen to have another one around?"

"*Well . . .*" he grinned at me. "I might have picked another one up for today. This being the grand finale and all."

I turned away so he wouldn't see my pleasure at this confession.

"Now that's hospitality," was all I said.

Owen disappeared, and from the floor just below, I could hear the sound of a popping cork. A moment later he was back with the bottle and two glasses.

We were in the master bedroom, where there was only the California king-size bed. No sofas, no chairs. He put the glasses on one of the night tables and sat on the edge of the bed to fill them each halfway.

"To you and me," he said, raising his glass. "A kick-ass team."

"I'll drink to that."

The wine was like velvet. He drained half his glass and set it back down. Then he lay back on the bed and laced his hands behind his head. I watched his biceps swell into hard knots and had to look away again.

"It looks good in here," he told me. "You know, you make every room look good just by being in it."

I closed my eyes, overwhelmed by how much I wanted this. All of it: the snow, the wine, the music, all the trappings of romance and seduction. A man who *looked* at me. A man who was excited to see me, who took pains to prepare for my arrival. How long had it been? What was Jim doing right now in his office at work? Did he even know it was snowing? Did he care? He had become soulless, mercenary, dead-eyed. I didn't want to go home to him.

"These roads are gonna be bad soon," Owen said.

I glanced out at the street. "They'll be okay," I said. "For me, anyway. I have four-wheel drive." I didn't need any reason to leave earlier than planned.

"Yeah, but when the hill coming into this complex gets iced over like it does, you'd still do better to stay off it."

"It sounds like you're saying I should leave now," I said, hoping I didn't sound as disappointed as I felt.

"Oh lord," Owen said. "Please don't let me be misunderstood. I was thinking just the opposite."

I tilted my head in bewilderment. "That I should wait until it gets worse?"

"That you should stay," he said. He sat up, smiled and extended his hand to me. "Stephanie. I'm just gonna go for it: Why don't you stay?"

Chapter 13

I STARED AT Owen. "What do you mean?" I asked after a long moment, though his meaning was clear enough.

"Don't go home. Stay with me tonight."

"But you have a girlfriend," I said, flustered.

"Not really. I've dated her a few times. It's nothing serious. I don't think of her as my girlfriend and I've never actually called her that."

"Well, your mom calls her that," I said, as if this were the central issue and not just one of countless things wrong here. After all these weeks of dancing on the edge of what was between us, Owen's directness was a surprise. I didn't yet know how I felt or what I would do. I was stalling for time.

"So that's her word, not mine," Owen said. "I mean, with no disrespect to my mom, I don't give her a running commentary on my social life. She sees me with the same woman a few times, and in her mind, we're an item. But I don't see her in my future, to be honest."

"Why not?"

"She's a party girl," he said. "You know. Likes to drink and have a good time, but there's not much going on beyond that. That's fun for a little while, but in the long term? I want a woman with direction." He paused before adding: "Someone like you."

I looked away. "Okay, but I have a husband."

"Yeah," Owen said. "Well, that I can't argue with. Does he know how lucky he is?"

"I don't know anymore," I said slowly. "I mean . . . things haven't been good lately. I'll say that much. I'll admit it: I'm tempted. But . . ."

Owen rose from the edge of the bed and cupped my face. I closed my eyes, overcome by the touch of his hand. Then I felt him leaning in, and I leapt back.

"Wait!" I cried, putting a hand up to keep him at bay. "Wait."

He stepped back and held up his own hands, as if to show he was unarmed. "Steph," he said gently. "Chill. Nothing's going to happen unless you want it to happen."

"I just—" I said. "This is too fast. I've never done this. I mean, I've never been with another man."

"In all the time you've been married?"

"In all my life."

"*What?*"

"It's true," I said.

Owen looked stunned. "How is that possible? Like. . . not even in high school or college?"

"I've been with Jim since high school. Since my sophomore year. We got married just after graduation."

"*Why?*" Owen asked. "Were you pregnant?"

"No! Nothing like that."

He shook his head, amazed. "Again, why? Were you raised crazy religious or something?"

"Ha. No. Nothing could be further from the truth."

"Then I don't get it," Owen told me. "You were so sure he was the one, and you just couldn't wait to be tied down for life?"

"It's hard to explain."

He cocked an eyebrow at me. "I've got all night."

I stood looking at him for a moment. How could he ever understand? He was Mae's son.

"Well," I said at last. "Essentially I wanted to be the opposite of my mother. I grew up watching her sleep with so many different men. I wanted my life to be nothing like hers. I wanted . . ." I trailed off.

"You wanted what?"

"To be pure."

The word hung in the air like a warning before he spoke again.

STEPHANIE THORNTON PLYMALE

"But I mean, how do you know if it's even any good with him?" Owen asked. "If you have nothing to compare it to?"

"I *don't* know," I said. "I never had the experiences most people have. Dating and different relationships and all that."

"Don't you ever wonder what it would be like with someone else?"

"Of course I do," I said. I felt my eyes fill with tears.

"Hey," he said. "Come here. I just want to hold you for a minute. Nothing else, I promise."

Slowly I moved to the bed. He put his arms around me and pulled me close. I rested my head on his shoulder, breathing in the faint fragrance of his clean shirt and his sweat. His scent intoxicated me.

"You're a beautiful woman," he said. "Let me show you how good it can be. I won't expect you to stay afterward. I mean, I know you can't and I get that. But let me make love to you."

All my life I had read about these moments in stories, watched them in movies. Where there was a friendship between a man and a woman, a friendship that had nowhere else to go because of some barrier that separated them. Sometimes the barrier had to do with religion or color or class, or marriage to someone else, or some ancient family grudge. In each of these stories, the moment always arrived when it was no longer enough to keep them apart.

I loved these moments in other people's stories. I never thought I would have one of my own, because I wouldn't allow it. No one was more loyal than me. *I* wanted to be pure.

I hated the word *purity*. It sounded priggish and prudish and regressive and sexist. But I didn't judge anyone else's choices. My friends' romantic decisions were nothing like mine, and that was fine with me. I just wanted, as I'd told Owen, a life that was unlike my mother's in every way, and to me that had always meant doing the opposite of all she had done.

Yet here it was. It was happening to me. I wished there were a way to pause the scene so I could just be inside it for a moment. I wanted to bask in it, breathe it in, so I'd never forget how it felt.

But this wasn't a movie. It was real life—*my* life. There was no slowing it down, no pause button, only Owen putting a hand on the back of my neck, bringing his mouth near mine once again. And this time when I twisted away, there was no turning back.

"No. I can't," I said in a sudden panic, almost tripping in my rush to get away.

"Steph."

"I'm sorry, Owen. I can't. I have to go now."

Owen sighed. He looked out the window, where the snow was still falling hard and fast.

"Baby, it's cold outside," he said, making me laugh even now, through my tears, as I bolted for the door.

OUTSIDE THERE WAS a hush to match the way I felt. Everything was muffled by the heavy snow. The streets were still and the sky was an otherworldly violet. The snow swirled around me and showered down in the sepia glow of the streetlamps.

It took hours to get home. The roads were as bad as Owen said they would be. Traffic all along the highway was at a near standstill as the cars inched along the road, swerving and skidding on treacherous patches of ice. My truck was equipped to handle these conditions, but I was stuck in the crawl.

On a regular evening, I would have found this maddening, but tonight I was grateful for the time. I'd come so close to stepping over the kind of line I swore I'd never cross. I was shaken and anxious, and yet my anger at Jim still flared and smoldered like a glowing pile of ash. I was so starved for connection, for affection, that it was making me into someone else, someone I'd promised myself I would never be.

When I stepped inside the house, it was as if I'd never left. Jim was in the same spot on the sofa, changing channels on the TV. He didn't even look away from the screen as he asked, "Where have you been?"

"I was finishing an installation at Owen's," I told him.

"I see," he said coldly. Owen had long been a fraught topic between my husband and me. It was as if Jim could sense the way I felt about him. "Well, nice of you to come home."

"You're right, it is," I said. "I almost didn't."

Now Jim turned his head to look at me over his shoulder. "What?"

"You heard me."

I pulled off my boots and left them by the door.

"I heard you but I don't understand."

"Then let me spell it out for you," I said. "Owen didn't want me to leave tonight. He invited me to stay there. I was very tempted to accept."

Jim snapped off the television and rose from the sofa to face me. Finally, it seemed, I had his full attention. He stared at me for a long moment before he spoke again. "You considered cheating on me?"

"I would hardly consider it cheating at this point," I said. "This relationship is dead. You're no longer a husband to me in any way and you haven't been for a long time."

"Whoa," Jim said. "Just—whoa. Are you out of your mind? I don't think you have any idea what you're saying."

"Oh, I do," I said. "Whether or not you believe it is another matter. But I know just what I'm saying, and I mean every word."

"Then maybe you don't understand what marriage is," Jim told me. "I mean, yes, things between us have been tough lately. Very tough. But in marriage, you take each other for better or worse. So no matter how angry you might be right now, or how angry you've made me, I'm still your husband and you're still my wife."

"Not for long," I said.

"What the hell does that mean?"

"It means we're finished, Jim. It's over. I've tried so hard, so many times, to talk about all this with you, and I'm tired of talking. I'm done." I hung up my coat, closed the closet, and turned to face my husband. "I'm leaving you."

Chapter 14

"STEPHANIE," JIM SAID. "What are you saying?"

"Which part don't you understand? I. Am. Leaving. You."

"You can't leave."

"Oh, I most certainly can."

"We're *married*," Jim said, as if genuinely puzzled.

"Which means I'll be filing for *divorce*."

"What about the kids?"

"What about them? Josh and Jeremy are out of the house. Andrea and I are used to having you gone all the time. I think it'll be a relief to everyone if we stop pretending you're a part of our daily lives."

Jim stared at me in disbelief. I stared back, calm and defiant.

"You're serious," he said. "I can't believe this. You're actually serious. Aren't you?"

"As the day is long."

"Okay, well, you're being insane. This is histrionic and over the top and honestly very hurtful. I get that you've been unhappy. I get that I haven't been accessible to you. We've gone through a really rough stretch this past year; I won't deny that. But Steph, good God, we've been together for decades. You're going to just throw it all away because of a tough year? It's obscene that you'd make a threat like that."

———

WE WERE UP for hours. Accusing and denouncing, blaming and berating, we raged and fought and cried for most of that terrible night.

"There's no way I could be lonelier by myself than I am in this marriage," I told Jim at one point. "I'm not going to live this way anymore. I still have half my life ahead of me. I'm not going to turn gray and die with a man who never takes his eyes off the money, who never comes home. Not because of a promise I made as a freaking teenager. I was nineteen years old, for God's sake. Not even old enough to drink."

"You were old enough to know what love was," Jim countered.

"You want the terrible truth, Jim? I don't even know if I loved you," I said. "What did I know about love? I was fifteen and totally alone in the world. I'd suffered so much trauma by then that I probably would have given myself to anyone who wasn't abusive. I mean, why get married right out of high school, who does that? I was just desperate for a clean, stable life."

"Well, you got that," Jim said. "You got what you wanted. Yes, we were young, probably too young to know what we were doing, but as it happens, it worked out."

"For you, maybe."

"But not for you? Stephanie, look around. Can you honestly tell me this hasn't worked out for you?"

"I cheated myself out of the most exciting years of life," I said. "When I was young and pretty and had no real responsibilities yet. I should have been out dancing and flirting and dating. I should have let myself have more romantic experiences before tying myself down for life."

"I didn't have those things either," Jim said. "Don't you think the same holds true for me? Don't you think it might have been fun for me to be a twenty-something guy who was tall and decent-looking? Making good money and driving a nice car?"

"You're still tall and decent-looking," I told him. "You're still making good money and driving a nice car. It's not too late! Go make up for everything you missed. Really, go have fun—if you even remember how."

"I don't want to," he said. "You're all I've ever wanted. That was true in my twenties and it's true now. I don't care what I might have missed."

"Well, I do."

I saw pain etch itself into Jim's face but it barely registered. I was saying terrible things and I knew it, but I couldn't make myself stop.

"Your family has never truly loved me as their own," I added. "That's another thing. Even after all these years, it's like I'm still on the outside, looking in. Your mother has never made me feel like a daughter."

"Oh, really?" Jim said. "Well, here's a little news flash: Your family isn't such a great prize either."

This brought me up short. There was no way to argue with that one.

"But you know what?" he went on. "I didn't marry you for your family. I married you for you."

And on it went. It felt dreadful on one level, and on another it undeniably felt good. As painful as it was to say these things out loud, as hard as it was to survey the wreckage of our marriage, I finally felt seen and heard and considered and unburdened, and I wasn't going back.

Toward morning, I went back out to my truck and drove away. I was desperate for sleep, but I knew I wouldn't be able to get any in the bed I shared with Jim. I wasn't prepared to face the weekend in our house in the wake of this mayhem. I wasn't yet ready to tell the kids, but nor did I have it in me to plaster a smile on my face and pretend nothing was wrong.

At four a.m. I pulled up to the Heathman Hotel in downtown Portland and handed my keys to the valet. Twenty minutes later, in a room high above the snowy streets, I drew the drapes closed and didn't wake up until late afternoon.

I DIDN'T LEAVE the room all weekend. I slept. I ordered room service. I cried. I sat by the window and watched the street. I imagined the second half of my life, the one without Jim.

It was easy to feel empowered at the house, with Jim following me around, begging and reproaching and remonstrating with me. Here at the Heathman, it was very quiet. Jim wasn't calling my cell. He wasn't texting.

I tried to imagine what was going on at the house. My rare absence would force him to be the primary parent for the weekend. I knew Jim would never let on to Andrea that anything was wrong. He'd be acting as if all were as usual. He'd drive her to the mall and pick up a pizza for dinner and invent some reason I wasn't there.

The silence and solitude of the hotel room were an unspeakable relief. I lay on the bed and watched the snow, much lighter now but still falling from the pearly sky. I imagined breaking this news to all of our children. Jim would never pretend a separation had been mutual. We could not trot out any script about how we loved each other very much but had reached a point in our lives where we both thought it best to live apart. I would be the villain, the one who left. I didn't know if the kids would forgive me or how this would affect them.

My main concern wasn't for Josh or Jeremy. They would surely be upset, but they were grown men. They weren't the ones who would be spending the next several years traveling back and forth between my place and his. Nor would they be navigating the daily havoc of our emotions as we each adjusted to single life after several decades spent together.

It was Andrea I worried about. She was still a child. She would be crushed by a divorce.

Jim had a special bond with Andrea. As reluctant and skeptical as he'd been at the prospect of adopting another child, he had given his whole heart to her from the moment she arrived.

I hadn't thought about that chapter of our lives for a very long time. It had been so fraught, so torturous, so filled with angst and anxiety and uncertainty. Once our new baby was safely in our home, I wanted to put the whole experience out of my mind and never think about it again.

Here in the hotel room, lying alone on that king-sized bed, I found myself letting the memory float up from the depths. Of all that Jim and I had been through together, Andrea's adoption was the most harrowing. It was a path I felt compelled to pursue, but my husband had found himself on it for no reason other than love for me.

———

THE DREAM OF giving a little girl the life I never had was always there.

Before I spoke it aloud. Even before I'd fully articulated it to myself. It was there when I was pregnant and when I wasn't. It would have been there even if one of those pregnancies had given me a girl. It was ancient and immutable. Sometimes it receded but it never left.

I was drawn to stories about the plight of female children around the world. The baby girls drowned at birth in China by their own mothers, because each family was allowed no more than one child, and boys were considered more desirable. The girls throughout the world who would undergo genital mutilation against their will. The three out of four girls in Niger who would be child brides, given in marriage to adult men long before they were adults themselves. There were so many ways for girls to suffer, so many ways for their lives to be foreclosed. Out of the path of that all-devouring tsunami, I would take one.

Where had this dream come from? It would be decades before I would associate it with myself, with my own past, in any way. It had just been inside me for as long as I could remember, like my own heartbeat.

Jim didn't share this dream. To him, our family was already complete. Our sons were the treasure of his heart, and they were enough. We'd been out of the baby phase for a long time, so long that it was hard for him to imagine starting it all—the diapering and bottle-feeding and daytime naps—again.

"I'm done," he told me often.

"I'm not," I would say.

Determined, I looked at foster and adoption sites—domestic and foreign. I discovered early that the temporary nature of foster care frightened me. To fall in love with a child and have to give her up, as Mama Bee had with me? I remembered how she'd howled when my mother came to take me away. The way she sank to the floor as if unstrung. I understood her agony now. I couldn't risk it.

I was afraid, too, of an open adoption, which was so encouraged within the U.S. I didn't want to share my daughter with a stranger. I imagined having to cultivate a lifelong relationship with a woman like my mother. I imagined having to explain her decisions, her whims, her state of mind to the child I might want above all to protect from her. I imagined the lifelong fear that she would not show up for visits, that she might have second thoughts about the adoption itself, that she might cast herself as my rival or victim. I was afraid to be at the mercy of another version of her. One of her was all I could handle in a lifetime.

For these reasons, I turned my sights overseas. I sought out online forums where adoptive mothers shared advice and support.

Every phase of the process—the dreaming, the research, the conversations with other adoptive parents, and finally the decision to set the quest in motion—was a solo venture on my part. Jim thought the whole idea was madness.

"Remember," I told him when we were finally on our way to an agency for the first meeting with our case worker. "Do not, under any circumstances, reveal any ambivalence during this interview. If you make it seem like I'm hijacking you here, I'll never forgive you."

"Except you are hijacking me."

"Yes. But keep that information to yourself."

WE'D BEEN WARNED, and yet there was no way for a warning to prepare us for how daunting and exhausting the adoption process would be, how invasive and intrusive and intimidating and expensive. There was paperwork, so much paperwork. There were interviews and home inspections and background checks.

During a low moment, a moment when it seemed that the nightmare of waiting would never be over, I had coffee with a friend who had since adopted from China. I cried at the table, and she took both of my hands in hers.

"I remember it all like it was yesterday," she told me. "They make you jump through dozens and dozens of hoops, and fill out reams and reams of paperwork, and fly thousands and thousands of miles, and pay tens of thousands of dollars. And then . . ."

Here her voice broke and suddenly she was crying too. "Then you finally show up at the designated place on the designated day *and they hand you a human being.*"

So IT WAS with us. One day, without warning or fanfare, the long-awaited email from the agency appeared like a miracle in my inbox. Attached was a photo of a newborn girl: tiny, sleepy-eyed, and nestled amid pink blankets.

"This is Andrea," the caseworker wrote. "She's a healthy and beautiful baby girl. Do you want her?"

Less than an hour later, I burst into my husband's office in the middle of his workday.

"Jim!" I cried.

He glanced up from his computer with a look of alarm. Tears were splashing out of my eyes as I thrust my phone at him, brandishing the photo from the agency.

"Our daughter is born!"

IN MY ROOM at the Heathman, I sat by the window and let myself remember how Jim managed to embrace me that day at his office.

When did the adoption turn from something I wanted into something *we* wanted? I never saw it coming. One Sunday morning, when I opened my eyes, Jim was lying next to me, already awake and staring at the ceiling. This was unusual. Usually he was out of bed well before I was, making coffee in the kitchen, bringing it to me in a mug. Today he was very still.

"Hey," I said, reaching over to touch his chest. "Good morning."

He turned his head without lifting it from the pillow and put his hand on mine. "My heart has changed," he said.

I regarded him for a moment in silence, bewildered. "What do you mean?" I finally asked.

"I think I can love this little girl," he told me. "And I want to."

Now I went still, hardly daring to breathe, barely able to believe what I was hearing.

"Are you . . . are you talking about Andrea?" I asked in a hush.

"Who else could I be talking about?"

"Do you really mean it?"

My husband looked straight into my eyes and tightened his grip on my hand. "I really mean it."

How can I describe the grace of that statement? It was among the most profound gifts of my life. From that moment forward, he was in all the way.

And yet the next six months were a hellish blur, a time I can hardly bear to look back on. The political situation in Guatemala worsened. Then a series of scandals broke, throwing a spotlight on the rampant corruption within the adoption industry, which involved children abducted and sold for money.

One morning in August, midway through a client meeting, a call from the adoption agency came in on my cell. From the caller I.D., I could see it was Rebecca, the director herself. I stood up, cutting the client off in mid-sentence.

"I have to take this," I said. I left the conference room and walked down the hall to my office. I would have walked out of the Oval Office if I'd seen Rebecca's name on my caller I.D.

"Stephanie," Rebecca said. "Are you sitting down?"

I sank into my desk chair, clutching the left armrest with one hand and my phone with the other. "I am now," I said. I felt myself starting to hyperventilate, and it was all I could do to stay upright. "What is it?"

"I have terrible news," she said. "Guatemala is suspending its international adoptions, effective immediately."

With the news that the entire adoption process was threatened, its completion uncertain, my life tipped into an unrelenting hell.

For the first time ever, I felt lost inside my everyday life. I spent whole days in tears. Some mornings I could not get out of bed. It was very hard to concentrate at work, and when I managed to show up for tennis matches, I lost—the only time in fifteen years of competitive tennis that I ever lost.

Each day I sought reassurance that Andrea's adoption, initiated before the suspension, would be allowed to proceed, and every day I was left frantic and uncertain. I followed the news of the region on an hourly basis. I hired a Spanish translator to assist me with phone calls to the PGN, the Procuraduría General de la Nación, the government agency overseeing foreign adoptions—and together we called them again and again, begging for updates, only to be told there was nothing new to report.

Summer ended and fall began. I took no joy in the crisp boots-and-sweater weather, the fiery leaves, the scent of wood smoke in the air, the electric beginning of a new school year. All the pleasures of the season—hot mulled cider, a fire in the fireplace, Halloween decorations appearing in all the yards—were like so much dust collecting on the sill of a window I was looking through.

Jim was as kind to me during these long terrible months as any man could be. He took over any tasks he could, at the school and at home. He loaded my truck and processed all my invoices. He helped the boys with their homework and made them dinner. Sometimes he held me in bed without saying a word, both arms around me, pressing my back to his chest, as if keeping me afloat on the raft of himself.

Thanksgiving that year was muted and sad. I went through the motions of creating the holiday dinner, but it was nothing but another chore to me. We were no longer a complete family. Our daughter was missing from our lives, as missing as one of those children pictured on the milk cartons of my childhood. How could we celebrate in her absence?

By the end of the month, I came to a last-ditch decision. If I could do nothing in my power to bring my baby to me, then I would go to her.

Chapter 15

HAVE YOU EVER been hospitalized for an illness or injury? If so, please list the circumstance(s) that resulted in a hospital stay.

I was applying to the Guatemala Immigration Department for a temporary residence permit, filling out the section on my medical history. I'd resolved to move to Guatemala in January if the process was still on hold. I'd met another adoptive mother in the same position as me, a woman who shared my despair. We'd made a pact to share an apartment in Antigua, to take over the care of our children from their foster families, and to be in daily contact with the PGN until our adoptions were official.

As I wrote the answers—*poison oak, broken arm*—I actually shuddered at the memory of each of these incidents. They both sounded ordinary, well within the range of commonplace childhood mishaps. But each one involved the kind of suffering I associate with torture victims.

I WAS IN the third grade when I broke my arm. It happened on the school playground at recess. I was nine years old and wanted to be a gymnast. It was the era of Nadia Comăneci's seven perfect tens at the Olympics, the year she won three gold medals at the Games, and the maudlin strains of "Nadia's Theme" were inescapable in elevators, in supermarket aisles, and in the repertoire of any girl learning to play the piano.

On the blacktop each afternoon, I loved to lose myself on the high bar. Recess was a respite from the rest of the school day, where I remained all but mute and mostly friendless. I still lagged in every subject; I remained barely able to read. I had thrift store clothes and a lazy eye.

But outside on the playground for a precious half hour each weekday, I pulled admiring eyes my way as I flew up and down and around the pull-up bar, doing flips and tricks and tumbles beneath the wide blue sky. My academic and social troubles faded. Nothing was left but the iron bar and my body and breath.

I thought I'd perfected the cherry drop, a trick where I hung by my knees and swung back and forth until I'd gathered enough momentum to flip free and land on my feet. Only this time, one of my feet got caught and I landed on my right arm. The explosion of pain was like nothing I ever felt before.

When a couple of teachers lifted me to my feet, I saw fear on their faces. My arm was dangling from the socket like a marionette's might if you cut the string. A throng of staff and kids followed as they ushered me to the office.

"Oh my goodness," said the school secretary, paling at the sight of me. "That looks like a very bad break. You poor thing. We'll call your mother right away. You can have a seat just outside in the hall."

I sat on the wooden bench by the office door, hunched over with tears sliding out of my eyes, cradling my hurt arm against my body.

"Mrs. Haskell?" I heard her say. "This is Helen Miller, calling from Forest Park Elementary School." I couldn't hear everything she said above the din coming from the nearby cafeteria, but I caught a few phrases: *I'm afraid your daughter Stephanie . . . rather serious injury . . . looks badly broken . . . will need medical attention.*

A moment later, she appeared beside the bench and knelt to meet my tear-stained gaze. "I just spoke to your mother," she told me. "She said she'll come right over and pick you up. Can I get you anything? Would you like a cup of water?"

I shook my head.

The clock on the wall said eleven forty-five. The pain in my arm was like a firecracker bursting each time I moved, so I sat as still as I possibly could, holding it close to my torso with my other hand, barely able to breathe. I heard myself whimpering like a kicked dog that didn't have the right to howl.

I sat there while the clock made its slow progress to half past the hour, then quarter till, then one o'clock. I sat there through English period and on into Social Studies; I felt the ringing of the bell inside my bone marrow. I sat there as the gym teacher, Coach Alex, led her class down the corridor and out to the track.

"You're still here?" she asked in surprise as the kids filed by me, staring at me with interest and alarm.

When I was still there half an hour later, Coach Alex stopped on the threshold of the office on her way back to the gymnasium. "Helen, can't you get ahold of anyone at Stephanie's house?" she asked. "That poor kid is still here."

"Oh my goodness," I heard Mrs. Miller say. "I did reach her mother, and she said she was coming. I'll call her again." And then, a moment later: "Mrs. Haskell, you're still at home? Didn't you hear what I told you before? Your daughter's arm is broken."

"All right, she said she's coming now," Mrs. Miller reported after she'd hung up again. "Of course, that's what she said before. I hope she means it this time."

Coach Alex trotted down the hall to rejoin her class, shaking her head as she went. I heard Mrs. Miller muttering to herself as she went back to working the mimeograph machine. *Gosh almighty*, I heard her say. *That woman doesn't seem right in the head.* It was one fifteen.

When my mother still hadn't shown up by two forty-five, Coach Alex announced she was driving me to the hospital. I had been sitting on that bench for over three hours.

"I didn't see any reason to rush over," my mother told me later. "It wasn't a life or death situation. I did come to pick you up when school let out, but you were already gone. Someone took pity on you, I guess."

My mother arrived to sign the papers authorizing surgery on my shattered arm. I would be in a cast for the rest of that year.

——

My OUTBREAK OF poison oak happened in seventh grade. It began on the Saturday of a three-day weekend: a prickly, insistent itch that started on my left leg, as if hundreds of frenzied fire ants were swarming over my shin. The skin flared bright red, and blisters broke out along the length of my lower leg.

"Look, Mom," I said, showing her the inflamed patch of skin.

"Ugh, that looks awful," she said. "Did you get too close to poison oak? Keep your hands off it."

I tried not to scratch, but it was almost impossible. The rash crept up my leg and over to the other. It laid siege to my torso, spreading across it like wildfire, moving to my arms and face. By evening, I was broken out everywhere.

"Mom, can you take me to a doctor?" I asked. I was maddened by the itching, feverish and bleary-eyed.

"You don't need a doctor," she said. "It's just a rash. Poison oak might be uncomfortable, but it isn't an emergency. It'll go away on its own."

I lay awake all night, crying, clawing at my own body, feeling as if I'd been laid low by a witch's curse. The itching sensation gave way to a full-body burn. The rash did not spare my private area, and by morning it was agony to urinate.

"Something's wrong, Mom," I sobbed, standing in front of her in the kitchen as she drank a cup of tea. "It doesn't just itch anymore. It hurts. It hurts so bad everywhere. It hurts to pee."

"You are fine, Stephanie," she said. "I don't have time for this. No one ever died from a poison oak rash."

"It looks bad, Florence," said her boyfriend at the time. I don't remember his name, just his slight and slouching form at our kitchen table, his red ball cap, and the five o'clock shadow dotting his jaw. I'll call him John.

His gaze found mine, and in that moment, I felt a flash of hope, because in his expression I saw mercy and concern: emotions that were missing in my mother's.

"Help me," I mouthed to him, eyes wild and begging.

"Tell you what, Florence," he said. "I'll just run down to the drugstore and see if I can get her something to put on it. I know you don't want to pay a doctor bill but I can shell out a few bucks for something off the shelf."

"You can get me a pack of Camels, if you're going," my mother said.

He came back half an hour later with a bar of Fels-Naptha.

"There was a lady at the pharmacy with three little kids," he reported. "I figured she would be a good one to ask. She said she uses this to get poison oak out of clothes. So it stands to reason it'll get it off your body."

I took the green and white box from him. Beneath the product name, it said Laundry Bar & Stain Remover. The yellow brick inside resembled a regular bar of soap.

"Go get in the bath and wash yourself all over with that," he said.

"Did you get my cigarettes?" my mother wanted to know.

Upstairs, my teeth were chattering as I stripped naked and tried to ease myself into the tub of warm water. The rash was like a live thing, a full-body scorpion burn. I knew better than to make the water as hot as I usually liked, but even the mild warmth was scorching on my blistered skin.

I stood in the ankle-deep bath, dipped the yellow bar beneath the surface of the water, and tentatively rubbed it on my arm. It was as if I'd poured acid on that spot, and I cried out.

"What is it, Steph?" John called from the hall outside the bathroom.

"It burns," I cried. "The soap. It hurts to wash with this soap."

"You gotta do it, honey," he urged through the closed door. "It'll be good for the rash."

I stood there shivering and sobbing, trying to work up the nerve to go on. It took me forever to wash myself all over and then stagger back to my bed, clad only in a towel. Bathing with that detergent felt like scouring myself with steel wool.

That evening, my blisters blew up into amber beads, like droplets of honey all over my body, sweating and leaking pus. I felt myself raging with fever, burning and freezing in wretched succession all night long. In the morning, my sheets were damp and sticky from the fluid oozing from all over my body. My eyes were nearly swollen shut, and tears leaked steadily from the slits they had become. A sickly odor like snot hung in a cloud around my bed, and every patch of visible skin on my torso and limbs was discolored, shading from deep ravaged pink to wine red to deep purple.

I felt the life leaving my body, and I knew I was going to die. It was a harrowing effort to pull myself out of bed and make my way down the stairs to my mother in the kitchen.

"Mom," I said. "Please take me to the hospital."

She looked taken aback at the sight of me.

"Wow," she said. "That is some rash. I never saw a poison oak rash like that. What did you do, take all your clothes off and roll around in it?"

"Mom," I said desperately. "If you don't take me to a doctor, I'm going to die."

"Okay," she said. "We can go a little later, I guess."

"Mom, please."

"Okay! I said I would take you. I'm having my tea now," she said. "Don't rush me."

An hour or so later, in the shotgun seat of her car, I clung to the armrest on the inside of the door and heard myself baying softly like an abused puppy.

"Stop being so dramatic," my mother said. "This is not easy for me. I could get in a lot of trouble showing up at the hospital again. Last time we were there Rick and I got busted for stealing pills."

I was staggering when we reached the hospital, leaning on my mother, barely able to drag myself along. My limbs felt weak and slack, and I was perilously dizzy. The moment we came through the emergency room doors, a triage nurse took one look at me and came running over, calling over her shoulder for a wheelchair. Another nurse brought one and—as if I'd just been holding on, keeping myself upright, long enough to reach safety—I collapsed into it. I wavered in and out of consciousness after that and can recall only sparse details of the next hour, overheard phrases that lodged in my mind, isolated images and impressions.

I remember the phrase *trauma call for twelve-year-old girl in probable septic shock,* and how swiftly I was wheeled into the trauma bay. And I can remember the conversation between the medical personnel and my mother as they took my vitals and began intravenous rehydration.

"How did she get such extensive burns?" the attending physician asked.

"They're not burns," she said. "It's just a rash from poison oak."

"Poison oak doesn't look like this," he said. "Was some caustic substance applied to her blisters?"

"We didn't put anything on it," she said. "Unless you count the Fels-Naptha."

"The what?"

"That's a stain remover," a nurse broke in.

"Stain remover?" the doctor repeated. He sounded baffled.

"It's laundry detergent," she clarified.

"We had her scrub her skin with it," my mother added.

"Good God!" the doctor exploded. "You scrubbed open sores with laundry detergent? Are you out of your mind? You could have killed her!"

It felt so unfamiliar and so good: the realization that someone was angry on my behalf.

I was admitted to the ICU and would remain there for a full week. No one was allowed inside my room without a gown and mask. I learned later that any infection I contacted during my time there might have been fatal. I was as vulnerable as a burn victim.

I liked being in the hospital. They had given me pain meds. I had three hot meals a day, and I thought the hospital food was wonderful. Every day my tray held unexpected treats like silk-smooth mashed potatoes, mounds of cut corn, butterscotch pudding. I could choose my drinks from a paper menu, and I loved the little bottles of juice and mini cartons of cold chocolate milk. I felt the same way about the free breakfast and lunch I was given at school every day, despite the humiliation of standing in a separate line for it. I felt nothing but covetous toward the canned vegetables, the gravy-drowned meat, the reheated french fries that tasted like sweat. Often I had nothing else to eat on any given day.

My bed in the hospital was comfortable, and there was a color television in my room. I loved sitting up in bed, propped up like a princess against the bank of pillows, changing the channels with the remote control.

The staff was kind. The nurses were soft-spoken and mild. When they bathed my body or changed the dressing on my wounds, they spoke in soothing tones and touched me gently. If I needed anything, day or night, I could press a button by the bed and someone would come and help me. I'll never forget what a pleasure it was to be surrounded by people who cared whether I lived or died.

When I had recovered enough to leave the hospital, I was sent to another foster home. For months afterward, I was streaked like a brindle dog, vast swaths of my skin discolored, mottled with shades of pink and lavender and mauve.

A FEW DAYS after I'd filed the paperwork for a temporary residence permit, another call from Rebecca lit the screen on my phone. I was in my home office this time. A painful rush of adrenaline surged through me. If God Himself had called me just then, I could not have been more breathless or frightened.

"Rebecca?" My voice was a pathetic squeak.

"Stephanie," she said. "Are you sitting down?"

The same words she'd used to open our last conversation, those terrible words I'd never wanted to hear again. I didn't think I could make it to my desk chair.

"What is it?" I whispered. My hand was over my face.

"Your adoption has been finalized," she told me.

Finalized. Finalized? I was so filled with fear I could not make sense of this sentence. *Finalized* sounded ominous, dark, like we'd reached the end of the road, like game over.

"What . . . what does that mean?" I quavered. My whole body was trembling.

"You've been cleared," she said.

"Cleared?" This, too, sounded bad—as if our application had been wiped out, erased.

"*The baby . . . is yours,*" Rebecca said, putting emphasis on each word as if sensing my incomprehension. "You can go to Guatemala at any time to pick her up." Tears came into her voice as she added: "And bring her home."

——

ANDREA HAD BEEN with us for more than a decade now, and Jim had doted on her every day of her life with us. What would she do if we divorced? How could I turn my back on the man who'd gone into hell with me to get her?

I was spent by the time I left the Heathman—spent of rage, of conviction, and even of any confidence that Jim would be glad to see me when I returned. He hadn't called my cell since I'd left or tried to get in touch in any way. I'd paid to stay in the room through the next morning, but I didn't want to sleep there another night. I wanted to go home.

The streets were cleared of snow when I set out for our house, but everything was still hushed, still sparkling. I drove slowly along the wide downtown avenues, the radio playing low, wondering what I would say when I came through my own front door.

It was ten o'clock at night when I let myself in. The house was mostly dark. The only light was coming from the kitchen along with the plaintive strains of a Black Sabbath song.

As I came near the kitchen, the unmistakable aroma of cigar smoke—cigar smoke?—and whiskey hung in the air. And then on the threshold of the room, I was faced with a very unexpected sight. Jim was sitting there in a white undershirt and boxer shorts, a glass of amber liquid in front of him, a haze of smoke wreathing his face. He hadn't shaved since I'd last left the house. His face was drawn, his eyes bloodshot and bleary. He looked ten years older than he had two days ago.

Suddenly I was overcome by the last thing I expected to feel: a rush of tenderness, of tender amusement. I bit my lip to keep from smiling.

"Really, Jim?" I said. "Drowning your sorrows in Maker's Mark and heavy metal? I mean seriously? Are we back in high school?"

I moved to the table and took the seat across from him. Tears slid out of his eyes and ran down his face and suddenly they were sliding out of mine too. And then he was out of his chair and on his knees beside me, his hands on my waist, his face pressed against my belly.

"I can't live without you," he said.

I bent forward awkwardly to hug him back, running both of my hands through his hair. "Shhh," I said. "We'll talk tomorrow."

"I'll do whatever I need to do," he said. "I'll go see a marriage counselor. I'll come home by six every night. Our family is my first priority. Nothing else matters."

"Shhhh."

"And you want to go on dates? I hear you. I do."

"Jim—"

"We married so young. You feel like you missed out. You want that novelty, the romance, the excitement. I get it. I want that for you too."

I sat back, disbelieving. Jim was so possessive. Was I hearing right? Was he proposing we open our marriage?

"So here's my promise to you: Whenever you get the urge for that kind of adventure, you can have it. Anytime. Fun and flirtation and dates. As much as you want."

"Jim . . .?" I asked. I looked down at him, stunned.

"You can go out on all the hot dates you want," he repeated, raising his wet eyes to mine. "With me."

Chapter 16

Dear Owen,

Obviously our working relationship has strayed into an awkward place, and over the last few days, I have been able to find clarity around this. The past several months have been a very troubled time within my marriage, and because of this I allowed my own professional boundaries to blur in a way that wasn't appropriate. I regret this deeply and feel it would be best to avoid further contact . . .

No. Too confessional; too intimate. Best to avoid any further disclosures about my personal life; best to be brief and to the point.

Dear Owen,

Given the circumstances of our last interaction, I've decided it would be best to end our working relationship. Fortunately, the work on your house is just about finished. I will arrange for the final delivery of your drapes, and . . .

This was no good either. It was too formal and stilted. It was right to cut him off completely, but I didn't have to be icy. We had both gone too close to the edge, and we both bore responsibility for that.

Finally, I decided to skirt acknowledgment of our last encounter altogether. I would just make it clear I had no intention of returning to his home.

Dear Owen,

Your drapes and pillows were delivered today, and I won't be able to drop them off. My husband Jim will be bringing them by late this afternoon.

JIM AND I were having breakfast when the drapes arrived on our doorstep. It was the first such breakfast we'd eaten together in months: facing each other in the sun-splashed kitchen, with coffee and eggs and toast on the table between us. It was hard to believe how good it felt just to begin the day this way. It had been so long.

When the doorbell rang, we were caught off guard.

"You're early," I said, upon opening the door to find one of the men from my workroom on the porch.

"Yes, ma'am," he said. "I have a delivery." He was holding a heavy stack of folded drapes sheathed in plastic. They were for Owen's master bedroom.

"What's this?" Jim asked, appearing in the foyer.

"Um," I said, flustered. "It's a shipment of drapes and pillows for a customer."

Jim took them from the workman while I signed the delivery form.

"Do you want me to bring them out to your truck?" he asked once the man had gone.

"Well—" I said. "I don't think I should be the one to deliver them. They're for Owen."

"Oh," said Jim.

"I mean, I don't think I should go back there."

"No," he said grimly, firmly. "I don't think you should either."

"I'll get someone from the company to take them over," I said.

"I'll take them over," Jim replied.

"You?"

"I'd like to."

I felt my forehead crease as I considered this. "*Really?*"

"Yes." His tone was unequivocal.

"Well. . . okay. If you really want to," I said. "You won't do anything unprofessional, will you?"

"Of course not."

I IMAGINED I would laugh about it someday: Jim's account, afterward, of how Owen came to the door looking like a guilty dog. How he asked my husband whether he'd like to see my handiwork, as if to prove my presence there had been merely professional. How Jim had taken an unlikely tour of the house, looking at the newly painted and furnished rooms and mustering pointed commentary from time to time.

"Wow. *My wife* sure knows how to put a house together."

"*My wife* is truly talented, isn't she?"

Yes, surely I'd be able to laugh about it someday. But not today.

THE SUN WAS just setting that Friday as my Uber pulled up to the curb in front of the Nines, a hotel in the heart of downtown Portland. Only one weekend before, I'd gone to another downtown hotel for a very different reason. Everything was different tonight. The snow had melted, the air was almost balmy, the sky was pink and I was in a little black cocktail dress.

I loved the look of the Nines lobby: an open atrium that somehow managed to feel intimate. I loved the vast purple area rugs, the high-glossed wooden tables, and the velvet furniture in jewel colors—wine, crimson, peacock, gold. As I stepped inside the entrance of the lounge, a tall and handsome man detached himself from the throng at the bar. He wore a midnight blue sports jacket and dark jeans. His shoes had been buffed to a high shine, and cuff links glinted at his wrists.

"Stephanie?" he asked. His voice sounded just a touch uncertain and yet hopeful.

I smiled at him. "Yes."

He broke into a dazzling smile in return. "I'm Jim," he said, extending his hand.

I clasped it briefly, watching my own hand disappear into his and feeling glad I'd just had a manicure. "It's nice to meet you."

"The pleasure is mine."

I actually felt nervous as I allowed him to guide me, with the lightest touch at the small of my back, toward one of the tables for two scattered around the lounge.

"I hope this won't sound too forward of me, but you're even more beautiful in person," he said.

I flushed with pleasure. "Well, aren't you charming," I said, dropping my eyes to the cocktail menu, unable to suppress another smile. "I hope you don't say that to all the ladies."

This was ridiculous, as ridiculous as my flirtation with Owen had been, and even more heady. The whole game had been Jim's idea.

You haven't had enough first dates? he'd said more than once during the week after I came home. *We can fix that.*

He spent the week planning this dinner, securing a reservation, arranging for Josh to spend the evening with Andrea, outlining the rules. We were strangers, set up on a blind date by friends, meeting tonight for the first time. We would exchange only the information about our lives that didn't include marriage or children. We would not break character throughout the planned portion of our evening and possibly not even after that.

He understood the allure of novelty, of unpredictability. He wanted to give that to me.

And it was working! I was actually looking at my husband as if for the first time, studying his features, his sense of style, the way he held himself. I liked all of it. He came off as confident but not presumptuous, gentlemanly yet down to earth. I felt a little flutter in my pulse each time our eyes met.

Jim closed his menu. "You run a school in town, a school for interior design, I believe?"

"That's right," I said. "The Heritage School, in the Mississippi district."

"I want to hear more about that," he said. "But first, how was your day?"

"It was very long and full, but everything went well," I said. "How was yours?"

And on it went. Jim asked me questions. He listened to the answers. He offered me the full intensity of his attention. He was thoughtful and sincere, a man of substance.

At the table next to ours, two women were having what appeared to be a girls' night out. I noticed the way they both stole glances at Jim throughout the evening. But he never let his gaze stray from mine.

"I don't usually do this on a first date," I said a few hours later, when Jim eased the car to the curb in front of our house. "But would you like to come in?"

THE NEXT MORNING, I woke up smiling. It had been a perfect evening, and now it was the weekend, and Jim was coming into the bedroom with coffee for me the way he always used to. Just then I heard my cellphone vibrating on the nightstand and looked over to see my mother's name on the screen. I realized I hadn't spoken with her in over a week.

"I'll call her back," I told Jim as the call went to voicemail.

"You know, I've been meaning to tell you: Your mom left four or five messages while you were away," Jim said.

Startled, I took the mug of coffee from his outstretched hand. "She did?" I asked. "Is she all right?"

"Oh, there was no emergency or anything, but she kept asking about a newspaper story," Jim told me. "She said: *Did Stephanie look up my story yet? It was in all the papers.* Do you know what she was talking about?"

I went cold all over again, just as I had in my mother's apartment.

"It's like I blocked it out of my mind," I said slowly. "With everything that happened over the last few days."

"Blocked what out?"

"My mom said something insane the last time I was there. I mean, I know better than to believe the stuff she says, but still."

Jim got back into bed to drink his own coffee with me, both of us leaning back against the headboard. "What did she say?"

"Well, she told me that she... was raped."

"Well, that's not news," he said. "I mean, we knew that."

"Yes. We knew about the rape outside the apartment she shared with Louie," I said. "But she said there was another rape."

"When?" Jim asked. "Where?"

"That's the insane part. She came out with this horrific story. I didn't believe her," I repeated. "I mean, we know my mom's a pathological liar. She's lied to me all my life."

"Sure," said Jim. "But what did she say this time?"

"Okay, she said that when she was a kid, she was snatched by some guys with a van. This was supposedly in Baltimore when she was eleven years old. She said they took her and her cousin to some building and kept them there for a long time, doing terrible things, unspeakable things, things she never wanted to think about again."

"Wow," said Jim. He set his cup of coffee on the nightstand beside him. "Was there anything else to it?"

"She said there were a lot of men. She mentioned the mayor's son. And an Indian who kept her alive with his love."

"Well, okay," Jim said. "That does sound pretty far out there."

"Yes."

We sat for a moment in silence, until finally Jim broke it.

"But still," he said. "Did you look into whether it checked out?"

"What do you mean?"

"That's what she wants you to do, right? She keeps saying it was in all the papers. If it really was a story of that magnitude, and if it really involved the son of Baltimore's mayor, there must be a record of it. If not, we'll know it's just another delusion."

"I haven't gone looking for any newspaper stories, if that's what you're asking."

Without another word, Jim took his phone from the nightstand beside him.

"Okay, your mother is, what, seventy-five now?"

"Seventy-six."

"So she would have been eleven in . . . 1953?"

"That sounds right."

"So first, who was the mayor of Baltimore in 1953?"

He wasn't asking me. He was typing into the search engine, which returned an answer within seconds: Thomas L. J. D'Alesandro Jr. I looked over Jim's shoulder at his Wikipedia entry. It said that D'Alesandro was the mayor from 1947 until 1959.

The mayor's son was there, my mother had said.

Jim cleared the search and began another: *D'Alesandro son gang rape 1953*.

The first link to come up was a blog about organized crime. The headline of the entry read: FBI Files: "Baltimore Mayor Thomas D'Alesandro Jr. Was 'Constant Companion' of Notorious Mobster Benjamin Magliano."

Again, my mother's words came back to me. *They were powerful men, society men. They had ties to the mob.*

I took the phone from Jim and began scanning the post for any mention of a rape. His search engine included a highlight feature, where keywords would show up in color. And midway down the page, there it was: the word *rape* in blazing yellow.

"Jim," I said. "Oh my God. Jim." I read from the screen: "The Piracci trial at which Mrs. D'Alesandro testified was immediately followed by a child gang rape trial against the mayor's twenty-year-old son, Franklin Roosevelt D'Alesandro."

My husband was visibly shaken.

"The FBI describes the ugly case in a January 30, 1961 memo as follows," I went on. "During the summer of 1953, Mayor D'Alesandro's son, Franklin Roosevelt D'Alesandro, aged twenty, was one of fourteen youths charged with having committed rape or perverted practices on two girls, aged eleven and thirteen, during July of that year."

That was as far as I got before I started to hyperventilate. It was as if an unseen hand had closed around my throat. I stared wildly into my husband's eyes, taking in ragged gulps of air, feeling as if I could not fill my lungs. My husband took the phone from my hands and pulled me tight against him.

"Jim," I cried. "Jim! What if she was telling the truth?"

Chapter 17

UNTIL THAT MOMENT, my mother had always been a two-dimensional character to me: the heedless, thoughtless, selfish free spirit. The wanton one, the capricious one, who did just what she wanted, and it was my fate to land wherever her whims blew her. My mother who flitted like a moth from one man to the next, always high, in a world of her own. My mother: the woman with no impulse control, no empathy, at perpetual war with the expectations of society.

For as long as I could remember, the story of my life went like this: My mother was the villain, and I was the victim.

But this revelation changed everything. I thought back to the day she'd touched on it for the first time. It was possible I'd goaded her into it. *You were never held captive in hell*, I'd said to her then, *trapped with sexual predators, used as a plaything by sick people, when you were no more than a helpless child.*

And she had said: *You're mistaken.*

What if my mother was a victim too? What if her formative ordeal was even worse than anything I went through? What if, unlike me, she was broken by it, her sanity crushed beyond recovery? What if my mother's multiple personalities had emerged in response to that trauma? What if it had frozen her in time, at age eleven? Agnes was eleven. I thought of all the times I'd wanted to flee from Agnes: from her petulance and fretfulness, her relentless need, her *childishness*. Her conviction that she was pregnant.

Jim and I spent the weekend scouring online newspaper archives for information about this crime. *It was in all the papers*, my mother had said. While that wasn't precisely true, it was in a lot of them: the *Baltimore Sun* and *Chicago Tribune*, the *Cincinnati Enquirer* and the *Cumberland News*, the *Morning Herald* and the *Daily Mail* of Hagerstown, Maryland.

Fifteen males ranging in age from fifteen to twenty-three were ultimately charged in connection with this crime. Some were charged with rape, others with "perverted sexual practices." The names of the men were: Franklin Delano Roosevelt D'Alesandro, Philip Sudano, Michael Sudano, George Baccala, and Armand Corridi. The names of the older teens were George Kincaid, Harry West, Francis Hart, Joseph Bednor, Michael Schertle, William Krug, and Charles Cooper. The fifteen-year-olds were not named in consideration of their youth.

These accounts were frustrating in their brevity, their dispassion, their lack of depth or detail or context. Taken together, they bear unequivocal witness to a few harrowing facts. On July 21, 1953, two girls aged eleven and thirteen were picked up in a car and taken by several men to an apartment on West Preston Street. There they were violated repeatedly by upwards of a dozen adult and adolescent males over the course of a week and a half.

The young men who violated my mother were white, wealthy society men. Fourteen of the fifteen defendants pleaded guilty, but the ringleader, the mayor's son, Franklin D'Alesandro, was acquitted after twenty-five minutes of deliberation by a jury of twelve men. None of the others served more than two months for the extended gang rape of two children.

I focused on that injustice as a way of not dwelling on the rape itself. Whenever I tried to picture that eleven-year-old girl, violated by so many men over so many days, my imagination bucked fearfully, shied sideways, skittered away. My own daughter was eleven. I could not let myself think about her in such a situation. If, as an adult, I could not even bring myself to imagine it, how could a young girl ever recover from it?

"I NEED TO go see her," I told Jim on Sunday evening. "Tomorrow."

He was holding me in bed. He'd been holding me for most of the past two days. We were both all but undone by what we'd learned.

"Do you want me to cancel one of my meetings and come with you?"

"It'll be better if I'm by myself," I told him. "I mean, she doesn't like you most of the time."

"True enough. But I hate the idea of you going alone."

"It's okay. It'll be different this time. Everything has changed for me now. I need to let her know that I finally understand everything."

"Just be careful," Jim said. "Everything might have changed for you, but nothing at all has changed for her. She's still dangerous and mentally unstable."

THE MOMENT I pulled into my mother's parking lot, the apartment manager emerged from his ground floor office and hurried over to intercept me. I'd met him once before, when my mother took the place and I had to co-sign her lease. He was a small, balding man who always seemed to be in a cold sweat under his ill-fitting suits. His name was Bart.

"You're here to see Miss Florence, aren't you?" he said. "I'm glad to see someone from her family. She's been out-of-control crazy lately. I don't know how much longer we can keep her here if this doesn't turn around."

"What's going on?" I asked. "What has she done?"

"She's been getting into fights with the other residents," he said. "Cursing them, spitting at them, pulling their laundry out of the dryer before it's finished and throwing it on the floor of the laundry room, screaming that it's her turn to dry her clothes. People are afraid of her. She's a liability for me, you have to understand."

"I do understand," I told him. "I'm sorry. I'll tell her she has to stop."

If she got kicked out of here, where the hell would she go?

I reached her apartment and knocked before realizing the door was slightly ajar. As usual, she was lying on the couch in her living room. Thinner and paler than ever, blue eyes blazing in her drawn face.

"Where have you been, Stephanie?" she demanded, pulling herself upright. "I haven't heard from you in days. I kept calling the house but Jim said you were away. Where were you?"

Had it really been just a week since I'd checked into the Heathman?

It felt like a lifetime ago. I sat down in the armchair across the coffee table from her.

"Jim and I were having some trouble," I told her, wondering why I was bothering to disclose this. "So I decided to spend a weekend apart from him. But I'm home again now. We worked it out."

"Too bad," she said. "You're better off without him."

Just a week ago, this would have sent me into a controlled frenzy. *Mom, that is so ridiculous*, I would have snapped. *You should be ashamed of yourself for saying that. After all he's done for you!*

But not today. Now I could sit there and remember she was mentally ill, with good reason. I didn't have to take it personally anymore.

"Mom, your story. The one you said was in all the papers," I said, ignoring her jab at Jim. "The one you told me to look up." For some reason I could not bring myself to say the word *rape*.

"What about it?"

"I did look it up. Jim and I found it together." I heard my own voice crack a little, saying this. "I read what happened to you, Mom."

She raised her head and met my gaze. "You read it?"

"I did. *We* did."

"Do you believe me now?"

"I do believe you, Mom. I'm sorry I didn't before."

She stared at me for another moment and then her face transformed before my eyes. Relief filled her eyes and softened her jaw.

"You believe me," she said, almost to herself. There was a note of wonder in her tone.

"I do. Jim and I, we both believe you. And I'm so sorry, Mom," I said. I started to cry.

She sat there without saying anything, eyeing me warily.

"I can't imagine anything more traumatic," I said, swiping at my eyes.

"I don't like to think about it," she told me.

"Of course not. Those men were evil."

"I never wanted to remember it."

"I understand. It was the most brutal thing that could happen to anyone, let alone a child."

Then without warning, my mother was on her feet and lunging at me, fists flailing.

"Stop it!" she screamed. "Shut up!"

I sprang from the chair, almost toppling it. I caught her by the wrists and tried to still her arms, but she wrenched away and came at me again. Her strength was shocking. As thin and frail and riddled with cancer as she was, I could not contain her. She managed to land several frenzied blows before raking at my neck with her nails.

"Get out!" she shrieked. "You heartless bitch! Get the fuck out of my house!"

No SOONER HAD she pushed me out the door than the building manager materialized again, as if he'd been lying in wait.

"Did Miss Florence attack you too?" he demanded.

"Oh . . ." I said. I struggled to catch my breath and compose myself. "She did, but it wasn't the first time, and it likely won't be the last." I was trying to sound flippant, but my hands trembled as I smoothed my hair back into place.

"Call the police," he said.

I made a gesture of dismissal, tears still running down my face. "No, it's okay," I said shakily. "I'm used to her. She's my mom."

"Please," he said. "I've called so many times, they don't take me serious anymore. But a classy lady like you, they'll listen to you."

"I don't know about that."

"For her own good," he urged. "It might be that she stopped taking her medicines. Maybe the police can make her take them. I'm afraid she'll hurt another tenant next, and then what?"

Reluctantly I pulled my cell phone from my purse.

"This is 911, what is your emergency?"

"I was just attacked by a resident of the Commons of Hawthorn Village," I told the dispatcher, referring to my mother's apartment complex.

"Bless you, ma'am," Bart said when I completed the call. "I need to keep all my renters safe, and I want to keep Miss Florence safe too."

Within minutes several police cars pulled into the parking lot, and at least half a dozen uniformed officers joined Bart and me on the sidewalk.

"Oh, that Florence," said a red-headed female cop. "What is she up to today?"

"You're on a first-name basis with her?" I asked. "It sounds like you guys are here a lot."

"We are," she told me. "We've had several calls about her these past few months, bless her cantankerous heart." She took a pen from her clipboard and held it poised over an incident report form. "All right, so what is your relationship to Miss Haskell? Are you her social worker?"

"I'm her daughter."

The cop did a double take. "Her *daughter*?" she repeated. "You?"

"I'm afraid so."

She and her partner turned to each other and exchanged glances of disbelief. While the policemen approached my mother's apartment, I stayed with the female officers, who cooed over my earrings, my handbag, and my shoes. "Honey," one of them said, "if I had to find Florence's daughter in a lineup, I sure wouldn't pick you."

"I've been hearing that all my life," I said.

"How did you . . . ?" She didn't voice the rest of her question, and I could only guess what it would have been. *How did you survive having her as a mother? How did you survive at all? How did you turn out like this? Well-heeled and presentable and apparently okay?*

"I bet you've been through a lot, growing up with her," she said.

"I have been through a lot," I conceded. "But as it turns out, so has she."

TWENTY MINUTES LATER, the cops had taken off. I'd declined to press charges.

"She seems calm now," one of the policemen said when he emerged from her place. "But the manager is worried about her, and to be honest, he's right to be. If we get another call like this, we'll have to commit her. She can't keep terrorizing her neighbors."

"I understand," I told him, as I'd told Bart not half an hour ago.

Now I eased open the door to her apartment once more and stood just inside the entrance, wary of going further. My mother was back at the far end of her living room sofa, huddled into the corner of it, a blanket drawn around her bony shoulders. She looked spent and small.

"Mom," I said. "Andrea will be getting out of school soon. I need to go pick her up. I just wanted to tell you that I love you."

She looked up at me. All the rage was gone from her face.

"I'm sorry I was mean to you," she said.

She looked so vulnerable. She looked like a child. I had never been able to look at my mother and see the vulnerable child inside her, but now I could. Had she been there all along?

"I'll come back soon," I told her. "In the meantime, Mom, please: You have to stop fighting with people. I know you like it here. I want you to be able to stay."

She nodded and dropped her gaze to the coffee table, where prescription bottles were cluttered alongside a makeshift coffee lid ashtray, an incense burner, and a paper bag from Starbucks.

"I need to hear more of your story," I said. "The one you told me to look up, but I'll wait until you feel ready to tell me."

"Next time," she said. "But come back soon. Don't wait too long."

"I won't," I promised. She didn't have long. We both knew that waiting was a luxury we couldn't afford.

Chapter 18

TWO DAYS LATER, the call came from Bart.

"I'm sorry, Miss Stephanie," he said, "but I had to call the cops on your mother again."

"What did she do now?" I asked, cringing at this news.

"She threw coffee at another resident in the gazebo," he said. "Luckily it wasn't hot enough to burn, but I can't have her here anymore."

"Wait," I said, clutching the phone with one hand and my head with the other. "It sounds like she needs an adjustment of her meds. That'll happen if she's committed to a psych ward, which is probably happening as we speak. She'll be in there for a few weeks, so you don't have to worry for now. Then she should be fine for quite a while once she's out again."

"For a while, maybe, but sooner or later she'll be up to her old tricks," he said. "When that happens, she'll be the same liability to me."

"Listen, she's not going to live much longer." Tears came into my eyes as I said this.

"I know she's sick, Miss Stephanie. I'm sorry about that."

"She isn't just sick," I said. "She's dying. Like I said, she'll be out of your way for two or three weeks and in the meantime, I won't let her payments lapse. Just—can we let her get treatment and see how she does?"

"I don't know," he said doubtfully. "I feel for you. I'm not a heartless man. But if she hurts someone, that's on my conscience too. I could be sued for all I'm worth."

"You've already done the right thing," I pleaded. "You had her arrested. They can't let her out if they believe she's a danger to herself or others.

It's her doctors' job to make that professional assessment. And if they're wrong, that's on them, not you."

I hated to hear myself badgering, begging, but I had to keep my mother's place in the complex. It might be the last place she ever lived. I wanted her to be able to die in a place she liked.

"YOU'RE QUIET TONIGHT," my husband said that evening. We were on the sofa in the living room, with my feet on his lap. It had been a long day. I managed to learn by noon that my mother had been committed to the Providence St. Vincent Medical Center in southwest Portland. I also managed to convince Bart to let her return once she was out, at least on a trial basis.

"I've been thinking," I said.

"About what?"

"This story about my mother changes everything."

"It's tragic beyond belief," he said. "But what does it change? Aside from the level of empathy we might have around her bad behavior?"

"It calls all her other delusions into question. What if all her crazy rants aren't as crazy as we've always thought?"

One corner of his mouth quirked up. "You mean, what if she's a direct descendant of George Washington?"

"I know you're joking," I said. "But I'm not. Seriously, what if she is?"

"Come on."

"I've always thought we were no one," I said. "I mean, we were strays. Drifters, grifters, lawless, homeless, and broke . . . but my mom is *smart*. She talks like an educated person. I went over to her place once when *Jeopardy!* was on and she knew all these obscure world capitals. How on earth would she know those?"

"All kinds of people are self-educated. She's always liked to read."

"It's more than that. She talks as if she came from some kind of high society. She's always complaining that there are no acceptable suitors in her apartment complex. *Suitors!* Who uses that word anymore?"

"That's still something she could have picked up from a book."

I sat there thinking for a moment.

"You know, when I was a kid," I said slowly, "and we were living in that motel? One day we were at the pool and she dove in and started swimming like an Olympian. I never forgot that. It didn't fit with what I knew of her life. How did she learn to swim like that?"

"It doesn't mean she descended from the first U.S. president," Jim said. "It doesn't mean anything. You taught yourself tennis, didn't you?"

"As an adult," I said. "An adult with time and money. It took time and money to become great at tennis, Jim."

My husband didn't answer.

"I don't know the first thing about my own heritage," I said. "I need to find out whatever I can before she dies. I'm going to visit her again tomorrow."

IT WAS RAINING when I drove to St. Vincent's the next morning, the kind of cold driving rain that falls relentlessly throughout the winter season in Portland. I was cold inside my car, though I was wearing a coat and the heat was on. I was filled with dread, the old icy dread of visiting my mother in a psych ward, though I knew this one would be better than other places she had been. After all, she'd been in the Oregon State Hospital, perhaps the most infamous psych ward in the country, the place where *One Flew Over the Cuckoo's Nest* was filmed.

Many years later, I would read an exposé of OSH in *The Oregonian*—a series of articles that won a Pulitzer Prize. Of the facility's maximum security ward, the reporters wrote: "This bleak stretch of dark cells built more than a century ago is more frightening, more inhumane, than any place still in use in Oregon's prisons." Elsewhere the writers referred to OSH as "a haunted house of a hospital."

I felt vindicated when I read those articles, as if my horror had been verified by an official source. But the truth is that no haunted house, no ghost story, no horror movie could be more ghastly than that place.

———

THE YEAR WAS 1986. I was nineteen and a newlywed, taking classes at Portland Community College. Jim and I were renting a modest apartment, and the simple daily fact of living with him instead of with my mother or a foster family still felt like a miracle to me.

My mother had come to the attention of the local police that wintry February after showing up at her neighborhood coffeehouse in a bikini. And the next day she pulled a knife on her boss, the man who ran the dry cleaning company where she was employed for six weeks. She was committed to the Oregon State Hospital, formerly named the Oregon Insane Asylum.

I drove from Portland to Salem to see her, alone in my little red Datsun. Jim offered to come, but I didn't want to subject him to such a place or let him see my mother that way. My siblings wouldn't help either. Isabella was just getting out of her foster home and she was estranged from my mom. I really never saw her after she was taken from the home after the assault. Pablo was incarcerated. Allan could not handle seeing his mother sick and in a psych ward and would turn to alcohol. Walter was in a foster home, and I didn't know where he was at the time.

It didn't look bad from the outside. It was a vast, three-story red brick building with a white spire at the center, immense and stately. A wide cement pathway led to a central entrance, and a trim green lawn carpeted the grounds on either side.

The matronly woman at the antechamber table barely looked up when I came in.

"Purse," she said.

"What?"

"Give me your purse. And your coat."

Wordlessly I complied, slipping my purse from my shoulder and pushing it across the surface of the desk. The motion felt deeply and dreadfully familiar. Where had I done this before? It took a moment for the answer to come: when I was being admitted to the dependent unit, surrendering the black plastic bag that held my meager possessions. Now, as then, I felt a sense of panic as the woman stashed my bag and coat in one of the lockers behind her desk before handing me the plastic tag that bore my locker number. What if I never got my belongings back? What if, once inside this place and stripped of my identity, the trappings of my regular life, they didn't let me go?

In one of my current college classes was a young man whose mother was among the first American women to be ordained as an Episcopal priest. Just a few days before, he'd told a story about his mother's visit, as a chaplain, to a psych ward in her city. Afterward, as she tried to leave, she was stopped by the guard manning the exit.

"No patients beyond this point," his mother was told.

"But I'm a priest!" she exclaimed.

"There, there."

Everyone laughed at this story, even me, but I could feel her fear, the claustrophobic unease that descended at the threshold of these places. I felt it grip me every time I stepped foot into one: *What if they don't let me out again? What if they know I'm her daughter and they think I'm just like her, that I belong here and they don't let me out?*

I pushed this thought from my mind as the woman spoke again.

"Empty your pockets," she said.

"I don't have anything in them."

"Turn them inside out."

I plunged my hands into the front pockets of my jeans and pulled the empty cotton lining into view.

"All right then," she told me. "Now, by law I have to do a body search on you."

Here I felt another flutter of panic, wondering if she was telling me to strip. If I had to be naked—even momentarily—to get into this place, I wasn't going in. She just came around the table and proceeded to pat me down, like a policewoman frisking a suspect.

"Okay, you're good to go," she finally said. "I'll have a guard bring you in."

She spoke into a radio, and a moment later a man in uniform appeared and motioned for me to come with him. I followed him to the set of sliding metal sally port doors leading into my mother's ward. It wasn't until the first door locked behind my back that he was able to unlock the second. The space between was like a cage in purgatory. Once I'd stepped across the threshold of the second door, the metal clanging shut, the patients on the unit seemed to appear from every corner.

Outside the ward, they probably wouldn't have looked alike, but in here their faces took on a terrible sameness. Even the younger ones looked wizened somehow: pale and slack, with pinched faces and sunken eyes, their hair hanging in limp and greasy strings. Several of the women were as skeletal as concentration camp victims. Each patient's body seemed to bear the marks of trauma and mutilation, ancient scars faded to white, cuttings and slashes and cigarette burns and gouges and bruises.

They were trapped within this catacomb, and each new person to come in might as well have been a visitor from another realm. They drew near in fascination, forming a silent ring around me like spirits of the underworld. And there within this cluster of wraiths was the figure of my own mother. To stand in their midst was to feel grief closing like a hand around my throat, choking me like floodwater in a clogged gutter.

It was a force of will to move to my mother's side and touch her arm.

"Mom," I managed to say.

She jerked away as if I'd burned her. "What do you want?"

"Florence!" said an orderly standing nearby. "You never told me you had such a beautiful daughter. Would you like to visit with her in the dayroom?"

My mother stood rooted to the spot, eyeing me with suspicion.

"Come," the orderly went on in a bright voice. "I'll walk over with you."

Reluctantly my mother detached herself from the throng, and together we trailed the orderly down the hall, through the patients' quarters and past the baths. I looked around at the decor that clearly hailed from another decade.

The ward was in a state of decay. The walls were buckling from water damage, and everything was peeling: the paint on the walls, the ceiling plaster, the surfaces of the sinks. All the hospital fixtures, it seemed, were leaking and corroded and rusted. Metal pipes ran in every direction: up the walls and along the ceiling and parallel to the floor.

Every aspect of the interior was industrial: the white bathtubs surrounded by dingy tile, the trough-like sinks. In the communal washroom, the toilet stalls had no doors. Just outside it, human excrement was smeared all over the water fountain.

The corridor housing the patients' rooms was long and narrow, with wheelchairs strewn here and there like wreckage. The windows were covered not only with bars but a layer of mesh as well, the kind that might be used to create the high fencing around outdoor tennis courts.

Each room was as small and spare as a cell. On every bed was a rough brown blanket with the words Oregon State Hospital in black capital letters. In some of these beds were patients who were strapped down, bound at the wrists and ankles with leather restraints. Some were thrashing in these bonds, and others lay as still as the dead.

Outside the rooms too were patients at every turn, some of them in palpable agony. One woman was sitting on the floor, plowing furrows into the underside of her own forearm with her fingernails. Another was wandering the halls, clutching her head and moaning. From time to time, a scream would ricochet down the corridor—another echo of the dependent unit.

Other patients were shuffling around in their hospital shrouds and slippers, and some looked as if they had just given up, slumped in chairs or on their beds as if their spirits had vacated their bodies altogether. How else to escape the sodden misery, the stagnancy of this place, with its reek of mildew and urine and canned cafeteria food?

As we rounded the corner, a young patient grabbed my arm, and it was all I could do not to shriek and recoil. Her dark hair was filthy and matted, sticking out around her face. She wore a hospital gown and oversized shades. The exposed part of her face was heavily and grotesquely painted. Her cheeks looked as if they'd been slapped with rouge she hadn't bothered to rub in. Bright magenta lipstick was smeared not only on her lips but all around them.

"Are you here to interview me?" she demanded.

"Not today, Judy," the orderly said. "Please stand back." To me, she said in a lowered tone: "She thinks she's a movie star."

Grudgingly the girl released me. My heart was pounding as I hurried away from her.

Finally, the orderly turned into the dayroom, and my mother and I followed. The walls were made of brick that had been painted white. The floor was covered with cheap linoleum patterned with dark and light squares. Tables and chairs were scattered around the space.

My mother and I sat down at one of the tables. I crossed my arms in front of me, clasping my own shoulders in an effort to stop shaking.

"What's the matter with you?" my mother sneered.

"It's hard to see you here," I told her. "I don't like it here, Mom."

"You put me in here," she said. "You and your husband."

"Mom! We had nothing to do with it. You pulled a freaking knife on your boss. We weren't even around."

"You two were in on it," she said. "You want me out of the way."

"That's not true at all," I said, starting to cry.

"You used to belong to me," she fretted, "but Jim took you away. Now you show up pretending to care, but you're just here to spy on me. So get out," she said, her voice rising to a scream. "Get the hell out of here and don't come back!"

She jumped up, tipping the table toward me with both hands. I scrambled up too, managing to dart out of the way before it crashed to the floor. Two nurses appeared in the doorway.

"Florence!" one of them called. "What's the trouble? You need to calm down."

"Get out!" she screeched again. The cords stood out in her neck. She came around the fallen table and lunged at me, both hands reaching for my throat.

I twisted away as the two nurses ran over and another stood out in the hall, calling for security. Within seconds, it seemed, a team of white-jacketed men closed in on my mother. She was howling and kicking and thrashing with her usual formidable strength. It took all of them to wrestle her arms behind her back and drag her from the room.

I crept along behind them, trembling uncontrollably, wanting to know what they would do with her. They made their tortured way down the long corridor, my mother's howls echoing off the walls, and disappeared into a room on the far end of it, a room they needed to unlock.

I paced the floor outside, shivering and weeping. I wanted to go home. I wanted Jim. But I couldn't even leave on my own. I needed someone to escort me out. After many long minutes, the door opened and everyone filed back in the room. Everyone, that is, except my mother.

"Excuse me," I asked. "Is my mom okay?"

One of the men turned to me. "Is Florence your mother? She'll be all right. She's in the seclusion room. We had to put her in restraint so she can settle down. You can look in if you want." He indicated a small window at eye level on the door.

I stepped up to the little oblong of glass and peered through it. The room had padded white walls and was empty of everything except a mattress on the floor. My mother was inside, still agitated, standing upright and jerking as if having a seizure. She was in a straitjacket, cocooned and limbless inside the white expanse of it, arms crossed in front of her and tightly secured, still snarling and spitting but unable to strike.

The sight of my mother in that straitjacket has been seared into my memory. Buckled in from throat to ankle, folded into herself like an origami figure. The image has come to me countless times since, in my waking hours and in my nightmares. The helplessness, the humiliation, and the terror of it are indelible.

THE PSYCH WARD at St. Vincent's was nothing like the Oregon State Hospital. The facility was modern and clean, the staff warm and welcoming. I still had to surrender my purse on my way in, but I didn't feel as if I were entering a prison.

Still, a psych ward is a psych ward. Many of the people in it are bereft and broken. Some are unnerving and some are terrifying. This one was no different.

The dayroom, at least, was sunny and somewhat cheerful. I sat down with my mother on one of the sofas.

"How are you doing, Mom?"

"I don't belong in here," she rasped. "What am I doing here?"

"Well, you got yourself into some trouble," I said. "I heard you threw a cup of coffee at another resident, back at home."

"That bitch," she spat. "I saw the way she was looking at me. It's her fault I'm here."

"I want to get you out of here, Mom, but we need to get your meds adjusted first. Then I hope like hell you can go back to your apartment. The manager isn't too keen on having a tenant who attacks other residents."

She eyed me sullenly from her corner of the sofa.

"How is it here, Mom? This is a nice place, isn't it?"

"I don't like it," she said.

"Why not?"

"These people think I'm nothing but a commoner," she said, her voice dropping to a whisper. "But I'm a descendant of presidents and kings."

She sat back against the armrest, brushing the hair from her face with one weakened claw. I looked at her, huddled there in her hospital gown. Never had she looked or sounded more lost. I locked eyes with her and leaned in, speaking low.

"Mom," I said. "This royal heritage of yours." I paused. "Of ours."

She cocked her head to one side and waited.

"Tell me about it," I said. "I want to finally know who I came from. Tell me about our family, mom. Please."

Chapter 19

My mother drew herself up on the couch. For a moment, she seemed to puff up with importance.

"My grandfather," she said, "was the most highly regarded and distinguished professor at Johns Hopkins University."

It felt ridiculous to put faith in these words, and yet there I was, leaning in, yearning. My whole life had been rootless. I wanted a connection to any past, any clan. They didn't need to have a whiff of prestige about them. I just wanted to belong to a family, a place, a people.

"Who was he, Mom?" I asked. "What was his name?"

"His name was Thornton," said my mother grandly. "Dr. William Mynn Thornton Jr."

"Wait," I said. "Let me write this down." I fumbled in my purse for a scrap of paper and pen. "William . . . what's his middle name?"

"Mynn," my mother said. "M-y-n-n. Thornton. Junior."

The skin prickled on the back of my neck. Just as when she had revealed the rape, she seemed ablaze with certainty and clarity.

"You said he was a professor," I said. "What did he teach?"

"Chemistry," she said. "But he lectured all over the country on all different subjects. He wrote a lot of published articles, and he even wrote a book."

"I'll look him up when I get home," I said.

"You do that," she said. "You'll find him. He was a great man."

"Tell me more," I begged.

"He married an artist. My grandmother's name was Florence Beall. She painted miniatures that were displayed in the Baltimore Museum of Art."

"Her name was Florence also?"

"Yes," she said. "My mother and I were her namesakes."

I wrote down her name as well.

"She came from a great family too," my mother went on. "The Bealls founded the Cotton Exchange. My grandmother and her sister had dazzling weddings. They were written up in all the society pages."

And here my hope was outweighed again by skepticism. "Mom, how did you stray so far from this family?" I asked. "We had no money while I was growing up and no relatives in our lives, except that one time when we went to see your mother in Mexico."

I flashed for a moment onto my memory of that strange old woman, with her single breast and her beer cans, sitting by the front window of her house most of the day. I could only remember her in fraying men's undershirts. There was nothing fancy about her.

"They cut my mother off without a dime," she said.

"Her parents? You mean they disowned her? Why?"

"She eloped with her chauffeur," my mother said. "It was a terrible disgrace."

And now hope disappeared altogether. Eloped with her chauffeur? It sounded like she was repeating the plot of a romance novel.

"She was from such a prominent, elegant family, and he drove a taxi," my mother went on. "And he was old enough to be her father. Think of the humiliation. They were positively scandalized."

"Mom," I said. "This sounds like an episode of *Downton Abbey*."

"You see, this is what you do," she said. "You beg me to tell you things, and then you don't believe me."

"I'm sorry," I said. "But I mean, that very thing just happened on a hugely popular TV series. Are you sure you didn't see that show and get confused?"

She glared at me. "I'm tired," she told me. "I think you should go now."

"Listen," I said. "I will look these people up. And if any of this is true, no one will be more excited than me."

She didn't answer. She wouldn't even look at me.

I rose to give her an awkward hug, which she endured but did not return.

"Get some rest, Mom," I said. "I'll see you soon."

When she still didn't respond, I saw myself out.

IN THE PARKING lot of St. Vincent's, I texted Jim.

Mom gave me two names. Dr. William Mynn Thornton Jr. and Florence Beall. Her grandparents?

The truth was that, beneath my skepticism, I was still embarrassed by my own hope. All my life I'd heard people refer to my family as the dregs of society. Was it possible that these prominent, pedigreed people could actually be my kin?

I'd always felt that Jim's family was superior to mine. I'd apologized to him for that so many times, though he had no need of such apologies and winced whenever I voiced them.

I come from nothing and no one, I'd say.

It doesn't matter, he always told me. *I hate when you say that. You're everything to me.*

And I knew he meant it. If Jim's family had any notions of his marrying up, I couldn't have been further from their hopes. This bride's family would not—as tradition would have it—be assuming the cost of our wedding. This bride's father would not be offering the promising young man a place in the family business. I was not an uptown girl.

JIM AND I had saved one thousand dollars between us for our own wedding. He was working for UPS, and I was waiting tables at Elmer's, a local diner. We were renting our own apartment and paying all our own bills with his paychecks and my tips. Every spare cent went into the wedding fund.

I lucked into what I thought at the time was an elegant dream of a wedding dress, and the memory of the afternoon this miracle unfolded will always be with me.

I'd just arrived at Elmer's for work when I saw Connie pull in across the lot. Connie was another waitress who'd gotten engaged a few months ago. We would be working the dinner shift together. She was a pixie-faced blue-eyed blonde who had always been kind to me.

I waved to her now, and she waved back. Then she took what looked like a wedding dress from where it hung beside the shotgun seat. It was still sheathed in plastic.

"Connie!" I said, going over. "Did you just pick up your dress? Oh, it's beautiful!" Only then did I notice that her face was splotchy, as if she'd been crying. "Connie, what's the matter?"

"I don't know what I'm going to do," she sniffled.

"About what?"

"Last Friday I found out I'm pregnant," she said. "Not only that, but I'm already three months along! I don't know how it happened. I thought I was being so careful, making him pull out every time."

"Oh, Connie!" I hugged her, not sure what to say. "Are you at least a little bit happy, though? I know you and Don want a big family."

"We do, but I wanted the wedding to come first. And it will, I guess. But I'll be just about ready to pop by then."

"Can't they alter the dress?"

"I asked about that. They said it doesn't have enough seam allowance to let it out much. It's one thing to take a dress in. But you can't really make it much bigger.

"My mother paid five hundred dollars for this one," she said. "I was so happy about this dress. I mean, look at it—isn't it pretty?"

This was the era of Princess Diana's wedding, and minimalism was not in. This dress was in keeping with the decade: It was made of white satin and dripping with lace. It had a lace-edged sweetheart neckline, puffed lacy bell sleeves, and a long lacy train.

"It's beautiful," I said truthfully. "It's the most beautiful dress I've ever seen. I'm getting married too, and I would give anything for a dress like this."

"Well," she said. "You can have it, I guess."

I stood very still.

"*What*?" I finally said. "No!"

"Why not?"

I felt my face heat up. The possibility of Connie giving me her wedding dress had honestly never occurred to me. Did she think I'd been fishing for it?

"Connie, no. I'm sorry. I didn't mean—"

"Oh, I know you didn't. But why not? I can't wear it."

"But can't you return it?"

"No, I can't. I already had it altered. Before I found out about the baby."

"I'll give you all I can for it," I said. "My budget for a wedding dress is one hundred dollars. I wish I could give you five hundred dollars but I just can't."

"I'm glad you'll get to wear it," she said. "At least it's going to someone I like."

Just like that, by sheer chance and Connie's grace, I had the dress of my dreams. That's where the fairy tale ended.

Jim and I had no idea where to get married. We opened the Yellow Pages, and the only place within our budget was a tiny wedding chapel in Aloha, Oregon. It was on the main highway and shared space with a bridal shop. The storefront faced the road, and the chapel was in the back. The venue offered a choice of clergy who could essentially be rented by the hour, and we chose a nice minister whose name I no longer recall. Jim rented a gray tuxedo with tails.

We had given no thought to wedding music. The minister suggested Eddie Rabbitt. Jim and I lit our unity candles to the recorded strains of his "You and I" on the chapel boom box. Our guests showered us and our car in white rice as we descended the chapel steps.

Our reception was a potluck at a friend's country club. To our peers, we were a curiosity. None of them were close to getting married and wouldn't be for a long time. Jim and I weren't old enough to drink yet, so we served soda. Toward the end of the party, his high school buddies threw him in the pool in his rented tux.

These same buddies had also decorated our car. They'd written "Just Married" in shaving cream on the rear windshield and tied tin cans to the back fender. By the end of that hot June afternoon, the shaving cream and rice had been baked into the car. In his sodden rental tux, Jim drove it to a car wash and the car got stuck on the tracks in the middle of the wash. He was drenched all over again while trying to get out.

I cringe now when I look at our photos from that day. The dripping gown, that hot eighties mess of satin and lace. My big hair and blue eyeshadow, the plastic flowers in the chapel. The high school classmates who didn't remain in our lives.

Yet when I recall that day, I also think of the Eddie Rabbitt song that played as we lit our candles. *Just you and I / Sharing our love together / And I know in time / We'll build the dreams we treasure / And we'll be alright / Just you and I . . .*

There was a certain prescience in that default wedding song of ours. All Jim and I had then was our love for each other. In time, as the song went, we would build the dreams we treasured.

We'd be all right, just he and I.

WHEN I REACHED our house, Jim was standing on the front porch. His face was ashen, and I couldn't read his expression, but I understood something momentous had happened.

"Jim!" I said. "What is it?"

"The names you gave me," he said. "Stephanie, it's true. They're real people. They're your grandparents."

He was holding two sheets of printer paper. On each one were a series of what looked like endnotes. And on each, Jim had highlighted a section of them in yellow.

The first read:

> *William Mynn Thornton, Jr. graduated from Hampden-Sydney College [B.A., 1904], the U. of Va [M.A., 1907] and*

Yale [M.A., 1912; Ph.D, 1914]. A Robinson fellow at Yale, he taught chemistry at City College of NY and he was chemist for Du Pont & Company. During WWI, he worked on gas-mask absorbents and related research in the laboratory at Johns Hopkins. He was later an associate in chemistry at Johns Hopkins and then research fellow at Loyola College. During the WWII era, he was a chemist at the Explosives Division of the U.S. Bureau of Mines. After the war, he was a research associate in the Department of Pharmacology at the U of Maryland until his death. He married in New York, NY [Feb. 5, 1916] Florence Beall [born in NY, ca 1884, died 1959]. He died in Baltimore, MD, Sept. 22, 1953. Child: Florence Beall Thornton.

The second read:

Florence Beall Thornton (born in Dela, Dec. 9, 1916) and she resided at one time in NY. She last resided at the U.S. Consulate in Guadalajara, Mexico, and she died Aug. 14, 1985. Children:
Florence Agnes
Allan Winfield

My mother and my Uncle Allan.

"Jim," I said, shivering in disbelief. "Where did these come from?"

"From a series of books called *The Washingtons: A Family History*," he told me. "Volumes 5 and 6. Which cover, respectively, generations nine and ten of the presidential branch."

We stood staring at each other. My husband looked as dazed as I felt.

"Stephanie," he said. "You're a direct descendant of the Washingtons."

Chapter 20

IN OUR KITCHEN a few moments later, with these two pages in front of me on the table, I felt my eyes fill with tears. Yale. Johns Hopkins. Such prestigious universities. All those degrees! A bachelor's, two masters', and a doctorate. I had always been so intimidated by people who'd attended prestigious schools, convinced of some innate difference between them and me.

But this was my own great-grandfather. My blood. A man of industry, intellect and science. It felt like Christmas, the kind of Christmas I dreamed of as a child. A gift so precious I hardly knew how to hold it.

I DON'T THINK I slept that night. I sat in Jim's study in a fever of research. I bought memberships to heritage and ancestry websites. I subscribed to newspaper archives and spent the darkest hours of the morning poring over the stories, clipping the articles. I scanned the fine print of society pages for the precious names of my kin. For many hours Jim sat across from me with his laptop, conducting his own search, joining other sites, trading content with me.

The most comprehensive account I could find of my great-grandfather's life was his obituary in the *Baltimore Sun*. The year was 1953. The year of my mother's rape. "Dr. Thornton Is Dead at 69," the headline read. As if he were so well known in the region as to not need identification by first name. What followed was an account of his extraordinary life. My great-grandfather was a polymath by anyone's estimation, with a long career in chemistry, minerology, geology, pharmacology, physics and other sciences. He was widely published, widely honored, tapped by entities as diverse as the government and the American Chemistry Society to produce research on various topics. He produced all this without ever stinting on his heavy workload at Loyola. The best and brightest students vied for a spot in his classroom.

The obituary ended with: "Funeral arrangements have not been completed. He is survived by his wife, a daughter and a grandchild."

And a great-grandchild who would have given anything to know him.

Next I went looking for my grandmother. The wayward daughter. The link between my mother and these men. The heroine of the TV-caliber melodrama. I found far less content about her, just a few scant clippings about her startling marriage. Here again, my mother's account was verified. My grandmother had indeed eloped with her chauffeur.

"Nature-Loving Cabby, Socialite Married" read the headline of an item in the *Courier-News* of Bridgewater, New Jersey.

> *BAR HARBOR, ME—(AP)—"A mutual interest in the great out-of-doors" set in motion a romance that resulted in the marriage of the socially prominent daughter of a Loyola, Baltimore college professor and a Bar Harbor taxi driver, the couple disclosed today.*
>
> *Florence Beall, 24, daughter of Professor W.M. Thornton, Jr., and Gilman W., 44, were married by a town clerk last Thursday.*
>
> *The bride spent the past few summers in this fashionable resort painting nature scenes. Gilman, former assistant superintendent of a Boston construction firm, became acquainted with the young artist while operating a taxicab for a local garageman and serving as her chauffeur.*

No wedding, just a visit to the town clerk.

There was no photo or likeness of her in connection with her marriage, as there had been for her mother before her.

No appearances in the society pages. No mention in the weddings of relatives. It seemed she had been cut off from her family completely, just as my mother had said. And not just cut off financially, but gone from the picture altogether. Cast away, exiled. Erased.

———

TWO DAYS LATER I was back at St. Vincent's, submitting to the drill I was so used to by now, turning over my coat and purse and cell phone. My mother and I sat once again in the dayroom. I took one look at her face and could see that she'd turned a corner. The crazy had receded. Her eyes were clear and calm.

"Mom, I've been in shock," I told her. "Every single thing you told me checked out. And I can't comprehend that this has all been a huge secret from me for almost fifty years. That in all these decades, you never said a word."

"That's not true," she said. "I told you I descended from kings and queens and royalty. You just wouldn't listen."

I exhaled sharply. "Well, okay, yes," I conceded. "Yes, whenever you were getting arrested, or committed, you'd yell these things. Yes, it did just seem crazy in that context. But I mean, you never *really* told me where and who we came from."

"Of course I did. But there's no point in arguing," my mother said. "It's not my fault that you paid it no mind."

"I'm paying attention now. Tell me, Mom," I begged.

"What do you want to know?"

"Anything you can remember."

"Well," she said. She drew herself up on the dayroom sofa. I could see it pleased her to be the keeper of these details. "Let's see. My grandfather was tall—six-foot-one, I believe—and handsome, with dark brown hair and hazel eyes. He was a very reserved person, although he liked to talk at the dinner table. He let me hang around in his study whenever I wanted. I would play with his weights and measures while he worked at his desk."

"Was he nice to you?"

"Oh yes. He loved me so much," my mother said. "He would give me a piggyback ride up to bed every evening and listen to my prayers and kiss me good night."

I closed my eyes against the wave of longing that broke over me.

"Wait," I said after a moment. "Every evening? You didn't live with him, did you?"

"Oh, yes. Until I was sent away. After—well, you know."

"So there were three generations in one house?"

"No, no. My mother didn't live there," she said. "Just me. My mother lived with her husband and, as I said, she was cut off from the family fortune. She and my father were terribly poor, and they agreed to let my grandparents raise me so I would have all the finer things in life— all the opportunities that came with their money and their place in society."

As smitten with my great-grandfather as I was, it was hard to hear that he'd turned his back on his own child. I wasn't ready to face that, not yet. I pushed it aside and pressed on.

"What was their house like?"

"It was lovely," she said. "It had three floors, and the top level was his domain. Grandma and I shared the second floor. She almost died in childbirth with my mother, and her doctor forbade her to get pregnant again. So after that, she and my grandfather slept in separate rooms. The servants lived on the second floor too."

"Servants?"

"I had my own maid," my mother said. Her face took on a dreamy expression, recalling this. "Her name was Mary. I had a little silver dinner bell, and anytime I wanted something, I just rang that bell and she would bring it to me."

I winced inwardly at her pride and entitlement and a sudden memory came to mind. My mother had a bell in adulthood as well. It had been part of her Buddhist shrine. She rang it at the start of her prayers. I hadn't thought about it in years, but she'd gone through a phase of ringing that bell whenever she wanted something. She rang it when she wanted coffee or tea or her herbs, or anything at all. I would fetch it like a dog every time. I hated the sound of that bell.

"I loved living with my grandparents. They treated me like a princess," my mother went on, pulling me away from my memories and back into hers. "Every Christmas they put up a magnificent tree. Each year it was decorated so beautifully, and under it were so many presents, you wouldn't believe."

Here again, for just a moment, I let myself flash back to all the Christmas holidays in my own childhood home, with no tree, no decorations, no family dinner, and not a single gift for anyone. No food in the cupboards as often as not, and sometimes no electricity and no heat.

Then just as quickly, I let it go. My mother had endured the unthinkable. It had broken her in ways I would never be able to fully quantify. As angry as I might still become with her, I could no longer condemn her, and I could never judge her again.

WHEN I CAME home after our visit at St. Vincent's, I turned my attention to the senior Thornton mentioned toward the end of my great-grandfather's obituary. The most extensive account of his life I could find came from the University of Virginia Library Online. He too was among the most academically versatile professors at his own University of Virginia, where he was appointed the first dean of engineering.

"By the end of his fifty-year stint on the faculty, Thornton's genius was legendary," the profile says. "Dean B.F.D. Runk later quipped that he could have taught any subject in the curriculum except medicine and 'if they gave him six months, he could teach medicine.'"

The university also has web pages devoted to the history of its engineering school. When the senior Thornton arrived there in 1875, he set out to modernize the curriculum. Instead of being content to lecture the students, as professors had always done in the past, he assigned the most current textbooks and field manuals to his pupils and lectured only to supplement their reading. He identified real-world engineering problems and prepared case studies on them for classroom discussions. In 1935, after his decades of tireless service, the school unveiled a new laboratory named Thornton Hall in his honor. He died just two weeks after its inauguration.

My great-great-grandfather's influence on the engineering school was pervasive for decades after his death. Every dean appointed before 1973 had been one of his students. Thornton Hall remains the central home of the engineering school today.

READING ABOUT THE senior Thornton, I felt galvanized by a sense of recognition. I'd brought such a similar vision to my own takeover, my makeover, of Heritage School—making my own curriculum as current, relevant and hands-on as possible. Now in the kitchen, a new conviction came to me, sharp as a sudden pain. *Thornton was my rightful name.* It belonged to me. These men were my true ancestors, in spirit as well as blood.

Thornton. *Thornton.* I loved the sound of it. I said it to myself under my breath like an incantation, like a one-word prayer, an amen. It sounded certain and resolute and self-respecting. It was an upright, stately, sterling name, and I wanted it.

And I would get it. I would change my maiden name to Thornton. I'd start the process tomorrow.

Overcome by this sudden clarity, lit by it, I set my printed pages about the Thorntons on the table and rested my left hand on them, as if on a stack of Bibles. The right one I raised in the attitude of an oath. There in the darkened kitchen, eyes closed, I addressed the spirits of my departed forefathers.

"I, Stephanie Thornton Plymale, do solemnly swear," I whispered, feeling woo-woo and foolish and yet fervently in earnest, "to uphold your commitment to education. I promise to remain devoted to the excellence of my own school, to the welfare of my students, and to a purpose-driven existence. I promise to reclaim the Thornton name, in letter and in spirit. I vow to be worthy of its reputation, to carry it forth with integrity, and to strive to do it honor all the days of my life."

Chapter 21

IT TOOK SIX weeks to change my name. Throughout those six weeks, and well beyond them, I thought about the Thorntons every day. As childish as it was, I had a fantasy of meeting my great-grandfather in some picture-book version of an afterlife. Would he recognize me as a daughter in spirit as well as in blood? Would he see all I'd done to escape the educational wasteland of my childhood?

I learned to read when I was ten years old. Somehow, some way, I was in the fifth grade without ever having learned the sounds of the alphabet. I should never have been allowed to advance each fall during those elementary years, but I was. With each grade, I was more isolated, the gulf between me and my classmates only widening as time went on.

My mother's live-in boyfriend of the moment was Daniel, and he had the distinction of being the only adult who ever seemed alarmed that I was failing at school.

"Florence, the kid is ten," he said. "She seems smart enough to me. Why can't she read?"

"Because she's lazy," my mother told him. "Time and again, I've done my best to teach her, but she won't even try."

My mother never tried to teach me, not once. She never even read to us when we were little. No *Goodnight Moon*. No bedtime stories. No nursery rhymes, no children's classics, and no fairy tales. We never even had a book in the house until Daniel moved in, and then we had one: *The Hobbit*.

It was a green paperback. On the cover was a dirt road cutting a swath through an emerald landscape. Here and there on the green slopes, smoking chimneys came up through the grass, hinting at subterranean homes. In the foreground, a wizard with a staff was striding toward a round blue door set into the hillside. The book was fragrant with mildew and yellowed with age, but it was intact.

Daniel was in his early thirties with hazel eyes and dark-blond thinning hair, long and usually pulled back into a listless ponytail. He worked at RadioShack and probably made just enough to cover our monthly rent.

I try to imagine where he and my mother could have met. Most likely in a bar. He always smelled of alcohol, but not in the rank and dangerous way I associated with Rick. It seemed as if he drank just enough to blur the edges of the day and tamp down any flares of wistfulness or ambition.

Daniel resolved to teach me to read, and he turned to the only book at hand. He would read a paragraph, and then I was supposed to read a paragraph. He read slowly for my sake, but it never took him more than half a minute to read his own lines. A paragraph could take me half an hour.

> *In a hole in the ground there lived a hobbit. Not a nasty, dirty, wet hole, filled with the ends of worms and an oozy smell, nor yet a dry, bare, sandy hole with nothing in it to sit down on or to eat: it was a hobbit-hole, and that means comfort.*

The opening to this book couldn't have been more captivating to me. It was a description of a true home, and even at the time, I was aware that ours fell short by its standards. The only furniture in our house was a mattress on the floor of my mother's room, and the television that Daniel had brought home from the store (my siblings and I slept on the floor with blankets). Daniel and I sat on that mattress each evening and together we sounded out the words, syllable by agonizing syllable.

As hard and tedious as they could be, I never shied away from those evening lessons. I was desperate to learn and grateful, so grateful, for his gentle correction and his patience. All that year, like every other year, I'd sat at the back of the classroom, trying to will myself invisible so I'd never be singled out or called upon. My inability to read was a shame that blotted out all other thought.

On Monday afternoons, the kids were shepherded to the school library in anticipation of Sustained Silent Reading, a half hour every day set aside for each of us to read whatever we wanted. Every Monday, I'd go to the fifth-grade section and pull a book off the shelf. I'd try to find one with pictures. During those eternal thirty minutes, I would sit with my book open in front of me, scan what pictures were there and pretend to read the words, staring at the meaningless print. Every once in a while, I'd turn a page.

Now and then I dared to look around, and even at a glance, I could tell no one else was faking it. All the other kids sat transfixed, eyes scanning the sentences before them, occasionally breaking into laughter. Text that meant nothing at all to me was speaking to them. It was holding them captive, letting them in on wild capers and confessions and secrets. The silence in the room was charged with concentration, engagement.

I wanted to be like them. I wanted my face to assume a look of absorption, one that wasn't feigned. I wanted this code in front of me to transmit the messages that the others were receiving. I would have given anything to be initiated into its mysteries.

It had always been like this. In second grade, every day after lunch, the teacher had read *Stuart Little* to the class for fifteen minutes, marking her place with an index card wherever she stopped and picking up where she'd left off the next day. I was mesmerized by the adventures of the tiniest member of the Little family, who resembled a mouse. Each day I waited eagerly for that treasured time, the most gratifying moments I'd ever known in a classroom. A few of the other kids, as hooked on the story as I was, weren't content to have the story parceled out in quarter-hour increments. They checked the book out of the library or begged their parents to get it and they read ahead. They were proud and empowered—they didn't have to wait like I did, for scraps to be dispensed at someone else's discretion.

But now—sitting on that mattress, curled against Daniel's warmth—

my life was being altered. Three-letter words were unlocked first, and then longer ones, with special consonant blends and vowels that made different sounds depending on the letters that followed them. Daniel wrote words in a notebook to teach me. We did drills each evening before turning to *The Hobbit*. I would read a column of words—*rat, mat, mad, car*—and then Daniel would add an "e" to the end of each one, a magic letter that stayed silent but hardened the preceding vowel so that *mat* became *mate* and *car* became *care*.

What was Daniel doing with us? Was he a fool for my mother, or did he just take pity on our family? Although he spent hours on that mattress with his arm around me, there was nothing predatory about him. I'd spent a year and a half in Ted's house by then, and I knew the signs. Daniel had no ulterior motive, no desire to violate a child. He was just being kind.

A lot of people would call him a loser. He was sad-eyed and soft-bodied in that red uniform shirt with the white "R" stitched inside a circle. Even at that age, I could see that my mother was using him for room and board, and he was letting himself be used.

He was a hero to me, and I'll be grateful to him until my last breath.

There was no breakthrough moment during these reading lessons. It wasn't like flipping a switch. It was more like the dawn seeping into a room at daybreak: first a ray and then a beam and finally a flood of sunlight, as I became able to decipher a word and then a string of words and then full sentences.

> *The next morning was a midsummer's morning as fair and fresh as could be dreamed: blue sky and never a cloud, and the sun dancing on the water. Now they rode away amid songs of farewell and good speed, with their hearts ready for more adventure, and with a knowledge of the road they must follow.*

With each piece of the code he imparted to me, another part of darkness was lifted. The lock on the door keeping me out had been broken and, just like that, I was inside the fortress, I was on the pirate ship, in the highest turret of the castle, at the royal ball, in a cove by the sea. I could time-travel along with everyone else. I could find out for myself how the story ended.

THE JUDGE HAD just signed my change of name decree when the call came from the psych ward.

"Your mother is experiencing a respiratory crisis," said a woman who identified herself as the nurse on duty. "She's losing consciousness from lack of oxygen. We would like your consent to admit her to the emergency room."

"Of course," I said, pushing through the courtroom door and stepping out into the hall. "Is she okay right now?"

"Without an intervention very soon, she's likely to die," the nurse said bluntly. "Can you meet us at the ER right away, so you can sign the release forms?"

In her new bed in the oncology ward of the same hospital, my mother was gray-faced and wasted. There was a tube in her nose and others running beneath her hospital smock and into her arms. Though her eyes were open when I stepped into the room, for a terrible moment I thought she was gone. Her gaze was cloudy and opaque, sightless and empty. But then her eyes shifted in my direction. It was like seeing a corpse stir back to life.

"Stephanie," she rasped. My name seemed to cost her a terrible effort.

"Hi, Mom," I said. "I came as fast as I could."

She reached out and plucked at my sleeve with one bluish claw. "Promise me," she whispered.

"Anything," I said, tears gathering at the corners of my eyes.

"Promise you'll bring me back to Bar Harbor."

I looked at her in confusion. "Bar Harbor, Maine?"

"Yes," she said. "That's where I want to be."

I stood there for a moment trying to imagine what she meant by this. Did she want to be buried there? Or have her ashes scattered there?

"What do you mean, Mom?" I asked. "You want to go to Bar Harbor when?"

"As soon as we can," she said. "Tomorrow if possible."

"Oh," I said. "Well, I don't know about tomorrow. But—"

"I want to go to the candy store," she said feverishly. "See's Candies. The best in the world. And I want to go to the country club. I'm sure I'm still a member. I think I can get you in."

"That sounds lovely, Mom," I said, bewildered. "All those things sound lovely."

"And I want to see William. It's been so long."

"William who?" I leaned closer to her, brushing her sweat-dampened hair back from her forehead. "Who's William, Mom?"

"He was my boyfriend from Before."

Then she closed her eyes, exhausted, and in another moment, she was asleep.

THAT EVENING, in bed beside Jim, I did an image search for Bar Harbor. The photos that came up on my phone were like a dream of summer: A-frame houses of clapboard and shingles, colorful buoys, lobster shacks, flower boxes in all the windows, and shops studded with the American flag.

The next morning, back in her hospital room, I could see at a glance that she was better. She looked calm now, and her breathing was even. A hint of color had come into her face, and the spark was back in her blue eyes. She looked lucid; she looked good.

"Mom, you're better," I said, drawing a chair up to her bed and sitting down. "You look wonderful."

This pleased her, I could tell. Even in a cancer ward, she wasn't above preening. "Do you think so?"

"Yes! Your cheeks are all rosy, and your eyes look so blue."

"Well," she said. "It's too bad there are no proper suitors around here."

I smothered a laugh. "Mom, speaking of suitors," I said. "Yesterday you mentioned someone named William. You said he was your boy-friend from Before."

"That's right."

"Tell me about him, Mom," I said. "Did you meet him in Bar Harbor?"

"Yes, I did," she said. "We went there every summer. My grandparents had a little yellow beach house. It was my favorite place to be."

"Was he your first boyfriend? How old were you when you met?"

"I was ten years old and he was fifteen. He thought I was older because I was so tall for my age. I developed early too."

"Was his family rich like yours?" I asked.

"Oh no. He came from a common family. His father was a mechanic."

This was a surprise. "And your grandparents didn't object?"

"They would have objected if they'd known about it. I kept it a secret from them. I was young, but I wasn't a fool. When he sent me letters, he wrote 'Willa' as the name on the return address. They thought it was a girl writing to me."

She and William talked on the telephone as well. She did the calling because his family could not have afforded the long-distance charges. Her own grandparents never mentioned the expense, if they noticed it at all.

"We stayed in touch for years," my mother told me. "He came to visit me at my mother's house in Florida. Even after he was married, we slept together whenever we saw each other." Her eyes went distant and misty. "He was the love of my life," she said.

"Is that why you want to go to Bar Harbor?

"Yes," she said. "It's the last place I was happy."

"Mom, you never told me any of this," I said.

"I don't like to dwell on the past," she said. "What's the point?"

"I know how hard it is to talk about," I told her. "But you suffered so much in secret, for so long, and your story is important. I don't want you to die without telling me your story."

"This again." She sighed.

"Please, Mom."

"You always do this. It's so cruel." She sighed again, but this time it was a sigh of resignation. "What do you want to know?"

"I want to know what happened to you," I said. "Please tell me, Mom. I'm listening."

IN EVERY POSSIBLE respect, 1953 was the ghastliest year imaginable for my mother. Her father died suddenly that June from stomach cancer. By all accounts, he spent his final days in excruciating pain.

Three months later, her grandfather died as well. The cause of death was heart failure. I believe, in fact, that he died of a broken heart—that what happened to my mother was the death of him.

The men who abducted my mother brought her to a windowless room in a low-rent apartment building on Preston Street in Baltimore. The room was little more than a cell. There was nothing in it but a bare mattress on a metal frame, with coils that creaked and groaned, punctuating every assault.

My mother would find herself in one cell after another for the rest of her life. This was the first, the one that led to all the others. When she crossed the threshold of that room, the part of her life that she calls Before was over. She would never be able to return.

They kept the lights off when they were with her and when they weren't. She had no way to know whether it was day or night. Very soon she lost all sense of time. Only later would she understand that she had been there for ten straight days.

These numbers defy comprehension. Ten days. Fifteen men. Eleven years old.

Eleven was the age my own daughter kept her stuffed animals on rotation, taking a different one to bed with her each night so all of them would feel loved. The year she cried herself to sleep after her guinea pig died. The year she wrote every evening in a diary with a horse on the cover and spent most of her birthday money on stickers.

The men were inconceivably brutal. They slapped her and kicked her and punched her. They spat on her and urinated on her and ejaculated on her. They taunted her and called her names. They violated every part of her body again and again. When she was finally hospitalized, her eyes were blackened, her entire body was covered in bruises, and she was bleeding from every orifice.

When I reach for a comparison, I can find none. As a child, I experienced recurrent sexual violation myself. But even in the worst of times, I knew where I was. I had a bed with a blanket and pillow. I had daylight. I had long stretches of normalcy in between, interludes of school and chores and time with the animals outside. I had only one abuser. He made me service him with my hands and my mouth, but he did not rip me open. He did not beat me, call me names, blacken my eyes or bloody my face.

Even putting aside the sexual assault, I can't imagine the terror of being taken to a dark room and kept there for days on end. I can't imagine the pain of a little girl who had no shred of comfort and no reprieve before the next man.

I try to imagine the fathomless black depths of an ordeal like hers, but I can't.

HER SINGLE SAVING grace in this hellhole was the Indian.

The Indian never left my mother's side. He held her hand. He held her gaze. In the deepest way imaginable, he held *her*, cradled her. Within the force field of his compassion, she could drift, give herself over and leave her body behind, below, on the bed beneath the men.

The Indian had long black hair. He wore faded jeans and a white t-shirt. Deep grooves were cut into his grieving face. Sometimes he wept over her plight.

Without him, she would not have survived.

Toward the end, he pulled the shirt from his back and ripped it into two clean white swaths of cotton. Then he used safety pins to tenderly fasten them around her privates. She was clad only in this makeshift loincloth when at long last, he lifted her into his arms and carried her out of that room, down to the street, and over to a hospital.

———

THERE WAS NO Indian, of course. The police raided the building and arrested the men on the premises. An ambulance brought my mother to the hospital, where she received—among other treatments—an immense dose of penicillin and a blood transfusion.

Why was her guardian angel a Native American? What did he represent to her?

I couldn't ask her this question, because right up to the end, she believed he was real.

WHEN MY MOTHER was able to leave the hospital, a judge ordered her transfer to the House of the Good Shepherd for Wayward Girls. According to her, this was for her own protection. Many of the men indicted for raping my mother had ties to the mob. The facility was meant to serve as a safe haven, and her whereabouts were kept confidential.

The Good Shepherd order had many of these houses around the country. After hearing her account, I found a description of one such home, taken from the social services directory of Newark, New Jersey, in 1912:

> *A Catholic institution for the moral and religious instruc-*
> *tion and training of wayward girls and women. Under the*
> *charge of the Sisters of Good Shepherd. Two hundred inmates.*
> *A laundry is maintained, the work of which is performed by*
> *the girls. Contract sewing is also done by the institution.*
>
> *There is a Magdalene Department for reformed penitents.*
> *The inmates are also instructed in undergarment mak-*
> *ing and general sewing. Girls received into the institution*
> *through the Catholic Children's Aid Association on recom-*
> *mendation of the courts and probation officers.*

It would seem The House of the Good Shepherd was a reform school of sorts. The girls in the home were considered inmates. Of all the places to send my mother for protection, why there? One clue would emerge six or seven weeks after my mother entered the House, when her just-developing breasts swelled painfully along with her belly. She was pregnant.

There was no discussion, ever, of the pregnancy. No one seems to have acknowledged its existence, let alone the possibility of its termination. Here, my mind reels. Because her doctors *must* have known. No medical professional would overlook that possibility in a pubescent female patient who'd suffered dozens if not hundreds of unprotected sexual encounters. They would have tested for pregnancy or, if it were too early for that, scheduled a future test for pregnancy.

Was it a Catholic hospital? That's the only way I can make sense of this picture—of a child victim of gang rape being forced to carry to term.

Three months into her stay at the house, my mother woke to find the bed beneath her soaked with blood. All that day and the next, great quantities of blood issued from *down there* as well as dense purplish clots and grayish-purple pieces of tissue. She lay in the infirmary bed and wept with pain and fear as this discharge kept coming, her midsection swathed in towels.

I try to picture my mother in that home for wayward girls, miscarrying alone. Once again, this is beyond my imagination.

Curiously, my mother's memories of the house held no tinge of bitterness or self-pity. "The house was very strict," she recalled. "We had to attend mass three times a day. But we were allowed to listen to music after the night mass. And the girls would dance. Oh, how they danced! They were wild. I loved watching them move like that. I envied them, to be truthful. No one ever danced like that in the high society circles I grew up in."

More curious still, my mother begged to remain in the house even when it was no longer mandatory. "I didn't want to leave," she told me. "I wanted to stay there and work as a secretary in their office. I even thought about becoming a nun if it meant I could live there for good. But

Mother Cabrini said the house wasn't the right place for me. She said: *You have to face the world again, my child."*

———

WHEN I WALKED out of St. Vincent's and into the parking lot, I was almost staggering. I felt weak with grief, crushed by all my mother had suffered, and stunned with a new recognition.

For the first time in my life, I understood Agnes, my mother's child persona. Agnes was always pregnant. Always crying, and frightened, and always clutching her belly. No matter how my mother aged—even when she was forty-nine, fifty-three, sixty-eight—when she was Agnes, she was pregnant.

I thought of how much I had always dreaded interacting with Agnes. Flow was frightening and violent and unpredictable, but the raw vulnerability of Agnes was its own kind of threat—more intimate, closer to home, and closer to me.

I'd held Agnes at a distance because I was afraid of her pain. If she ever surfaced again, I would hold her close.

BY THE TIME I reached home that evening, I had my heart set on offering my mother the one thing she still wanted. I spent long hours online that night, researching travel accommodations for the terminally ill, trying to imagine how a trip to Bar Harbor could be managed. We'd have to fly, of course. I had a very busy schedule over the next several weeks, but I could find a way to clear a few days. We would take all her pain meds, and I could learn how to monitor her oxygen levels. I would rent a wheelchair and push her around the streets of her old vacation town. We could sit by the bay and have cups of chowder. Yes, it would take a lot of arrangement and effort, but it was her dying wish, and if anyone could make it happen, I could.

On my way back to the hospital the next morning, I took a detour that would bring me to Lloyd Center, a mall on the north side of town, where there was a See's Candies shop. I hadn't been there since my late teens, but the two-pound assortment of chocolate was in the same plain box I remembered—almost all white, printed only with "See's Famous Old Time Candies" in black and gold script. On the left was a graphic of a little cottage with a smoking chimney, on the right a cameo portrait of Mary See. The design probably hadn't changed since my mother was there, and for that, I was grateful. The idea, after all, was to offer her a remnant of her long-lost happy childhood.

When I stepped off the elevator and onto the oncology floor, a doctor was just leaving her room, and I rushed up to him. I would secure his permission for a trip to Bar Harbor, and then I would surprise her with the marvelous news.

"You can't possibly be serious," the doctor said. "*No*, she can't fly across the country in her condition. Even if her medical needs didn't defy plane travel, which they do, she's in no shape to make a trip like that." He sounded angry, as if I'd proposed that my mother take trapeze lessons.

"Are you sure there isn't some way?" I pleaded. "I'll do anything to make it work. I don't care how much it would cost."

"You don't seem to realize how fragile she is," he snapped. "If she had a life-threatening episode on the plane, there would be no way to help her unless they made an emergency landing. It would be terribly irresponsible to risk that."

I dropped my eyes so he wouldn't see them filling with tears. "It's just—can you understand? I'm her daughter and this is her dying wish."

"I'm afraid you're the one who doesn't understand," the doctor said. "Forgive me for being so blunt, but even here in the hospital, your mother might not survive the week."

IT TOOK SEVERAL minutes for me to compose myself enough to enter my mother's room. When I did, I saw that she'd taken a turn for the worse. Gone were all the markers of improvement from the day before. She was visibly feverish again: sweating, dull-eyed and agitated.

"Miss Florence is not so well today," said a young nurse who had just come in, as if reading my thoughts. "I thought we were out of the woods yesterday, but her vital signs aren't looking good right now."

I set the shopping bag from Lloyd Center on the floor and put the back of my hand to my mother's forehead. She swatted it away. "She feels warm to me," I said.

"Her temperature's up around one hundred and two," the nurse confirmed.

I dropped into the chair beside my mother's bed and bent to open the shopping bag. Then I set the box of See's Candies on her bed table and lifted the lid. Her eyes lit up, but she made no move to take one. In that moment, I realized the doctor was right. Bar Harbor had been a pipe dream all along. She was past eating chocolate. She was past eating chowder. She was not getting on a plane. She couldn't even sit up.

She was dying. My mother was really dying.

"I can't wait to get out of here," she said. "Stephanie, can you get me out?"

I moved my chair as close to her bed as it would go and spoke in a low, conspiratorial tone. "Mom, your stay here is almost over. I know how hard it's been. But you'll be somewhere much better very soon, I promise," I said, my throat tightening as I spoke. "You'll be in Bar Harbor."

She beamed at me. "The doctor said I could go?"

"You can go. You'll be there very soon," I said again. "And this time, you'll never have to leave."

Chapter 22

WITH MY MOTHER'S death so close at hand, a longing to find other family members took fierce root within me. I knew she had a younger brother named Allan. My mother had mentioned him from time to time over the years. I'd never thought to ask much about him before, but now I began to press her relentlessly.

"Mom, when's the last time you spoke to your brother?"

"Not since you were little."

"Where is he now?"

"Oh, I couldn't tell you," she said. "Last I knew, he was with that awful woman. What's-her-name? It's Beth, I think."

"How was she awful?"

"Oh, she was so uptight that time we stayed with them."

"You mean on our way to Mexico?"

"Yes. They lived in southern California then. Maybe they're still there. You can look them up: Allan and Beth Mulligan in San Diego."

"I REMEMBER YOU," Beth told me stiffly over the phone. "So you're all grown up now. Well, of course you are. It's been more than forty years. But I have to tell you, I didn't think you'd survive another six months. Are your other brothers and sisters alive?"

"What?" I said, caught off guard. "Um, yes. That is, most of them are. Allan died a few years ago."

I felt a deep pang, saying this of my brother. He was the one with whom I'd been closest by far. It was hard to believe she'd asked this question so casually, as if inquiring about a litter of animals.

"Well, how's that for irony?" she said. "Allan was the only one we tried to save."

"Save from what?"

"From your crazy mother. I'll never forget all the crap she pulled with us. Letting me drive around with all those drugs in my car, holing up in our house for at least a week and barely lifting a finger to help out. I was sure you kids were going to die, hanging around with her. When you all took off again, I offered to keep one child with us. We didn't have space for more. We took Allan because he was my husband's namesake. I thought, *Let us spare one of them, at least.*"

"I see," I said, not knowing what else to say. "So, do you know where my uncle is?"

"No, I don't," Beth told me. "Somewhere in Mexico is all I can tell you."

"Do you know which city?" I wondered if he could be in Guadalajara, in his mother's old place, or near it.

"Honey, I've got no clue. I haven't talked to him in years."

"Oh." My voice went high and cracked with disappointment.

"Don't cry," she said. "There's a friend of his who'd probably know where to find him. His name is Tom Shaughnessy, and he coaches high school football." She paused before offering, "I'd ask him myself, but I have my pride."

"Wait a minute," I said, scrambling for a pen. "Let me write this down." She gave me the name of the school where he worked.

"Listen, if you find Allan, tell him to call me," she blurted, just before hanging up. "I hate to admit it, but I miss that son of a bitch."

"HE'S BEEN IN Mexico for the past few years, but he can be hard to track down," Tom told me when we spoke. "He likes to spend time off the grid."

I'd emailed him late at night, at the address listed beside his name in the school's online directory. He called the very next day.

I closed my eyes, weak with my yearning for more. "But you do have an address? A phone number? *Something?*"

"I'm not supposed to pass it on to anyone. He doesn't want his ex to track him down," Tom said. "But I'll tell you what I'll do. You give me *your* phone number and I'll pass it along to him the first chance I get."

I wanted to argue, to beg for direct access, but I couldn't let myself come across as hell-bent or unhinged.

"I understand," I said reluctantly. "All right, then, if you think that's best."

"The thing is, like I said, he disappears for long stretches of time. So it might take some weeks for me to reach him. Please don't take it personal if you don't hear back for a while."

So I'd been warned, but it didn't keep me from hoping. All that day and the next and the next, I kept the phone nearby at all times, even when I was in the shower. I kept it on during business lunches and work meetings. I didn't silence it upon going to sleep.

A week went by and then another. My mother did not die. She recovered from her crisis and left the hospital, defying the predictions of everyone involved in her care. She returned to her apartment, and I turned to the task of securing hospice services for her. The school year went along at its usual hectic pace, and gradually Allan faded from the forefront of my thoughts.

IN MID-APRIL, after much discussion with Jim, I invited my mother to our home for Easter Sunday. It felt like the right time to risk a family visit. The kids hadn't seen her in many years, and I knew that after this weekend, they might never see her again. They had grown since she last saw them, too. They weren't vulnerable children anymore, and my mother was frail and ill.

On this occasion my optimism was rewarded. The whole afternoon was like a dream to me. Jim drove across town to pick up my mother while I cooked at home. When she arrived, I could see that she'd gotten all dressed up for the occasion. She wore a flowing lavender blouse and skirt, and her hair was tied back with a lavender ribbon. She had taken pains with her nails and makeup. She looked like any respectable grandmother.

While I put holiday dinner on the table, she sat on the sofa with our dog curled in her lap. She looked happy and content. If it weren't for the oxygen tank beside her, the scene might have been an ad for a retirement magazine. Each of our kids took a turn sitting with her, telling her details of their lives and showing her photos.

Eventually, Josh brought out his guitar and played her a few songs he had written. Her face lit up from the first few bars, her longtime passion for music clearly strong within her still. She was rapt with admiration for as long as he played, and she clapped her hands with delight at the end of each song.

I'd made a pineapple-glazed Easter ham, scalloped potatoes, and a salad strewn with flowers. It was hard for my mother to eat, but she took appreciative nibbles of everything and even tried to help me with the dishes afterward. We spent the rest of the afternoon on the porch, just enjoying the warmth of the day and the feeling of peace between us.

It was a day with no abusive words, no hurt feelings, and no self-pity. No blaming, no berating, no criticism, and no rage.

When she got tired, Jim took her home. They made a stop at her local pharmacy to refill a few of her prescriptions, and when they reached her building she thanked him. It was such a small, everyday thing—a man driving his mother-in-law home after a visit—but even this was a rare piece of grace. My mother had always hated Jim. Such simple kindness, rendered and accepted with gratitude, would not have been possible in the past.

When I fell into bed that night, I was filled with a rare sense of satisfaction. In that moment I felt as if I'd not only survived my own childhood, but transcended it, healed from it. After all these decades, I'd gotten my mother to tell her own story, and I'd helped her heal too.

I felt as if I had finally resolved our relationship. I'd built a life of stability and beauty, and invited her into it, and here she was. Here we were.

Not even one week later, still basking in the glow of that beautiful day, I went to visit my mother, and she told me I looked awful. She said my dress was all wrong for me and I'd gained too much weight to go sleeveless. She said I was a terrible mother and my kids were spoiled and Jim was the devil incarnate. She railed at me for not driving her home myself, and for letting her account run out of money. (I had full financial responsibility for her after I took guardianship.) She cursed the day I became her guardian and pushed me out of her room.

I drove home in tears, forced to face a bleak truth I'd tried to deny: It was not within my power to transform my mother, and it never would be.

THE VERY NEXT morning, when I pulled the car to the curb outside my school, my phone began to vibrate with an unidentified call. I never answered such calls. I don't know why I took that one.

"Hello?"

"Is this Stephanie?" It was a man's voice, low and unfamiliar. I could not imagine who it might be.

"Yes, this is Stephanie," I said. "Whom am I speaking with, please?"

"Stephanie, this is your Uncle Allan," he said. "Has my sister died?"

I sat in the car and spoke to him for almost an hour. I was making myself late for work, but I was afraid to let him go even for a brief time. What if he never called back? It was too soon to ask him to trust me with his number.

"I was so happy to get your message," he said. "As Tom told you, I like to be off the grid, so I didn't get his email until this morning. I'm sorry your mom is so sick. I haven't talked to her in a real long time."

"She'll be glad to know we connected," I said, though I had no idea if this was true.

"I love my sister," he told me, "but we have nothing in common. She was always heavy into smoking and drugs. I'm a dedicated runner and

I've always lived clean and healthy. She married a good man and then cheated on him with every deadbeat and loser who crossed her path. She left him for that scum, Rick." He spat my former stepfather's name as if it were a rotten chunk of apple.

"It killed him," he recalled. "*She* killed him. She might as well have shot him through the heart. I love my sister, but there's a demon inside her. She burned our mother's house down, did you know that?"

"*What?*" I said, shocked. "No. No, I didn't know that."

"Well, she did."

"When was this?"

"It was after she got out of that convent home she was in," he told me. "She was living with our mother, but she didn't like it there. She was used to a fancy house and fancy food and her own servants. Our place wasn't good enough for her. It was small and poor and shabby compared to what she was used to. The food our mother cooked wasn't to her liking. She was a serious swimmer—she'd been on the swim team at her prep school, Bryn Mawr—and we didn't belong to any country clubs."

"Why did she live with the Thorntons, while you stayed with your mother?" I asked.

"Because they only wanted her," Allan said. "They didn't want me."

"I don't know why they wouldn't," I said, feeling a pang for the child rejected by his own grandparents. "I'm sure you were an adorable little boy."

"I looked like him," Allan told me. "Like my father. Gilman. They hated him because he was just a regular guy."

He sounded bitter, and I didn't blame him.

"They never forgave my mother for marrying him, and she never forgave them either," he added. "Did you know she got rid of all their possessions in a yard sale?"

"A yard sale?"

"They disowned her, but when they were gone, there were no other heirs. She was their only child, so their entire estate went to her after my grandmother died. Their art collection was worth millions. Your mother's doll collection alone was probably worth a million. They had an original piece of art by Botticelli."

"No!" I said, shocked again.

"Yes, ma'am, as God is my witness. And priceless antiques from all over the world."

"And it all went to her?"

"Every last piece. Now, I can understand her loyalty to my father's memory. But why not use the money in ways that would have pleased him? He loved nature and animals and favored conservation. She could have endowed all kinds of outdoors or wildlife organizations in his name. But no. She dragged that fancy European furniture and their art collection and their family heirlooms out onto the front lawn and sold it all for next to nothing. Just about gave it away to anyone who came along."

"I can't believe that," I murmured, aghast and more than a little heartbroken at the idea of such flagrant waste. I myself would have paid good money for just one remnant of anything they'd owned.

"My sister had so many kids," my uncle said then. "Which one are you? Are you one of Louie's?"

"I don't think so," I said. "She told me Louie wasn't my father. I don't know who my father is."

"Doesn't surprise me," he replied matter-of-factly. "She probably doesn't know either. That's how she was. Pardon me for saying."

"That's okay," I said. "I know how she was."

How can I describe how it felt to find him? It had taken months to uncover and corroborate my mother's story, and even now, it still felt so far-fetched, so unreal. But here was someone who knew it all, someone who shared my family history and my blood. Someone who understood where I'd come from.

I talked with him until the battery of my phone flat-lined. Just before I was forced to hang up, he asked for my mailing address, and I gave it to him. Then I sat for several dazed minutes behind the wheel, staring at the rain on the windshield and smiling.

My uncle had called. My uncle had called! It was the kind of thing other people said all the time, but that simple pleasure had never before been mine.

———

"MOM, YOU'LL NEVER guess who phoned me today," I said that evening as soon as I arrived at her place.

The last few weeks of hospice had been good to her. When she left St. Vincent's, she'd weighed eighty-seven pounds, and now the scale hovered around one hundred and two. Her pain was under control, and she was even able to spend time outside.

She looked up at me from the couch as I dropped into the nearest chair. "Who?"

"Your long-lost brother Allan."

A smile lit her face. For a moment, she didn't look ravaged or old or sick.

"You found Allan? Where is he?"

"He went to Mexico, just like your mother. I spoke to him on the phone this morning for almost an hour," I said. "Mom, he told me you burned your own mother's house down. Is that true?"

"Yes, it is," she said without hesitation. There wasn't a hint of apology in her tone.

I hadn't really doubted it, and yet I felt myself stiffen with renewed shock.

"*Why?*"

"I didn't want to be there anymore! I never wanted to live with her in the first place. I loved my grandparents' home. I was miserable at my mother's."

"So your solution was to burn down the house?" I asked. "How did you do it?"

WHEN THE TRIALS were over—after none of the defendants received more than two months in prison for the prolonged abduction and gang-rape of two children—my mother was not sent back to her grandparents' stately home in Baltimore but to her own mother's home in St. Petersburg, Florida. Her grandfather had died during her time in the Good Shepherd

Home for Wayward Girls. The judge ruled Baltimore unsafe for my mother. My grandmother blamed her parents for her daughter's ordeal. She believed my mother never would have been abducted if they'd been more watchful and aware.

For years, the price my grandmother had paid to give my mother a better life was estrangement from her. Now, her daughter was back in her house, but by then my grandmother was in a bad state. By all accounts, she never really recovered from her husband's death. She moved through her days in a kind of malaise, spending a lot of time in bed or staring out the window. She passed most of her evenings in a local bar, where she'd pick fights with other patrons and come home bloodied.

Some of the details my mother revealed about her mother's life were of poverty and depression: Her house was dark and dreary, dirty and unkempt. Others revealed sheer eccentricity: She enrolled in the local black college, for instance, and the family received death threats in response. She had, according to my mother, at least twenty dogs.

"Mom," I said. "Come on. *Twenty dogs?*"

She swore it was true.

In any event, the rage inside my mother grew to be like a wild, clawing thing. So much had been taken from her. She'd been stripped of her girlhood, her innocence, her grandparents and home and future—all in the course of a single, unimaginable year. She felt trapped in this dreadful house, this dreadful new life, unable to abide it.

So one afternoon, after my grandmother had gone elsewhere, my mother let all the animals out of the house. She walked through each of the rooms, pouring kerosene. Then she stepped onto the porch, knelt on the threshold of the front door, and lit a match.

There was a popular lake within walking distance of their home, with an area marked off as a local beach. My mother spent the day at the swimming hole, as she called it, while my grandmother's house burned to the ground.

———

TWO WEEKS AFTER my phone call from Allan, I came home to find a flat parcel on our porch, leaning against the front door. It was wrapped in heavy brown paper and festooned with purple Mexican stamps.

Dear Steph, began the letter I found inside, a letter written on wide-ruled paper in the shaky hand of a seventy-one-year-old man, *I would much like to be your friend/uncle—I have few friends and no relatives I am in touch with.*

The next few lines provide his contact information, including two email accounts and a mailing address.

I really liked the man who was not your father—when I was seventeen, I spent my summer in the Bronx with your mother and Louie. I worked in his restaurant. He was very good at what he did. He was a great cook and people liked him. Beth and I spent our honeymoon in San Francisco with your mother and Louie. It was 1968—were you alive then? I didn't pay much attention to you kids.

Louie had another very successful morning and lunch diner for working men. I don't think Louie was crazy—he had a beautiful young wife whom he loved very much but she kept having children who were not his. It is hard to imagine how much that must have hurt him. Beth had an affair and it almost broke my heart and she didn't have another man's child. Suicide seems a natural reaction to that kind of pain—a man doesn't have to keep taking the slings and arrows of outrageous fortune. I thought he was a good man. Please don't judge him too harshly.

He'd enclosed a photograph of Louie at work, possibly on a break, wearing his tall chef's hat. The date printed into the frame was July 1967. He was seated with one arm slung casually over a chair in the foreground of the picture. Beside him on a nearby table is a cup of coffee.

I stared at this photo of Louie for a long time. The man staring back at me looked tough, burly, and resolute. He had a certain authority, even a certain majesty beneath that puffed white hat. Both the letter and this picture conjured a very different image of Louie than the one I'd harbored all my life. The tragic figure in my mother's story had been a kind of hapless cartoon character, in thrall to a reckless beauty, easily manipulated, drinking himself to death in a roadside motel.

Here in the letter and the photo, though, was an upright man, steadfast and hardworking, honest and competent. A man who'd bought me a dress just before dying. I felt awash in sorrow suddenly, for him and for myself. He was right there, ready and willing to be my father. I could have grown up with a man who loved me.

My relationship with your mother is strange. As I told you on the phone, fate led to your mother going to live with my grandmother in Baltimore. We never got together until my father died in 1952. After that, my mother and I took the Greyhound bus to Baltimore for two weeks at Christmas and a month in the summer at Bar Harbor, Maine or Watch Hill, RI. After your mother was raped, she came to live with us in St. Petersburg, FL—this was 1953 or 1954. This picture is how I best remember your mother.

Here I felt jarred by his words. *After your mother was raped.* Such a casual corroboration of the story she'd told me. I never doubted my mother was one of the unnamed girls in the newspaper stories, but it still felt momentous to have confirmation from a family member.

The photo he enclosed of my mother was breathtaking, the most beautiful one I'd ever seen. She was in a blouse and skirt, leaning against a tree. She looked prim and girlish with a slight smile, downcast eyes and soft brown curls. Her face was angelic. It was an alternate vision of her: fresh-faced and wholesome, serene and sane.

I want to tell you so much but just now I have to run. I will continue in my next letter—I promise.

Love ya,

Uncle Al

Chapter 23

THE PACKAGE ON the porch held one additional item, one that would send me down yet another rabbit hole, yield several more nearly sleepless nights. It was a brief and wildly entertaining account that seemed to have issued from an old-school typewriter. It was the story of yet another formidable branch of my family tree, one I'd heard of in passing but never dreamed had any connection to me. A story with the intriguing title of "One and a Half Elephants."

ONE AND A HALF ELEPHANTS

In the decade before the American Revolution, a man named Peter Grubb Jr. was making a good living from an iron mine and foundry in Sullivan County, Pennsylvania. It wasn't until the war came that he learned how to really make money. He went into munitions. He patriotically sold cannon and shot to Washington's impoverished Continental Army on credit. The name Grubb might well have been on the honor roll of American Revolutionary heroes along with Lafayette, Paine, and Franklin, had he not also sold cannon and shot to the British through Tory sympathizers in Broome County, New York.

I put my uncle's pages down to do an internet search of Peter Grubb Jr. He has his own Wikipedia entry that identifies his occupation as ironmaster. He and his older brother Curtis were the proprietors of Cornwall Ironworks, after which the town—initially part of Lancaster County—was eventually named. Its mine was, at one point, the largest one of its kind in the world, and it would produce continuously for 236 years.

His father, the senior Peter, was the one who discovered the vast deposits of exceptionally pure magnetite ore in that region. At the time he had been a stonemason in search of quarrying stone. Once he had acquired the ore-laden land and assembled the necessary components to harvest it, he built the Cornwall Iron Furnace and the nearby Hopewell Forges, which were eventually taken over by his sons.

Their contributions to the Colonial forces during the American Revolution are indeed considered significant. George Washington paid a personal visit to Cornwall to inspect their operations. Both Peter Jr. and Curtis Grubb also served as Union militia colonels.

Eventually a rift between the brothers drove them into competition with each other. Peter Jr. purchased an additional tract of land that he named Mount Hope, where he built his own charcoal furnace. Today the Mount Hope Estate is a national landmark in Lancaster County.

> *This is the story of how I happen to be living off Grubb's money today. It was told to me by my mother as it was told to her by my great aunt, Carter Thornton. My mother assured me that this story is mostly true. Jesus, I'm proud to be descended from a man like Peter Grubb! Can you imagine a man having the foresight and business acumen to sell cannon to the winners on credit and collect gold on delivery from the losers?*
>
> *His grandson Clement Grubb didn't seem to have inherited any genius for making money. During the first thirty years of his stewardship of the family fortune, he was no more than an uninspired caretaker. There was only slow, conservative*

growth—nothing to parallel the spectacular coups of his grandfather. But the acorn doesn't fall far from the family tree. Clement simply hadn't found his war yet.

Providentially, American history provided him with a financial wet dream. The Civil War was such a spectacular slaughter that the Grubb Ironworks had all they could handle just catering cannon for the North. Of course, he would have preferred to play both sides. He was as admirably even-handed as his grandfather. By the end of the war, he was one of America's first multi-millionaires.

A separate search for Clement Grubb revealed that he was indeed the grandson of Peter Jr., entering the family business at the age of seventeen and becoming the manager of Mount Hope Estate the following year. When he died, Clement was reportedly the richest individual in Lancaster County.

But Clement wasn't the yikes his father had been. He realized that money was no longer enough—he had to have class. So he sent his daughter to Europe to buy him some.

In the second half of the 19th century, a symbiotic relationship developed between the great families of Europe and America. Europe, fighting a lost cause against creeping democracy, was a great refugee camp of bankrupt nobility while America was teeming with bumpkin nouveau riche. Great alliances were forged based on fair value trade—cash for respectability. Mary Grubb was as devoted to her father as she was beautiful. Within three months of her introduction to European society, she was engaged to a French count.

But I am not descended from a French count. To tie my genetic thread to the Grubb blood money, we have to backtrack a little. When the Civil War broke out, a wealthy cotton farmer named Jeremiah Beall sent his three sons off to fight with the First Georgia Volunteers. The oldest son, Jesse Beall, was vaporized by a grapeshot cannonball in the Battle of Knoxville. Do you suppose the shrapnel was manufactured by Peter Grubb? There are wheels within wheels in the Great Mandala. The youngest son, James Beall, had his right leg shattered by a runaway caisson less than a week before the end of the war. The third son, Joseph Bond Beall, fought in nearly every major campaign of the war and never even caught cold—much less any stray Grubb ordnance.

After Appomattox, James and Joseph were reunited at their father's plantation in Pembroke, Georgia. James Beall's leg was such a mess that the local doctors said it would have to come off. Despite the honor attendant to losing a leg for the South and the assurance of his brother that amputees were getting so much pussy in Savannah that he was considering having a limb of his own amputated, James was adamant that he was going to keep both legs or he'd just as soon give up the whole package.

Here I laughed out loud, even as I felt a deep pang over the sly, brash, irreverent uncle I'd never known and might never know. I wished he were telling me about our family at my dining room table, or on my patio over a bottle of wine.

Old Jeremiah Beall had so much cotton money that even the financial drain of losing an essentially privately funded war had not seriously depleted his fortune. So in desperation, the brothers took passage for Europe to find a doctor who could mend the leg. Joseph was trucking James from specialist to specialist all over Europe the same spring that Mary Grubb was shopping for a title to give respectability to her father's wealth.

All of the doctors agreed that the leg was finished and would have to go—all, that is, except one. A London orthopedist told the brothers there was a doctor in New York who was mending shattered bones with metal pins if James would allow himself to be operated on by a Yankee. James surprised the doctor and his brother when he declared that he harbored no ill feeling for the Yankees since they had merely defended themselves when he had tried to kill them.

The brothers booked passage on the next ship for New York. The morning that the ship was to leave London, Mary Grubb was on the promenade deck when Joseph, dressed in his Confederate captain's uniform, carried his crippled brother up the gangplank. Mary told her aunt, who was her chaperone on this European tour: "I love my father more than Cordelia loved Lear and my only purpose in life is to bring him honor, but if I can't have that handsome rebel, I know that I will die." Three days out of London harbor, they were married by the ship's captain. One of their daughters was Florence Beall, who was my grandmother.

But that's hardly enough, is it? You want to know how James Beall's leg turned out. And you're starting to doubt the veracity of the Beall fortune. If the Bealls had so much money, why is the Grubb money so important to me today? The doctor in New York repaired James' leg with a series of silver pins and he made a miraculous recovery. He never again ran the high hurdles but he was left with only a slight limp, for which he acquired an ivory-inlaid ebony walking cane, just for the style of it.

The Beall brothers were such a success in New York society that they stayed on and founded the New York Cotton Exchange. They were so successful as cotton brokers that by the turn of the century, they were each just as rich as their father, Jeremiah Beall, or old Peter Grubb.

I can find far less on the Bealls than I can on the Grubbs. In the *Biographical Annals of Lancaster County, Pennsylvania*, Joseph Bond Beall is cited as the owner of several cotton plantations in the south. He was indeed the father of my great-grandmother Florence Beall, who married William Mynn Thornton. The couple surfaces in several of the society pages of the day. And in their wedding announcement in the *Washington Post* in 1915, it's noted that "Miss Beall's father, the late Joseph Bond Beall and her grandfather, the late Jeremiah Beall, were among the organizers and charter members of the New York Cotton Exchange."

Joseph and Mary Beall lived quite well, but within their millionaire means. Unfortunately, James tried to make the name Beall synonymous with ragtime opulence on a scale with Carnegie or Brady. He acquired the largest private zoo in America—over one hundred and fifty species, including three elephants. He married a cousin of Eleanor Roosevelt (as did Eleanor, whose rapacious spending was only exceeded by that of her husband's mistress, a hoochie-cooch dancer he met at the World's Fair).

The financial pressure of such a lifestyle was more than even a multi-millionaire could bear and in desperation, James began raiding the portfolios of investors in the Beall Brothers Commodity Brokerage. Eventually his perfidy came to light and the ensuing scandal bankrupted both brothers. Unable to live without money, James hanged himself in the Park Boulevard apartment of his mistress in Atlantic City. Joseph and Mary Beall retired from New York society to live the

*rest of their days happily and uneventfully in Sullivan
County, Pennsylvania.*

*When my mother turned twenty-one, she and her cousin,
Tucker Smith, inherited the proceeds from the estate auction
of James Beall. After the descent of a locust swarm of ancient
creditors, all that was left free of liens and encumbrances
were the three elephants from James Beall's private zoo. My
mother and Tucker Smith sold the elephants to Frank Buck,
who put them in his Bring Them Back Alive Wild Animal
Show. My mother used the proceeds of the sale of her one
and a half elephants to finance two years' study at the Art
Students' League in New York City.*

Frank Buck is real enough and his menagerie of wild animals is well
documented. I don't know whether the sale of elephants funded my
grandmother's art studies, but I love the idea of it.

I also don't know how many hours I spent on ancestry and genealogy
sites after reading my uncle's account. Enough to trace the Grubb lineage all the way back to Sir Henry Vane Jr., my eighth great-grandfather,
who served as the governor of the Massachusetts Bay Colony and supported the creation of Harvard College.

While reading about Sir Henry, I thought about how Harvard had
always been a source of fascination and longing for me. To my mind,
it represented the pinnacle of intellectual excellence. I studied their
branding and logo when I took over the leadership of my own school,
and when I created my own branding, I modeled the "H" in Heritage on
the "H" in Harvard.

I don't know how to describe the way my uncle's story opened yet
another treasure trove of ancestors for me. I don't know if I'll ever meet
another person who can relate to the surreal feeling of uncovering such
an illustrious family history after so many formative years of internalizing
the labels that others had always applied to my family: *indigent, low-life,
white trash.*

The only place I've found a narrative similar to mine has been in the fairy tales I read to my children when they were little. In those stories, this kind of reversal is a recurrent motif. Some child of fortune is cursed, or under an enchantment, or whisked away at birth for protection, and lives as a commoner among the poor until the spell is broken and the truth is revealed. Then the beast turns back into a prince, or the royal girl is restored to the highborn place she was torn from.

There's always a pretense within the fairy tale that such a girl can go back, return to her place of origin, and be seamlessly reinstated in her rightful life.

My ancestors as far back as I can trace seem to have cherished the very same values I've revered all my life: industry, innovation, education, and art. Like a homing pigeon, like an animal who instinctively crosses forests and streams and highways to return to its home, I have found my way back to where my phantom counterpart might have been if no child had ever been gang-raped, if all had not gone terribly wrong.

However, nothing is as simple as a fairy tale. While I cherish my newly discovered family roots, if only for the fact of finally having a lineage, I recognize that this knowing comes with a price. My connection to one of the founding families of our nation elicits both pride and disgust. The expansion of the American empire and that of my ancestors was built on the backs of the enslaved and the land of the dispossessed. Many of my ancestors profited enormously off of the struggle of others in order to guarantee their constant place in society.

If it's true that this iron dynasty is in my blood, then it's also true that like the iron itself, I was indelibly forged in the furnace of my childhood. I will always be a kid who was born out of wedlock, a foster girl, dirty and illiterate. I will always be the daughter of a woman the world considered a whore. And in some deep and secret way that no one who knows me would ever guess, I will always be cold, I will always be hungry, lost and silenced in a classroom, and half-blind from neglect. I will always be homeless, watching the sun rise over the ocean in the morning, delighted in spite of everything by the pink in the sky.

Chapter 24

IN THE WAKE of finding my uncle, my thoughts kept turning back to my strange conversation with his ex-wife Beth. *Are your other brothers and sisters alive?* she had asked. And then, upon hearing my answer: *Well, how's that for irony? Allan was the only one we tried to save.*

It was impossible to connect with my mom's brother Allan without thinking of my own brother Allan. His namesake, as Beth had said.

I've chosen to write as little as possible about my brothers and sister. The truth is that while most of them *are* still alive, the circumstances of our childhood hurt them in ways they have not been able to transcend. I have no desire to hurt them further. They deserve their privacy and dignity.

But Allan is beyond pain now.

Allan was my favorite brother. He was the one who introduced me to Jim. Would I even have looked at Jim in the first place if Allan hadn't told me he was cool? It's possible that I owe him my marriage, which is to say it's possible I owe him everything.

Allan was the oldest of my mother's six children, and sometimes I think he suffered the most. In my earliest memories, he was the boy almost swept out to sea as he descended those ocean cliffs to gather seaweed, putting his body between us and starvation.

He was the only one I really had in the family, the only one who was protective of me, who looked out for me. When I was frightened at night, he would lie down next to me in bed and say, "It's okay, Tef. Don't be afraid." *Tef* was what he'd called me as a little kid and it's what he called me until his last day.

We lived in rough neighborhoods throughout my childhood, but because of Allan, I was never the target of local bullies for long. If ever I had reason to be afraid of other kids, I only had to let him know. *Don't even come near my sister again*, he'd tell them, *or you'll be hurting*. And after that, they always crossed the street when they saw me coming.

Isabella was tougher than me, but Allan's protection extended to her too. I don't know how he got hold of a gun, but after Isabella was assaulted, he went looking for Rick with every intention of killing him. He blamed our stepfather for what happened to her, since it was his friend who hurt her. But Rick disappeared in the aftermath of her assault. He fled to Arizona and joined the Peyote Way Church of God, a cult in the Aravaipa wilderness that regarded peyote as a holy sacrament.

I'm thankful now for Rick's escape. It's what kept my brother from dying in prison. It allowed what happened later to come to pass. Rick and Allan would meet again.

WHEN MY SIBLINGS and I were taken to the dependent unit, the separation of children by gender—girls on one side of the building, boys on the other—was a harbinger of all the trauma to come. There was no fear for me in being separated from my mother. The terror set in when I was separated from Allan, the only protective presence in my world.

I would not see him again for more than a year. Like me, he was sent to an abusive foster home, where he was regularly beaten with a belt. It's hardly surprising that he fell in with a troubled crowd of kids in high school, and before the end of his freshman year, he and his friends were convicted of breaking and entering, as well as theft from private homes. Allan was sent to a juvenile detention center, a place even worse than his foster home. He was gang-raped during his time there, and the shame of that would gnaw at him for the rest of his days.

When my siblings and I were returned to our mother after our time in foster homes, Allan was not among us. He was still in juvenile detention.

I have no memory of my mother ever calling, writing, or visiting him. He tried calling us once or twice, but he could only call collect and she wouldn't accept the charges. When we moved to Portland, she just left him there, as easily as she'd left him with his aunt and uncle ten years earlier.

Six months after we moved, he was released from the facility. My mother hadn't seen him in well over a year, but it never occurred to her to pick him up. I don't know how he would have joined us in Portland if his parole officer hadn't bought him a bus ticket.

As AN ADULT, Allan was the smart and capable one. He could fix and operate any computer, and eventually he worked in tech support. In the workplace my brother was a model of competence. He loved every job he ever held in IT. He was very good at what he did and valued by every employer he had.

He was very handsome, too: dark-haired and dark-eyed—a dead ringer for Cat Stevens. He had a weakness for country music and liked to wear cowboy hats. Women were always wild about him, but as a romantic partner he was hapless and hopeless.

He had a memory like flypaper, and he carried all our childhood carnage with him at all times, with nothing blocked out or hazy or erased. He remembered every worthless man my mother ever brought into her bed. He remembered their names, their tattoos, their scars, and their cigarette brands. He remembered every wretched apartment we lived in, every brutal school and each frigid windy empty day on the beach. My love for the Oregon coast, my desire to spend as much time there as possible, was a mystery to him.

"What's wrong with you?" he would ask. "After everything we went through in Mendocino, how can you love the beach?"

He would never brave such conversations without an open bottle of liquor. He had to be drunk to talk about our childhood.

Allan was a chronic alcoholic. Our mother, who never went a day without her "herbs," or her acid if she could get it, seemed to somehow regard his alcoholism as a weakness that was beneath her. According to her Allan began drinking at the age of nine. His first taste of alcohol was one of Louie's Spanish beers, and later he raided Rick's stash of Steel Reserve and Thunderbird. It's hard to imagine a child developing a taste for beer, or any alcohol really, but he must have noticed that it made him warm, made things blur, and helped him sleep.

My brother married young. His first wife's name was Lynn, and she was the administrator of an insurance company. She wore huge dark-rimmed glasses, and her dark shoulder-length hair framed her face like an Egyptian headdress. Their relationship was fraught from the start. Allan had poor communication skills, and he was wildly averse to confrontation. When an argument arose, no matter how minor, he would disappear. Walk out the door and come back drunk.

Lynn had a take-charge, do-it-all, intensely managerial character. She kept meticulous books at work, and she kept perfect order in her home, but she could not control my brother, and it maddened her. She loved Jesus and hated alcohol, but she couldn't get him to church or away from the bottle. In a way, she was the good mother Allan never had, but years too late.

They had a beautiful daughter named Rachel. She was born with retinoblastoma, and her eye was removed soon after birth. The sight of his baby girl with an empty eye socket sent Allan to the corner bar, and he didn't come home for two days. In his own way, he was a wonderful father, affectionate and gentle. He was always playing with Rachel and loved to take her places. He snuggled her and read to her and let her ride him around like a pony.

He may have been a wonderful father, but he was an untenable husband. His inability to stay in the room when emotions ran high and his continual return to liquor as his only source of solace drove Lynn to divorce him by the time Rachel was four.

———

His SECOND WIFE was Carol, and with her, he had a beautiful daughter named Cindy. Carol was nothing like Lynn. From time to time she would call me and announce: "I'm sending Cindy to stay with you for the summer." Then she'd put her little girl on a plane and fade into radio silence for the next several months. She never called, never checked in.

Carol was the bad mother he'd always had; she was, in fact, very much like ours. They were soon divorced as well.

I REMEMBER THE day I got the call from the hospital. I was at the local organic market, filling my cart with grapes, wine, strawberries, and brie when I learned that Allan had been taken to the nearest ER after a grand mal seizure. I left the cart where it was and ran out to my car.

Even after learning the diagnosis was brain cancer, it was rare to see my brother without a cigarette in his mouth and a beer in his hand. When I nagged him about it, he'd say: *The tumor can't grow if I feed it nothing but nicotine and beer.* Eventually we joked that maybe he knew something his medical team didn't, because he lived for years beyond their most optimistic predictions—more than a full decade. His doctors marveled at how long he held on. The phrase they used time and again was *unheard of.*

It's hard to know how to feel about his decade of survival. He suffered in ways no human being ever should. He had countless debilitating seizures, after which he'd temporarily lose the use of an arm or a leg. He had two brain surgeries, chemotherapy, radiation, and steroid shots. The steroids swelled his face until it was almost unrecognizable. He was hospitalized over and over, sometimes for weeks. He developed pancreatitis and was in the ICU for seventeen days, on a breathing machine during the worst of it. Sometimes I secretly hoped he would die and finally be free of pain, but he held on. He fought to stay. At the tail end of this very dark span of days, a most unlikely angel reappeared on his path.

If I'd thought, during the years they were married, that Lynn was the good mother Allan never had but years too late, it would turn out that she had just turned up in his life years too early. Her persona was an exquisite fit for both of them when he was dying. During the last several months of his life, my brother and Lynn were reunited, and they finally achieved the relationship they'd never managed to inhabit in wedlock.

Lynn and I were never close, but what she did for Allan while he was dying was among the most beautiful things I've seen a person do. When he needed full-time care and had no insurance and no money, she set up his bed in the middle of her one-bedroom trailer and attended to his every need until he went into hospice. This arrangement was deeply, undeniably gratifying to both of them.

Lynn finally had all the control she'd always longed for. Allan was fully present with her for the first time in their lives together. He was no longer able to walk out. He gladly joined her for church on Sundays, and he even accepted Christ as his personal savior. It brought him a measure of peace he'd never known before.

For her own part, Lynn became a completely different woman— soft-spoken, accommodating, and tender—as if this were the role she'd been waiting to embody since they'd met. Alcohol had destroyed their marriage, but she even brought him beer toward the end: all the beer he wanted. She accepted his chain-smoking. She let the air inside her trailer turn blue with cigarette smoke.

"He's dying," she would say. "Let him have whatever he wants." It was as if being needed by him in this way had transformed her, lit her from within.

AT THE VERY END, during his last days, when Allan could no longer eat or drink or speak, he clutched an empty orange water bottle around the clock, even in his sleep. It would fall to the floor whenever he had a seizure and when he came to, he would gesture aggressively for me to give it back to him. If he could tell me, I'd have asked what it meant to him. Since he couldn't, I can only imagine that the feeling of a bottle in his hand was his lifelong association with comfort, and that on some level, any bottle was better than no bottle.

He had so many seizures at the end. He couldn't make anyone understand what he wanted. His legs began to turn black. On his last day, he went into a series of convulsions, and a hospice worker asked me to leave the room while they tended to him. I went out to get a cup of coffee, and when I came back, a sheet was over his face.

WHAT CAN I say about my brother's life? It was dark and hard and sad. It was soaked in alcohol and sorrow. Filled with suffering from start to finish.

It was also stoic and brave and redemptive. He was a godsend of a brother, a good worker, and a loving father. He was a broken soul and yet a gentle one. He was a far better parent than the one he had.

He internalized his grief. He tamped down his rage. He self-medicated with beer and nicotine.

He did no harm.

Because of Lynn, his most important affairs were in order before he departed. He got to make up for lost time with his daughter. They all wanted to be together, and they were. It was the best and closest-knit version of family he'd ever known. He told me before he died that Lynn and Jesus had healed his heart.

I'll always be grateful to her in a way I can't put into words. She offered him shelter at the end of his road, inside a trailer instead of a bus, but the same elements made it a true home: light and warmth, order and comfort. Devotion, provision.

Love.

Chapter 25

THE DEATH OF my brother Allan was one of the two hardest losses I've suffered in my life.

The other was that of my stepfather, Rick. I can only imagine how unlikely it sounds. It sounds unlikely even to me as I write it.

For most of our acquaintance, Rick was a drunk and a junkie. He was in and out of our lives, in and out of prison. He cheated on my mother and beat her often. He wrecked two vehicles while I was inside them, driving one of them straight into an oncoming car and rolling the other.

On both occasions, I walked away without so much as a scratch. In a way it was a metaphor for my love of him. Throughout my formative years Rick was a terrible man, and yet somehow my love for him survived it all, untouched and intact.

LIKE MY MEMORIES of my sister's assault, I can only recall Rick in a series of mental snapshots. He was in and out of our lives so randomly and haphazardly, it's hard to order or make sense of his appearances.

In my earliest memory of Rick, he and I are hitchhiking in the rain. We get into and out of many different cars. He keeps me close to him in these cars. At some point, we stop off at a bar, an old vintage-looking bar with a piano by the front window.

A catchy song is playing on the jukebox. The song is "Yellow Submarine" by the Beatles. While Rick is getting his whiskey, I go and sit at the piano. I touch its cracked and yellowing keys and within a few minutes, by sheer instinct, I'm playing along with the song. There's nothing to it. I know exactly how to reproduce the tune. I do it over and over.

I'm only three or four years old, and this feat draws a small crowd of startled onlookers. No one is more surprised than Rick.

"Holy mackerel!" he whistles. "How did you do that?"

I remember the delight of being celebrated, if only for a few moments.

I don't know why Rick and I were hitchhiking alone. This was during the time we lived on the beach, but I don't know where we were going. We ended up in someone's hippie house in the forest. I'm guessing now that it was drug-related. Maybe a dealer lived there. Maybe it was easier for Rick to hitch rides with a little girl in tow—maybe it made people less afraid to pick him up.

I don't know how I was able to play the piano when I'd never seen or touched one before. I don't know why I've never touched a piano since. You would think that once I could afford to try anything I wanted, I would revisit the piano and cultivate it as I did tennis. But no.

I do remember feeling—in a way I could not articulate then and can barely put into words even now—that I didn't belong in the life I was living, that I had been abducted somehow, kidnapped into it, and this strange talent was evidence that I belonged to another time and place, other circumstances. I had a rightful long-lost life, one that included a piano teacher, perhaps, and this inexplicable skill was from that other, better place, like something I'd stashed in a sock and smuggled out along with me.

MY MOST REVELATORY encounter with Rick—the time I glimpsed the man divested of his shadow, if only for the briefest interlude—came when I was thirteen. He broke character on that day in a way that foreshadowed what would come later. It was the day my memories of the house on Creekside Drive came back to me.

After I left the home of Ted and Lorraine, I pushed all that had happened there out of mind, dropped it like a stone into black water, and let it sink beneath the depths. I didn't think of it for years. I spoke of it to no one. It was as if none of it had happened.

I'll never know what triggered the memory: the creak of a door or a floorboard, a man's tread in the hallway outside my room, or possibly nothing at all. I only remember sitting straight up in bed as if shocked by a bolt of electric current. It was a little after four in the morning. Just that suddenly, for no reason I could fathom, I remembered it all: Ted's hot hands, his rank breath, the seamy odor of his bedsheets, and the dreadful things he'd made me do.

I lay there for hours, shaking and sick as the sky went from black to dark blue to pink streaked with orange. I lay there as everyone else in the house got up and went out about their Saturday morning. I heard the sound of cartoons from the living room television. I heard a neighbor mowing his lawn.

I could not imagine rising from the bed and resuming my life. The memory of Ted, of his hands and his mouth and his privates, felt like a stain I would never be able to wash away. I felt frantic to blot him out, to erase him again as he had somehow been erased before. I needed a doctor, a drug, a cudgel—something.

At long last I made my way downstairs to where my mother was drinking coffee in the kitchen. She was alone at the table.

"Mom," I said unsteadily.

She looked up at me without speaking.

"Mom, I have to talk to you."

"What is it?"

"I remembered something bad that happened to me."

I have a vivid recollection of the look on her face just then. She regarded me not with alarm or concern but irritation. "What are you talking about?"

I started to cry. "It was in that foster home I lived in after you were committed. The one in Santa Rosa. The man in that house—he did bad things to me, Mom."

"Stephanie. What are you saying? What kind of things?"

"He made me touch his private parts," I told her, almost choking, barely able to get the words out. "He even made me put them in my mouth."

My mother leapt from the table so fast that coffee sloshed over the rim of her cup. She actually put her hands over her ears, like a child. "Stop it, Stephanie!" she shouted.

"Mom," I said, frightened.

"I cannot handle this," she yelled. "I can't! Don't say another word! Don't ever speak to me of this again." She slammed out of the house.

I stood there as if rooted into the linoleum, feeling like I might die of shame. At some point, Rick appeared on the threshold between the garage and the house.

"What's the matter?" he asked.

I stood looking at him, tears running down my face, unable to answer.

He tried again. "What's wrong with Florence?"

"She got mad about something I told her," I managed.

He motioned me over, and I went to him.

"What did you tell her?" he asked.

Rick sounded different than usual, and it took me a moment to figure out why. He wasn't drunk, and he wasn't high. He was all there. His eyes were focused, and his voice was steady.

When I failed to respond, he repeated his question. "What did you tell her?"

"She said never to talk about it again."

"Never talk about it to *her* again, maybe," he said. "But you can tell me. What is it, honey?"

And so I found myself telling Rick exactly what I had just told my mother. And when I'd finished, he did not cover his ears. He did not get angry.

He stared at me with an expression I had never seen on his face. In his eyes were terrible awareness, understanding, and agony. Then to my astonishment, he began to cry too. He pulled me to him and held my head hard against his chest.

"Baby," he wept. "Oh, my poor little girl."

I was as surprised as I'd ever been. Could this really be happening? Was this my stepfather?

"Rick?" I asked, my voice muffled against him.

"I'm sorry," he keened. "Jesus Christ, I'm so sorry. It was my fault. All of it was my fault."

How can I convey how it felt to finally be heard and seen? To have an adult take *ownership* of the things that had happened to me? To hear a grown man's voice breaking with regret for it? To be wept over?

I can't. The relief of that moment, the validation, and the marrow-deep gratification—it defies explanation. In a movie, Rick would decide to get sober at that moment. In real life, it was just a glimmer of what was possible for him, a glimmer that wouldn't resurface for another decade.

I WAS IN my twenties and newly married when Rick's truck pulled to the curb outside our house in Hillsboro. I was surprised by his knock because I wasn't expecting anyone. When I came to the door, my former stepfather was standing there, unshaven and unsmiling, his hat in his hand. He did not say hello.

"I want to get clean," he said. "Will you help me?"

I called AA and found a meeting within the hour. I told him I would go with him that day and every day for as long as he wanted.

The first meeting was in the basement of the Lents Baptist Church in Southeast Portland. There was coffee, cookies, and folding chairs arranged in a circle.

When we went around the circle, introducing ourselves, I said, "I'm Stephanie, and I'm here to support my stepfather, who's not ready to speak yet." This happened at each meeting for three straight days. But when we were walking in on the fourth evening, he touched my shoulder. In a low voice, he let me know he was ready. When it was his turn to speak, he finally said the words that would begin his recovery.

"My name is Rick," he said, "and I'm an alcoholic and a drug addict."

I can't think of that evening without tears coming into my eyes. There is something inexpressibly profound about the moment an addict owns his sickness.

And they enfolded him into their ranks then, replying back with the same words, spoken in many voices: *Hi, Rick.* It was this jumbled chorus that would hold and steady Rick through the hard months to come. A circle of strangers who spoke as one, offering him their simple acceptance.

Rick did everything by the book, down to the last detail. He attended ninety meetings in ninety days. He accepted a sponsor—a slightly older man who'd been clean for many years—and was fastidiously accountable to him at every step of his recovery. He undertook each of the twelve steps as if they were sacraments. He embraced the eighth and ninth steps with the faith of a fanatic.

Make a list of wrongs done to others and be willing to make amends for those wrongs.

Make direct amends to such people wherever possible, except when to do so would injure them or others.

Rick's sobriety was a miracle in my life. It was proof that people can change.

He took responsibility for every bad thing that had happened in our lives: The sexual abuse I suffered in my foster homes was his fault; the terrible things that happened to Allan were his fault; Isabella's assault was his fault. He owned it all.

He became a different person—gentle, reliable, accountable, and so desperate to make amends that he would never be done making them. He would do anything I asked. Whenever I wanted to paint my house, for instance, he would show up and do it alone and for free. He was no less invested in making amends to my siblings. My oldest brother had hated him for years, but he and Rick grew to love each other like a true father and son before Allan died. He was like a grandfather to both of Allan's daughters.

He did his best to be a father to my other siblings as well. He offered his time and gave his money whenever any of us needed anything. He came to both of my sons' games and cheered himself hoarse on the sidelines. He took my husband golfing and bought him a set of clubs.

He told me often that my coming to AA with him was the best thing anyone ever did for him. He asked how I could possibly love him after all he'd done. He told me I was beautiful, inside and out. He said this over and over.

There was a certain purity to his penance. He would do anything we asked, and he never said no. Another man so consumed by guilt and shame might have chosen to end it all, but Rick reasoned that he was worth more to us alive than dead. He took a vow to be of service to all of us for as long as he might still live.

Even after he'd been sober for years, he'd give money to homeless drunks so they could buy alcohol. I couldn't understand this and said so.

"Of course you can't understand," he told me. "You've never had the shakes."

RICK'S DEATH WAS very sudden. He had a heart attack in the shower, and forty-five minutes later he was gone. I got the call on a Saturday afternoon, just as I was about to climb into our hot tub. My younger brother, Walter, told me he'd been found dead on the bathroom floor.

I cried at least once a day for more than a year after he died. Sometimes I wonder at the depth of my own grief for him. I've come to think it has to do with the fact that my mother never once took stock of the damage she'd done, let alone owned it or sought forgiveness for it. So he became something of a stand-in for her—he performed the atonement that she never could or would. He was the one adult with whom I had lifelong continuity who showed emotional investment in me. Who'd borne witness to how it had been for me. The only one who could say firsthand: *I know what you went through; I know how you've suffered and what you overcame.*

On the morning of his funeral, a homeless woman came up to me in

Starbucks, drawing closer than a stranger would. With no alarm at all, I let her reach out and touch my face.

"You're beautiful," she crooned. "I can see you're beautiful inside and out."

It was Rick's mantra to me, and in that moment, I had no doubt that the message was from him. The gift of it knocked me out, rocked me from the roots of my hair to the soles of my feet. It was a moment as otherworldly as the one in that vintage bar, at the piano, when music flowed from beneath my hands with no explanation. That was my first memory with Rick, and this would be my last: both of them shimmering, glittering with mystery.

Chapter 26

WHENEVER I TOOK stock of what I'd learned about my roots, I was struck by all that had been revealed in just a matter of months. I'd found out more about my family history in this brief interlude than in the forty-eight years preceding. I'd learned what happened to my mother, discovered my connection with the Thorntons, and traced my lineage to the Grubbs. I'd even found my uncle.

But there was still an absence at the heart of it all, a space that remained hollow and melancholic. It was an ache that flared every third Sunday in June, or when I watched Jim with Andrea. I felt it when brides were given away at weddings and when I was faced with family history forms in any medical office.

It was there whenever someone said: *You have such an exotic look, are you Portuguese? Catalan? Turkish? Greek?*

I'd laugh. "Oh, I'm a mongrel," I'd say. "I'm a mix of things." I could never bring myself to say: *Maybe?* To confess: *I don't know.*

It was time to look for my father.

ALL MY LIFE, my mother had told me that the dumpster rapist was my father. When I was very young, I believed this, and the shame I felt was like a live thing writhing inside me, coiling like a cobra up from my gut and into my throat. By the time I was in my teens, it was clear to me that my mother had a very intermittent commitment to the truth. Whatever she said on any given day might be a mash-up of invention, distortion, half-lies, and a dash of what actually happened.

The story of her abduction and gang rape had turned out to be true, for instance. Her connection to the Washington family was true. Her lineage on both sides was as rarefied as she'd always claimed.

She also told countless outright lies. Like the tales she'd told all my life about my younger brother Dominic.

Dominic had disappeared just after Louie's death. He was still just a baby, less than a year old. He was there one day and gone the next, and when my siblings and I pressed our mother about it, we would hear a different story each time.

"Dominic was very sick. I did everything in my power to help him get well. I sat by his bed around the clock and fed him soup and toast. I chanted over him the whole time, but he died anyway."

Did I ever accept this story? I'm not sure. I could not imagine my mother sitting by a sick child's bed for even five minutes, let alone feeding him, doting on him, and caring whether he lived or died.

"Dominic had cancer," she might say on a different day. "Leukemia. He was in the hospital and had all the best doctors, and they did everything they could, but they couldn't save him."

This also rang false. My childhood memories were hazy in places and blurred in others, but if my brother had been hospitalized with cancer, I was sure I'd remember something of it.

"Dominic was kidnapped," went the third and most frequent explanation. "He vanished without a trace. How was I to know, that morning he went out to play, that I would never see him again? I called the police, of course, and detectives spent months looking for him. But the clues that came in about him led nowhere." Sometimes she added, "I cried myself to sleep every night after he went missing."

My mother always brightened when offering these accounts of his disappearance. It was clear that she enjoyed the tragic role and knew her lines. She invoked every cliché of the desperate or grieving mother when she talked about him, as if she were trying on a story she'd read in the tabloids.

Growing up all I knew for sure was that Dominic was gone, and despite the soap opera script she might trot out on any given day, my mother did not mourn him. I'd heard grieving mothers talk about their lost children. *It's the worst pain a woman can ever feel, and it never goes away*, they said. *You learn to live with it, but it's always there.*

My mother was not in pain. She wasn't suffering over her missing son. On the issue of his disappearance, I had the sense it was best not to press her too hard, lest I disappear too.

It was also best to be needed, indispensable. Best to do her bidding in all things and to be of use to her at all times. So that my place in her orbit would be assured. So that I would not vanish as my brother had.

I was thirty years old before I learned the truth. My brother Allan called one day without warning and said, "You're not going to believe this, but I found Dominic."

I couldn't make sense of this sentence. Found Dominic? What did that mean? Had Allan found his police report, his file, his underground cell, his grave? If I'd never quite believed the tales of his illness or abduction, these were still the images I'd come to associate with his absence.

"Dominic?" I repeated. "You mean our brother?"

"*Yes*, our brother. I found him, Tef."

"Found him where?" I asked, my voice going high-pitched and frightened.

"He's living in New York City. In the South Bronx," Allan told me. "He just got out of prison."

"Oh my God," I said. "Then Dominic is *alive*?"

"Alive and well," Allan said. "At least, he's well as far as I know."

"What happened to him?" I demanded. Where in God's name had he been all these years?

"Louie's sister Alma adopted him soon after he killed himself," Allan said. "She wanted a child and couldn't get pregnant."

I stood clutching the phone with both hands, stunned and breathless, as Allan filled in the details. Alma was devastated over her brother's death, and she pined for a baby, so when she and her husband came to pick up Louie's ashes, they decided to raise his infant son as their own.

She'd always told Dominic that his real mother was crazy. She supported this claim with a true story: Just after he was born, our mother had run down the street naked, holding him and screaming, *You can't kill me because I'm already dead!* Dominic grew up believing he'd been rescued from a madwoman.

At the end of this long explanation, I had one more question. "Did Mom know where he was the whole time?"

"Of course she knew. She let them take him. Just like she let Uncle Allan and Beth take me that time," Allan told me. "She didn't care."

MY MOTHER HAD lied about Dominic and a thousand other things, and I'd long since come to believe she was lying when she said her rapist was my father. According to her own story, the rapist was pale with bright green eyes. My mother was pale with bright blue eyes.

My eyes and skin and hair are dark. My mother's fair skin has always burned without protection, whereas the walnut color of my skin only deepens in the sun. For most of my life, I believed I was half Puerto Rican, even though I look very different from Isabella, Pablo, and Dominic. In any case, I thought it most unlikely that two pale-skinned, light-eyed people had created me.

Do-it-yourself genetic testing had swept the nation that year. It seemed that everyone I knew was bent on discovering all the facets of their ancestry, even without the central question of a parent's identity. So I too sent away for a kit, spit into its saliva collection tube, returned it in the prepaid mailer, and waited for my results to arrive.

IN THE MEANTIME, I began a search for William.

William, my mother's first love, her true love—the one she called *the love of her life.* The one who represented the last true happiness she'd ever known. It was her quest to find William that drew her to New

York from her mother's home in Florida, only to find upon her arrival that he'd gotten engaged to another woman that very morning. This engagement did not keep him from succumbing to her charms that day any more than his marriage would in the future, whenever their paths might cross.

With so many trysts over so many years, wasn't it possible that I'd come from one of them?

He wasn't hard to find. The last my mother knew, he was in Minnesota, and that's where I found him in the first nationwide directory I tried online. The age matched—he was an old man now—as did a previous residence in Smithtown, New York. Jim sat next to me on our living room sofa and held my hand as I made the call.

William answered on the third ring. "Hello?"

My heart was banging in my chest as I said, "Hi, my name is Stephanie, and I'm looking for William."

"Well, you found him."

It was hard for me to read his voice. He sounded proud, tired, and wary.

"I'm trying to track down an old friend of my mother's," I told him. "Have you ever known a woman by the name of Florence Agnes?"

There was a startled silence on the line for a moment. Then in a guarded tone, he said, "Yes, I have."

I sank back into my corner of the sofa and nodded at Jim. "Then you're the right William," I told him. "I'm her daughter."

"Well, isn't that something," he said. "Forgive me for asking straight out, but has she passed?"

I heard it, then, unmistakably: the fear in his voice. God knows how long it had been since he'd seen or heard from my mother. It had likely been many decades. Even now, she mattered to him.

"Not yet," I said. "She has end-stage lung cancer, and she doesn't have much longer to live, but she's still with us."

There was a barely audible sigh of relief.

"You've kind of caught me at a funny time," he told me then. "Would you mind if I take down your number and give you a call back tomorrow?"

———

"I COULDN'T SAY much with my wife in the room," he said the next day when he called me back. "She's always been jealous of Florence. And, well, I can't say I blame her. I've given into temptation a time or two, and God help me, I could never resist your mother."

"I'm sorry," I said. "I don't want to create any trouble between you and her."

"We'll be all right," he said. "We've been through worse. I had an affair with Florence early on. I don't know if she ever said anything about that."

"My mother says a lot of things," I said. "Some of them are true and some aren't. That's why I'm looking for people who knew her. It's hard to know what's real."

"I hope I'm not giving away any secrets of hers, but we were together a few times even after I got hitched. I'm not proud of that, but like I said I found her irresistible."

William and I talked for twenty or thirty minutes. He sounded lit with the reminiscence of his younger years and the memory of my mother's beauty.

"Florence was the loveliest woman I ever knew," he told me. "The kind of girl you'd see in an advertisement for Ivory soap: innocent and pure and high-class. Oh, I loved walking around town with Florence on my arm. I knew I was the envy of every man I saw.

"I was sixteen, going on seventeen that first summer. She was eleven but she told me she was fifteen, and she looked fifteen. She was at least five-foot-two and she was all filled out. I know it sounds crazy but it's true. Some girls grow up early, I guess, and your mother was one of them."

I felt a little squeamish, hearing these details. At eleven, my own daughter looked nothing like a fully developed woman, nor was she interested in dating yet. It was hard to think about an eleven-year-old lying and running around with a young man almost out of high school, with no responsible adults the wiser. Where were her grandparents?

"Do you know what happened to my mom the summer after you met?" I asked.

Here his voice dropped a register, as if the subject of rape was as unmentionable now as it must have been then. "Are you talking about . . . how all those men had their way with her?"

"Yes," I said.

"We never really talked about it," he said. "She told me it was over and that I was never to mention it in her presence. I never did, but it just about ripped my heart out. Those guys were lucky I wasn't in the courtroom when they went to trial."

"What was it like to see her afterward?" I asked.

"I'll be honest with you," he said. "She wasn't the same. She wasn't any different to look at, but that girlish, innocent sweetness was gone."

In some terrible way, it was reassuring to hear testimony from a stranger that reinforced my mother's story. Allan had corroborated her account, but it was still good to have reinforcement from an outside source. If nothing else came of our conversation, I would still be glad I had contacted William.

"Listen," I said, toward the end of our call. "My mother told me that you and she were lovers for years. I've been looking for my father, and I'm wondering whether he might be you."

There was dead silence on the line. I could almost feel his panic gathering in the space between us.

"What year were you born?" he asked after a very long pause.

"1967," I told him. "July 2."

In his exhalation I heard pure gratitude.

"It's not me, honey," he said gently. "It couldn't be. I was overseas from the summer of '66 straight through to the next spring. I came home on Easter Sunday in '67. You can ask your mother. I did two tours back to back over there, in Vietnam."

I didn't blame him, but it was still wrenching to hear his relief as he repeated, "I'm not the one, honey."

———

FOR WEEKS AFTER finding William, I was unable to shake a sense of sadness. The fear in his voice had depressed me. In my fantasy of finding my father, we were both overjoyed. He was thrilled to have a daughter like me. The man in my daydreams considered me a miracle and a gift.

"Listen, Steph. The way William felt, it had nothing to do with you," Jim told me. "You have to know that. He's married, and he was cheating on his wife every time he went to bed with your mom. It could blow up his marriage if he suddenly had a daughter with another woman. At the very least, it would be the kind of drama no man wants to deal with at home."

I knew Jim was right. I knew it wasn't personal. I knew my mother had likely been a sore point between William and his wife for decades, and this would have been the last thing he needed. Yet I couldn't help wondering: If I were lucky enough to find my real father, would he feel the same? Would I be the bastard child, casting a shadow over his chosen family?

This sadness lingered until the afternoon a link appeared in my email inbox and one of the mysteries that had been with me for nearly half a century was resolved.

I was not Puerto Rican. Or Portuguese or Greek or Catalan, or any of the other "exotic" nationalities that people had guessed over the years.

I was 38 percent Italian.

MY MOTHER WAS in a hospice facility in Southeast Portland, a place called Gracelen Terrace. For the most part, the staff was gentle and caring. They greeted me warmly whenever I came in, knew each patient by name, and were responsive to calls for help around the clock.

Even so, there were echoes of every other institution my mother had been in. The odor of human incontinence hung in the air. Screams tore the quiet at regular intervals. The demented, the sick, and the dying were at every turn, and some were in agony that no level of attention could relieve.

As always, I'd done my best with my mother's room. I'd made up her bed with a pink velvet coverlet. I brought decorative pillows for the padded seat along the window. A purple orchid plant presided over the end table by her bed, and around it, I'd arranged beautifully framed photos of her grandchildren.

When I came into her room an hour after receiving my ancestry results, she was sitting up in bed doing a word search puzzle.

"Mom, I need to talk to you," I burst out.

She looked up and met my wild gaze with no apparent alarm. "What is it?"

"I took a DNA test so I could get a genetic analysis," I told her. "Everything I've learned over the past few months has been about your side of the family. But the other half of my ancestry has just been a blank. You don't know what it's like, Mom. You know where you came from, who your people are, who your father was. You can't imagine how much it hurts not to know."

She stared at me from beneath her bluish eyelids.

"I'm half-Italian," I told her. "My father must have been Italian. I need to know who he was, Mom."

"Really?" she asked. "Italian?"

"Yes."

"Well, that changes things," she declared. "That certainly narrows it down."

"Did you have an Italian lover?" I asked. I was holding my breath.

"Yes, I did," she said, a little grandly. She was enjoying this. It was a game to her, and she held all the power.

"Mom!" I all but howled. "You have to tell me who he was!"

"All right, all right, don't make such a fuss," she said, pleased to be in possession of something I wanted so badly. "Sit down and I'll tell you."

I sank into the nearest chair and pressed my fist hard against my mouth. "What was his name?"

"Oh, I don't remember that."

I wanted to seize her by her bony shoulders and shake her. I wanted to fall on my knees in front of her bed. I wanted to scream.

"*Who was he?*"

"There was an Italian diaper salesman at the hospital where I gave birth to Isabella," she said. "Morrisania Hospital in the Bronx. He would get to know the new mothers and sign them up for his delivery service. Then he'd come around once a week. He came around to see me more often, though." There was a sly note in her voice as she said this, as if savoring her own naughtiness even now.

"You went to bed with this man several times a week and you can't remember his *name?*"

"It was so long ago," she said, without a hint of apology. "He was a lovely man, though, that I can tell you. He was clean and he dressed nicely. He smelled like Old Spice and his clothes were always pressed. He made me feel good, and he had an Italian accent all the new mothers loved."

"What did he look like?"

"He had tan skin and dark eyes like you. His hair was dark too, and he kept it slicked back from his forehead. He whispered Italian in my ear whenever we made love and it drove me wild. He called me *bella, carissima.*"

"This is more than I need to know."

"His wife was pretty when they got married," she went on, ignoring me. "But after she had their two kids, she let herself go. I felt sorry for him."

"You remember *all* this, but not his name?"

"I've always been better with faces," she said. "And he was a handsome man. Congratulations, Stephanie. You should be happy."

Chapter 27

IT WAS A relief to know my father was not the dumpster rapist—to bring a definitive lid down on the lie that had dogged me my whole life. Though I hadn't fully believed it in some time, it was still a mercy to have my mother finally disown it.

I liked hearing my father described as handsome and charming and courtly. I liked that his eyes and complexion resembled mine.

But I hated that he was nameless and would remain nameless. I hated that I couldn't even *imagine* how to seek more information about him. A few years ago, I'd learned that Morrisania Hospital had closed in 1976. Even if it hadn't, there would never be a record of a random diaper salesman from decades ago. I would never know who he was.

Relief, pleasure, intrigue, loss, and desolation: I felt like a stone skimming the surface of the water, flitting from one emotion to the next.

AT HOME AGAIN, I headed for my office, resolving to catch up on email while I had the house to myself. As soon as I opened my inbox, I saw it: a notification from the ancestry site. It had found a relative of mine: Lucia Fiore. Her page on the site listed a residence in Staten Island.

Predicted Relationship: Second Cousin

Confidence: Extremely High

I stared at her name for almost a minute before I opened Facebook, typed her name into the search bar, and clicked on the lone profile that surfaced. The moment I saw her page, I felt my heart clench: The city beneath her name was indeed Staten Island. At least three generations were accounted for in her profile photo. I took in the dark-haired, dark-eyed smiling faces of several beautiful young women, a couple of children, and one older man.

The two children were Lucia's. The older man was her father, and everything about him was lovely. He had a lean, trim figure and high-boned, clean-shaven face. His silver hair was swept straight back to reveal a gentle widow's peak. There was laughter and kindness in his eyes, and he held himself with a simple dignity.

Within moments, a family drama unfurled before my eyes: The patriarch of this clan was in the final stage of kidney disease, and they were searching for an organ donor. To this end, they had created a slideshow, a two-minute montage of the older man doting on his family. There was grandpa with the kids: at the beach, in a park, on a boardwalk. In every photo, he was cuddling them, buying them ice cream cones, or teaching them to ride bikes.

Lucia had written:

My father's favorite saying is "Family Above All." Growing up, our family has always been my father's #1 priority and still is to this day!

I closed my eyes against my own yearning and jealousy. I couldn't let myself imagine what it would be like to have a father like him. I would not let myself go there. It was senseless. It was pointless.

And yet. Could he possibly be? How accurate were these tests? The women in that picture could so easily have been my half-sisters. We had the same eyes, the same hair, and the same bone structure. A genetic test for popular consumption wasn't likely to be foolproof. Maybe I was more closely linked with this family than it predicted.

What if that were indeed the case? The man's blood type was O+. What was mine? I didn't even know. *Would I donate a kidney to a virtual stranger?* I would if he were my father.

They would surely accept and embrace me then. They would reason that I was blameless, while my mother, elderly and skeletal and dying, would be no threat to anyone anymore. I saw myself recovering in a hospital bed, thronged by weeping and grateful women. There would be talk of how God worked in mysterious ways.

It was such a rosy fantasy that I clicked on the page they had created for prospective donors. Within a minute, I felt a pang of the sharpest disappointment.

The man was only sixty-one: too young to be my father.

I sat very still at my desk. He was theirs. He wasn't mine. Or if he was mine in any sense at all, it was only in the most distant and tangential way.

But wasn't even that worth investigating? The whole family looked lovely, and they might be the only blood connection I'd ever find on my father's side. Maybe they would know exactly who he was.

A diaper salesman at Morrisania? I imagined one of them saying. *That was my cousin Vinny!*

One thing was certain: I'd never know unless I asked. And how could I not ask?

Lucia had posted her mother's phone number within the paragraph so anyone who might want to be tested could talk with her directly. My hands were trembling as I dialed her cell.

"Hello?" It was, as expected, an older woman's voice, but a warm and maternal one.

"Mrs. Fiore?"

"Yes?"

Here I began the fumbling, uncertain ritual—it was a ritual to me by now—of explaining this unlikeliest of calls. "My name is Stephanie," I said. "I got your number from your daughter's Facebook page. She posted it in connection with your husband's . . . health situation."

"Yes?" she said again, but this time she sounded breathless with excitement. Naturally she thought I was a prospective kidney donor.

"I was on your daughter's page for a different reason," I added hastily, hoping to head off her expectations. "You see, my mother is very sick, in fact she's in the final stages of lung cancer."

"Oh, I'm sorry."

"Thank you," I continued. "I guess because she's dying, she recently told me a few things she's kept secret all my life. She told me she had an affair with an Italian man from the Bronx, a man I've come to believe is my father."

"Oh my," she said, sounding confused.

"So I've been searching for him, and just today I learned from an ancestry service that your daughter and I are related."

"Oh, oh," she said after a moment. "Oh my heart. What are you telling me? Are you saying my Sal could be your father?"

"*No*," I said, alarmed. "Not at all! I'm saying my father might be his cousin. Or *your* cousin, for that matter."

"I always wondered if there could be someone else," she went on, as if I hadn't spoken. "Oh, but my heart can't take any more trouble. Not this. Not now. There's too much to bear already."

"Mrs. Fiore," I cut in. "Please! There's absolutely no chance of that. Your husband is sixty-one. I just turned fifty. He was eleven years old when I was born."

"Glory be to the Father, and to the Son, and the Holy Ghost," she said rapidly under her breath. "And thank you, St. Joseph. You frightened me, honey."

"I'm sorry," I said sincerely. "I was just calling to see whether you might know of a cousin—on your side of the family or your husband's—who was living in the Bronx in 1967. I know that for a while, at least, he was selling diapers at Morrisania Hospital."

There was a long pause. "I don't know about that, honey," she finally said. "Sal doesn't have much to do with the rest of his family. It's a long story, but I don't think we ever knew anyone who worked at a hospital or sold diapers. His father had a check-cashing business."

"I see," I said slowly.

"He's at the hospital right now," she told me. "He's on nocturnal dialysis, you see. That means he gets it while he's asleep. But I'll ask him when I see him. I'll be visiting him in the morning."

"I appreciate that," I said. "I'm so sorry to even show up at a time like this, Mrs. Fiore. I just don't know where else to turn. Your daughters are the only lead I have in connection with my father."

"You poor thing," she said. "Of course we'll try to help you, sweetheart.

Like I said, I'll talk to him in the morning and if we can think of anyone, we'll let you know."

After hanging up with Mrs. Fiore, I wanted to crawl into bed and pull the covers over my head. This was it. I was done.

I couldn't go on like this: lurking on the fringes of happy, intact families, tugging on the sleeves of wives and daughters, timid and apologetic and begging for scraps. Even if they were polite to me, even if they were kind, to them I would always be unwanted, unwelcome—a threat.

Jim and Andrea came home with a pizza, and I sat with them until Andrea went to her room to do her homework. Then I told Jim I could feel a migraine coming on.

"I'm just going to lie down for a little while," I said. "If I fall asleep, we'll talk tomorrow, okay?"

Then I lay in the dark with my arms around my pillow and stared at the ceiling. When Jim eventually came to bed, I pretended to be asleep. I lay awake for many hours after my husband fell asleep himself. I felt as angry as I'd ever been.

I was angry that it had taken my mother more than fifty years to tell me the truth about my father. I was angry that she didn't even remember his name, that I had nothing to go on and no way to find him. I was reduced to these humiliating overtures and set up for rejection again and again. She had been so heedless and selfish. Even now, she didn't get it. She didn't understand my anguish, or she didn't care.

The following day, I left work at three to return to my mother's hospice facility. By the time I pulled into the parking lot, I really did have a headache. I had barely slept, and it seemed that all the tension of the last twenty-four hours had gathered between my temples and behind my eyes.

"Mom, all my life you told me that my father was the dumpster rapist," I said not a moment after walking through her door. "Do you have any idea what kind of shame that made me feel? Why would you tell your own child such a vicious lie?"

She was in the padded rocking chair by the window filing her nails, and she barely looked up. It was as if she had been expecting me and my outburst all day. "Louie would have killed me for sleeping with other men," she said placidly. The nail file didn't falter for a moment.

"But you kept it up long after he was dead."

"Well, I guess after a while I started to believe it myself."

"Mom," I shot back, *"you invented a blood link between me and a rapist,* and the irony is there were so many wonderful *real* relatives you somehow never saw fit to mention! I have a legitimate connection with the Thorntons, for instance—people I could be so proud to claim as my own! But you hid that from me all this time. *Why?"*

I wasn't expecting a real answer, so it startled me when my mother blurted: "Because after I was raped, I was garbage to them!"

I was surprised into silence. For a moment it was so quiet I could hear the snip of the gardener's shears outside the window.

"Is that true, Mom?" I asked after a long moment.

"Yes, it is."

"Did you feel they blamed you?"

"I don't know about that. All I know is that it ruined me in their eyes. They never looked at me the same way again." To my amazement, her eyes filled with tears. "They could hardly look at me at all," she added.

"That's terrible, Mom," I said, stricken. "I didn't know that. Now so much makes sense to me. Why you were always running away. I didn't know. You never told me."

"I don't like to remember it," she said.

"I understand," I told her. In that moment, I also understood something else: Even if my father hadn't been her literal rapist, I was still in the deepest sense a product of rape—her gang rape. All her children were. We were the result of her self-abdication.

"No, you don't," my mother told me. "Honestly, Stephanie, you can't understand what I've been through in my life."

"Yes, I can." I said, surprised by the vehemence in my voice. "I have been through a *hell* of a lot in my life, Mom. I was sexually abused, too. Maybe not for ten straight days in some hidden room, but on an ongoing basis for more than a year in my own foster home, by the people who were supposed to take care of me. I've been violated, I've been homeless,

I've been hungry and cold and afraid and alone. I lost sight in one eye because you never took me to a doctor. I've been through plenty in my life, Mom, and I had to get through it by myself. I had to process it all on my own."

She was quiet then. I dropped onto the window seat next to her bed, spent. After a long moment, she met my gaze and nodded.

"We are both survivors, Steph," she said. "We have that in common, I guess. We don't have much, but we have that."

At this, whatever was left of my rage evaporated.

"Yes," I said softly, "we do have that, Mom."

"And you're right. I've spent my whole life running from what happened to me."

"Mom, we can both stop running now. We have the truth, and now we don't have to run anymore."

This sounded so good to me as I said it that I almost expected to hear violins swelling into song. At that moment I felt like the heroine of my mother's story as well as my own. As if I'd freed not only myself from some intergenerational cycle of wretchedness, but freed her as well.

But driving home after my hospice visit, I was struck by how deftly, as always, my mother had turned the tables on me. I'd come in fired up and furious, intent on finally confronting her about the sadistic lie she'd told me throughout my childhood. Wanting her to acknowledge the ways I'd suffered at her hands.

She'd turned it around, made it all about her—about all that she had suffered, her own victimhood. I'd ended up comforting her as usual. At most, she had extended her survivor status to me and offered me a space beneath that umbrella. She had taken no responsibility for her part in it, and she never would.

I had to accept that she simply wasn't capable of accountability. It wasn't even a matter of choice. If my mother could live differently, then surely she would. Who would choose to be broken and alone at seventy-six? Who would choose a life of psych wards, jail cells, chaos, poverty, and estranged and angry children?

My mother's trauma had broken her. She had never really recovered. She had no capacity for love or introspection. As I'd learned in the wake of her Easter visit, no transformation had taken place on her part. With so little time left in her life, I had to face the overwhelming likelihood that none ever would.

Chapter 28

AT FIVE THIRTY in the morning on December 29, my bedroom door creaked and our dog barked. The call came just a moment later. I like to imagine that my mother paid me one final visit as she departed from this world.

All my life I've heard stories like this, of otherworldly dispatches, coincidences too outlandish to have happened by chance. A framed photo of a friend falls over on the night table, its pane of glass cracking into a mosaic. A phone call follows within the hour, to relay the news of that friend's death—at precisely the moment the photo fell.

A woman hears her sister saying *goodbye* so clearly that she actually looks around for her, even though her sister lives across the country. Again, the call comes soon afterward, and again the time of death matches the inexplicable communiqué.

Sometimes the case for a visitation is more of a stretch:

All her life, she loved monarch butterflies. It was her thing. She had monarch-patterned scarves, monarch stationery, a monarch brooch. Well, the last time I visited her grave, a monarch landed on the edge of her headstone and stayed there for the longest time. I knew it was her.

Or: *I knew she had sent it.*

It was a message. A sign. That she was okay. That she was still with me.

I have a secret weakness for these stories. I tend to believe them. I've climbed out from the crushed insides of two totaled cars without so much as a scratch. If I can feel divinely protected after a childhood like mine, how can I feel skeptical about someone else's butterfly messenger?

I like to imagine my mother sweeping by our house on her journey from this world. My childish imagination has her floating by in a mist of stardust. She peeks in on me, tucked snugly between Jim and our dog, and feels reassured, as a mother should.

My need to invent a watchful and attentive mother is strong even now. My need to believe in a transformation endures. But as wishful as it sounds, I do think a transformation finally took place. The last weeks of my mother's life were unlike any other time during our half-century together.

WHEN HER MEDICAL team told me that my mother was actively dying and it was time to move her to hospice, I chose Gracelen Terrace for its cleanliness and natural light, its tranquil neighborhood and well-kept grounds, and because somehow it reminded me of the motel where my mother had been a maid, the last place our family felt secure and happy.

Gracelen Terrace is a long, low-slung building in Southeast Portland. If you took four or five houses from a Monopoly game, laid them end-to-end, and painted them white, leaving only the trim in its original green, you'd have the nursing home. Lilies and flowering sage added splashes of color by the entrance. Beside the birdbath in the courtyard, a stone angel peered at her own upturned palms, which hovered before her face as if supporting an invisible book.

As with all the other places she had lived since her diagnosis, I decorated her hospice room. Knowing how she hated fluorescent tube lighting, I brought in a floor lamp and a desk lamp, both with pink shades to bring a warm glow to the space. I brought luxurious bedding, bright throw pillows, a small velvet armchair, and half a dozen framed photos.

She had reached out one day to touch my faux fur coat with a look of yearning, and so I brought in a throw for her that was made of the same material, cream-colored and kitten-soft. After every sponge bath or bedding change, someone would tuck the throw back in around her body. She loved the feel of it beneath her fingertips, stroking it even in her sleep.

Each week I brought in freshly cut tulips, always in the same color—a flaming and luminous pink. The same shade as the ocean sky at dawn, my childhood color of hope. Even as the sun was setting on my mother's life, I hoped it would rise in the better place that the chaplain said she was destined for. I prayed he was right about that, but it wouldn't take much. Any place was better than the world as my mother had known it since 1953.

ONE EVENING DURING this time, I spoke with my son Josh, who had moved to New York City. He too had recently taken part in a deathbed vigil. He and several of his musician friends had gathered for a few days at the bedside of a female friend dying of bone cancer.

"She wanted us to sing for her, so we did," he told me over the phone. "We sang her out, we sang her on her way."

"That's so beautiful," I whispered, struck both by the visual and his phrasing.

We sang her out. We sang her on her way.

I was no singer, but I could love my mother out. I could love her on her way.

ON HER LAST lucid evening, she and I went to an Elvis concert in the dining hall after dinner. The impersonator was a middle-aged man with all the usual accoutrements: sequin-studded white jumpsuit, dyed-black pompadour and sideburns, dark shades and heavily ringed hands. He swaggered around the floor, crooning the lyrics of "Love Me Tender" and "Blue Christmas," serenading old women in their wheelchairs and high-fiving the elderly men. My mother loved it. I felt a surge of joy every time she laughed at his antics or clapped with appreciation. She still loved music, however it came.

"Stephanie," she said in her room just afterward, as I was getting ready to leave. "Hand me my purse."

She was sitting in her nightgown on the edge of the bed, bare feet dangling over the side.

"Sure, Mom," I said, taking the beaded macramé bag from the dresser and setting it down beside her. "What do you need?"

"And my shoes."

"Your shoes?" I asked, confused. Was she thinking of trying to go somewhere? "Do you mean your slippers?"

"No, my moccasins," she said, referring to the shearling-lined shoes she hadn't touched in weeks.

"Mom, what do you need shoes for?" I asked. "It's bedtime."

Even as I said this, I was bringing them to her. Obeying her was a habit it seemed I would never break.

She set the shoes beside her on the bed and then began pulling things out of her purse: a lipstick, half a roll of cough drops, loose change, and a lone key. One by one, she shoved them into the toe of her left moccasin, out of sight.

"There," she said. "A perfect fit. That's much better, don't you think?"

"Better than what?" I asked, hearing my voice go high with alarm. "Mom, what are you doing?"

She looked at me, then back at her shoes. A puzzled expression crossed her face.

"I don't know," she said after a moment. She shook her head. "I don't know what's wrong with me."

"That's all right, Miss Florence," a nurse said from the doorway. "You just got confused for a second. Pay it no mind."

The nurse breezed in, took the shoe from my mother's hands, and shook the contents back into her purse. Then she took my mother's chart from where it hung at the foot of her bed and made a few brisk notes.

"Stephanie, honey," the nurse said, "stop in at the office and see me on your way out, if you would."

"I'm sorry to have to say this," she told me a few minutes later, after my mother had gone to bed, "but the cancer has reached your mother's brain. From here on out, she's going to keep having spells where she's not making a whole lot of sense. You need to be prepared for that, honey— she's not going to be the same."

———

SHE'S NOT GOING to be the same.

And she wasn't. She was different, so different. While these words had been meant to warn me—so I could brace for unfortunate changes—the truth is that for a brief and luminous interlude, she became the mother of my dreams.

Her eyes widened with delight whenever I walked into her room. She reached out to take my face between both of her hands. She said my name as if she savored the very sound of it. She thanked me, over and over, for everything I did for her.

Her gratitude was like an opiate. It took so much of my pain away. It eased the chokehold of sorrow that set in whenever I crossed the hospice threshold. She said over and over that I'd made her room beautiful. She told me I made her proud. She said she loved me.

She said she loved me. How can I express what it was like to hear those words from her? I'd been waiting for them all my life, and now I hovered around her like a thirsty cat lingering by a drainpipe, wanting above all else to hear them again.

The moment I was showered and dressed in the morning, I would run down to my car and drive to Gracelen without stopping for breakfast. The staff began bringing me meals each day, and I'd eat them beside my mother's bed. I'd stay by her side well into the evening, working during her naps, leaving only after she seemed to be asleep for the night, a moment which came earlier each visit.

And finally the day arrived when she didn't wake at all. She was asleep when I arrived and, hour upon hour, she stayed asleep. Her breathing was steady but her eyes never opened.

After that, she was asleep each time I came. The nurses said she was essentially comatose and would likely remain so until she passed.

IT HAD BEEN two years since I'd learned of my mother's lung cancer. I'd known she was going to die for all that time. In some ways, I'd waited for it—for the blessed end of her mood swings, her middle-of-the-night calls, her intermittent abuse and incessant demands.

But to have her slip into oblivion so soon after her turn toward tenderness was a special kind of agony. I felt as bereft as I had ever been. When I woke in the morning, my face was damp with tears. I went around all day leaking at the eyes, hardly noticing enough to wipe the tears away, and Jim told me I whimpered all night in my sleep.

True to our family form, my mother outlived the hospice doctor's prediction by many weeks. More than a month after she checked in, a nurse named Jane cornered me as I was leaving for the evening.

"Stephanie, do you have a moment?" she said. "There's something I've been wanting to ask you."

"Of course," I said, thinking she wanted to discuss some aspect of my mother's medical care. When I sat down facing her at one of the tables in the common area, I was startled to see accusation in her pale blue eyes.

"Stephanie," she said in a tone of prim reproof, "you aren't keeping your mother here, are you?"

"What do you mean?" I asked, looking at her in bewilderment. Hospice was, by definition, a patient's final destination. Where else was I supposed to bring my mother? "People come to hospice to die, right?"

"Exactly," Jane said. "So why hasn't she died?"

"Excuse me?"

"She was supposed to die three or four weeks ago," Jane said. "So why is she still alive?"

I remained so dumbfounded by this line of inquiry that it took me a moment to find words. "I don't know what you're asking me," I said. "Her doctors said she was actively dying and that it was time for hospice. If you think there's been some mistake and she was brought here too soon, that's something you should take up with her medical team, not me."

"I don't think her doctors made a mistake," she said. "I think *you* are standing in her way. You won't let her go."

I sat there with my mouth open, unable to believe what I was hearing. *Who was this woman? Was she out of her mind?*

"You're seriously blaming me because my mother isn't dying fast enough for you?" I finally managed.

Jane folded her arms across her chest. "I had a feeling you'd get mad at me," she said. "But I have to speak my conscience. That poor woman is suffering, and there's no sense in keeping her here any longer. You need to release her."

"How can you—" I was so flustered I couldn't speak without sputtering. "This is so unprofessional! I can't believe—"

I watched her lips turn white as she pressed them into a thin line. "I've been doing this a long time, honey. I'm just calling it like I see it. I'm sorry if you're offended by my honesty."

I rose without another word and fled the building. How *dare* she? What business did she have calling herself a nurse? Did she talk to all family members this way when patients didn't die according to her timeline?

I thought about reporting her to her supervisor. I considered filing a complaint with the hospice and another with the state medical board. I still wonder if I should have done any of these things. As it was, I went out and cried in my car, drove home with shaking hands, and raged about it to Jim. But underneath it all, I wondered whether she was right.

The next day, though I refused to look at Jane or return her greeting, I pulled my chair up close to my mother's bed, took her bluish hand as she lay comatose, and began speaking the words I'd rehearsed throughout the sleepless night before.

"Mom," I said in my gentlest voice, low and resolute, "you know I love you so much, and I always have. I've felt so close to you during these last few weeks, and it's made me so happy. But I know you're in a lot of pain and it's not going to get better, and I want you to know that it's okay to go."

My heart felt as if it were skittering around like a dying thing itself—something crushed and stunned and flailing. But my mother's breath didn't falter, nor did she show any other sign of hearing what I'd said. If on some level I expected her to be snuffed out somehow, like a candle, in response to my words—well, that wasn't happening.

"You had a hard life, Mom, and I know you're having a really hard death too," I went on, "but very soon, all your hardship will be over."

My mother didn't stir. Her eyes didn't flutter. Her labored breath did not falter.

"One of your nurses, the one named Jane, she thinks I'm keeping you here," I told her sleeping form. "She thinks it's past time for you to go, and that I won't let you."

It was as if I wanted my mother to wake up and take my side, share my anger at Jane. She didn't, of course. I all but recoiled, hearing the words I'd just said out loud: *She thinks it's past time for you to go*. They sounded cold and peremptory and ugly, and I was furious with myself for relaying them, even to an unconscious woman.

I strode out of her room and down the hall, looking for Jane. The facility was small, and it wasn't long before I saw her stocking a supply cart on the far side of the corridor.

"My mother will die on her own time, whenever that might be," I flung at her, as if there had been no break in our conversation since the night before. "She doesn't need my permission or anyone else's. She certainly doesn't need *your* intervention."

I stalked away before she could answer or see that I was shaking.

Jane avoided me after that.

DECEMBER DRAGGED ON, and I continued to come every day, living in what began to seem like infinite limbo. My mother did not die, and she did not wake up. Spending nearly all my waking hours within the hospice walls began to feel unsustainable. My body hurt from sitting all day. My heart ached from the sorrow around me, pressing in on me from all sides.

The looming fact of Christmas added another layer of dread. I hated the tinsel-heavy plastic trees scattered around the place, inside the entrance, the visiting room and dining hall. I hated their artificial and garish colors. They reminded me of every institutional Christmas of my life: in the dependent unit, hospitals, psych wards, and jails. It depressed me to see the nurses in their red plush Santa hats with sagging white pom-poms, and to hear tinny Christmas music on the sound system in the visiting room.

Yet there was nowhere else I could imagine being. Hour after hour, I sat by my mother's bed. Leaning toward her from a hospital chair had begun to hurt my back, so the staff lowered her bed as far as it would go and I sat beside it on the floor, on the imitation sheepskin rug I'd brought from home. I had a certain sense of completion, sitting on the floor at her side: I had been her servant in life and now I was her servant in death. But I was no longer a child in servitude. I was a woman yearning, with all my heart, to be of service.

"LISTEN, HONEY," Jim told me a few days before the twenty-fifth, "I have the highest respect for your choice to visit your mother every day. But I hope you'll make an exception on Christmas Eve and Day, and just be fully present in our family celebration."

"Of course I'll spend most of it here with you," I said. "But it's all right if I visit her for just a little while, isn't it?"

"Well, that's what I'm asking," he said. "I'd like you to take a break, just for the holiday. When you come home after your time with her, you're always tired and sad. Can we just have Christmas away from all that? For the kids' sake?"

"They're not actually kids anymore," I said, irritated. "I mean, really, Jim. I promised my mother I'd be with her up to the end, and any of these days could be her last."

"Steph," my husband said gently. "She won't even know you're there."

"We have no idea what she knows," I snapped. "Maybe she doesn't consciously know what's going on, but what if she can hear me, or even just sense my presence?"

"You've been there every day for more than five weeks, hon. She wasn't supposed to last more than one."

"Wow, Jim," I said. "You sound like Jane."

"Whoa," my husband said. "I mean, just— whoa. That's not fair."

"Isn't it?" I retorted. *"She wasn't supposed to last?"*

"Stephanie, I saw how your brother held on well past what anyone would have thought possible. To my way of thinking, this could go on a very long time. I know you made her this promise, but you have a very full life—running a school, getting another one off the ground, and parenting. Spending all your time there for weeks or even months on end just isn't realistic, especially when she's not even conscious."

The fury I felt was beyond anything reasonable, but there it was.

"I'm the one doing it all," I countered, my voice rising to a shriek. "I get to decide whether it's realistic, all right? I only get one shot at this, Jim. She'll be dead soon enough, I promise. And then she'll be dead forever."

My husband paled at this. He held up a hand in concession. "Okay, honey. I'm sorry. You do what you need to do."

So I'D WON. On Christmas Eve, I arrived at Gracelen with a beautifully wrapped box and Andrea in tow. In the box was a white faux fur wrap. In my very irrational fantasy, the matriarch and her daughter and granddaughter would sit down together for a holiday dinner, after which she would open the present we'd brought.

How can I explain expecting to find her in the dining room with all the other families, awaiting the Christmas banquet and gift exchange? I actually scanned the room and felt confused when I didn't see her.

"Merry Christmas, Stephanie! Oh my goodness, is this your daughter? What a beautiful young woman," said Mara, one of my favorite nurses.

"Merry Christmas, Mara," I said. "Do you know where my mom is?"

She looked at me with a startled expression. "She's still asleep. Still unresponsive," she told me. "Which is of course to be expected."

"Of course," I managed after a moment, feeling deeply foolish.

"But I don't blame you for hoping you'd get a Christmas miracle," she hastened to add, squeezing my hand. "I would feel the same way. I'm sorry I don't have better news."

Andrea and I made our way down the hall and into my mother's room. As Mara had said, everything was unchanged. She was asleep in her bed, her face ashen and gaunt against the pillow. One skeletal arm was flung out as if to welcome me, but there was a finality about her closed eyes, as if they had been sealed shut.

I sank down onto my place on the floor, by her side. Andrea took the chair.

"Merry Christmas Eve, Mom," I said. "I brought you something. I hope you don't mind if I open it, because I want you to have it now."

Carefully, I pulled the paper from the box, lifted the lid, and took the wrap from where it was nestled between layers of tissue. As gently as I could, I slipped one end of it beneath her neck and angled it around her shoulders.

"Isn't it soft, Mom? I wanted it to keep you warm and cozy."

I felt wildly inhibited with Andrea there, unable to talk to my mother freely as I usually did. My daughter looked uncomfortable as well. She looked down at the floor, or around at the walls—anywhere but at my mother or me.

"Mom," she asked after a few minutes, "can we go now?"

"Not yet, honey!" I said. "We just got here."

"Do you think she's going to wake up soon?"

"No, I don't," I said. "I don't think she's going to wake up at all."

"Then I don't get it," my daughter said. "Dad was right. What's the point of sticking around if she doesn't even know we're here?"

I felt a howl gathering inside me, one I could not unleash. *You wanted to come*, I railed silently at my child. *I didn't ask you to be here. You asked me to bring you along!*

"Tell you what," I said instead. "We won't stay long at all today. We'll leave in just one hour. Okay?" Even as I said this, I was wincing inwardly at the idea of so brief a stay. What kind of woman abandoned a dying mother so soon on Christmas Eve?

"A whole *hour*?"

———

I DIDN'T VISIT her on Christmas day. I wanted to, but my family prevailed. The nurse on duty that day said she never woke up, that she surely wasn't aware of having no visitors. But I spent the day in a state of miserable impatience, waiting for it to pass so I would be free to take my place at her side once again.

I went to her the day after Christmas, and the next, and the next.

Very early on the fourth day—at five thirty that dark December morning—my bedroom door creaked and our dog barked. The call came just a moment later. I like to imagine that my mother paid me one final visit as she departed from this world.

The nurses said her passing was easy and peaceful.

"EVERYTHING ABOUT HER death, about her entire hospice stay, *was* easy and peaceful," Jim told me that day. "You healed her heart."

"I don't know about that," I said.

"She was so different than she'd ever been," he insisted. "So happy to see you every day. So thankful for all you were doing. She was finally capable of showing love, and it was because of what you did for her, Stephanie—the work you did to uncover her story, your willingness to understand her and forgive her."

I closed my eyes against the longing that broke over me then, the longing for his words to be true.

"You healed her heart," he repeated.

It was the most seductive thing he could have said. It was what I wanted to believe more than anything. Sometimes I do believe the difference in her was due to a shift within her psyche, rather than a symptom of the cancer that had reached her brain. Just the same way I sometimes believe in otherworldly signs, like messages in the form of a monarch. Other times I believe a butterfly is just a butterfly.

I'll never know for certain if I really healed my mother's heart. But there *are* a few things I can be certain about:

My mother did not die alone.

Whatever might have brought it about, during the last few weeks of her life, the two of us were together in that fabled place of love and gratitude that had been my dream forever.

I'd found a way to be the love I didn't get.

I loved her out. I loved her on her way.

In all of this, I had healed my own heart.

Epilogue

WHEN MY DAUGHTER was five years old, I read her a children's book about a very long dachshund called Pretzel, who rescued another dog, Greta, from a deep hole. When the story was over, Andrea started to cry.

"What's the matter, honey?" I asked.

"A picture in that book made me feel sad," she told me.

Instantly I knew the picture she meant. When Greta, depicted as a much smaller dachshund, was trapped in the hole, she wept so hard that her tears gathered into a huge blue puddle at her feet.

I reminded her that Greta ended up safe and sound—and married to Pretzel, no less, with a litter of puppies.

"But she was in there crying for a long time," Andrea said.

"So it made you sad to know she felt so scared and alone?"

My daughter nodded.

"I understand. But remember: In the end, Pretzel saved her, and they lived happily ever after."

Andrea was quiet for a moment, and I allowed myself to believe she had been consoled. Then she replied:

"But there are big holes like that all over the world."

I fell silent in astonishment.

TWO MONTHS AFTER my mother died, as if fate had decided to spare me from dealing with both of them at once, I found my father.

The path to discovery was convoluted, full of loops and dead ends and mirages. It was crowded with New Yorkers, Italians, and Australians: all the far-flung branches of my father's family tree. It held exhilaration and deep sorrow, tenacious days and sleepless nights. It was seven or eight weeks of full-throttle obsession.

The process of finding him was far too complicated to recount, but in the broadest strokes: The ancestry site continued to turn up distant relatives, and I continued to be incapable of turning away. Many were less than forthcoming, but others were willing to assist with my search. They talked with their own extended families and sent a series of leads. A few weeks in, I made contact with a woman named Debbie, whose own subsequent DNA test identified her as my first cousin. She confirmed that her uncle Giuseppe was a salesman for Jack N' Jill diapers in the Bronx.

He had been dead since 2006.

I KNEW ALL ALONG, of course, that he might very well be gone. It wasn't a shock, but it was still a blow.

The dream of the archetypal father died hard. The one in which there was a man in the world who would claim me as his own. Who would be overcome by the sudden gift of a daughter in his midst, fully formed and needing nothing from him but his paternal pride. The one where I garnered all the phrases people used to describe a father's tenderness for his daughter: *the apple of his eye, the treasure of his heart, the balm of his old age.* The dream of having a parent who actually loved me.

I begged my cousin to tell me anything she could remember about him, but she could only recall a day spent driving through the streets of our Bronx neighborhood in search of Giuseppe's car. "My mom and his wife—my Aunt Maria—were best friends," she told me. "So when Maria was sure my uncle was cheating on her, my mom helped her look for him, even though it meant busting her own brother. We spent hours driving up and down, but we never caught him."

She sent a single photo of him. It was black and white and cracked and faded, and in it, my father wears a dark suit jacket, light shirt, and patterned tie. He looks game but impatient, unsmiling. His dark hair is trimmed short and slicked back, close on the sides and forming a slight crest at the crown. He looks a little like Andy Garcia in *The Untouchables*: taciturn, mysterious, and New-York-glamorous.

How can you lose something you never had? I don't know, but I look at his photograph and I ache with the loss of him.

Debbie also reported that Giuseppe and his late wife had two children: a son and a daughter. Their names were Joseph Jr. and Carol Lynn, and both were alive and residing in Scarsdale to the best of Debbie's knowledge, though she hadn't spoken with them for years and had no contact information to share.

The idea of another brother and sister was a potent consolation, and I set out to find them myself. What followed was the strangest, hardest blow of all.

In New York in 2019, decades into the internet age, I could hardly find a shred of information about either of my half-siblings. No social media pages, no LinkedIn accounts, no professional listings, no community or political affiliations. Moreover, no one from any place they'd lived or worked was willing to speak with me. The two of them might as well have been ghosts, or figments of my imagination.

An exhaustive online search finally turned up an obituary for Carol, dead at fifty-seven. It bore nothing but her name, age, date, and city of death—July of 2016 in Scarsdale—and the name of the funeral home that had seen to her arrangements, Sinatra Memorial. The guest book had been signed by a single acquaintance, a Michelle Caruso.

Carol was a beautiful, friendly, funny, full of life person I knew. I will think and miss her a lot. My heart goes out to her family.

Debbie found contact information for Michelle and tried to connect with her by phone. She reported that Michelle hung up on her, after telling her never to call again.

Sinatra Memorial provided me with the phone number of her only known relative, my half-brother Joseph Jr. I must have called that number, and all the other ones I could find in association with him, a hundred times. No answer, ever. No voicemail. No nothing.

Next I dialed Michelle's number again myself, unable to fully accept Debbie's report of her hostility. She'd written that message in the guest book, hadn't she? Carol could hardly have offended her since, given that she was no longer alive.

A man answered, who identified himself as Michelle's boyfriend. I said I was the half-sister of Joseph Tobacco Jr. and that I was trying to track him down by searching out anyone connected with his family.

"No!" the man bellowed so loudly that I actually jumped in fright. "No! No, no, no! *Never* call this number again, do you hear?"

Then he hung up on me, as Michelle had done with Debbie.

Finally, in desperation, I hired a private investigator.

Two days later he called to say that Joseph Jr., too, was dead, as of 2018. The medical authorities believed that both brother and sister died by suicide. By the coroner's best estimate, Joseph Jr. had taken his own life on his sister's birthday. His body wasn't found for another full week, and then it was by the police, who'd had to break down his apartment door. The P.I. gave me the name of the funeral home that had accepted his body.

The undertaker told me the county welfare office had conducted a search for his next of kin and found no one. They cremated his remains and disposed of all his possessions. The city provided him with a "welfare funeral and burial." No one came.

I DON'T RECALL just what I said in response to my daughter the evening we read the story of Pretzel, but I do remember thinking she'd spoken a terrible and irreducible truth. There are big holes like that all over the world, and sometimes we don't get out of them.

The hole that swallowed my mother was so deep and dark she never truly emerged from it. All of my living siblings are in holes of their own.

I might never know why my two paternal half-siblings seem to have been submerged in darkness as well. It's impossible not to suspect abuse in some form. Two suicides, two unattended funerals, two human beings so isolated there's hardly a record of their having lived—that kind of twinned pathology doesn't happen by chance. It was hard for me to believe that it could happen at all. How did that depth of social estrangement come about? As bad as my mother's children had it, not one of us is without connections, attachments, or entanglements.

I was shocked by the depth of my own grief for people I had never met. But if blood counts for anything, they were just as close to me as Allan, Pablo, Isabella, Dominic, and Walter. They shared a single parent with me, no less than the siblings I grew up with.

I was a year too late in Joseph Jr.'s case, three years too late in Carol's. For weeks I was haunted by this. If only I'd found them sooner, could I have made a difference? Might I have stopped either of them from taking their lives?

Nothing could be more pointless than wondering about this. I'll never have that chance or know those answers.

I still don't fully know how I escaped my own hole, the one that seemed to be yawning in wait for me since the womb. I can list the circumstances I credit for saving me, but they amount to no more than my own ever-shifting conjecture. Emotional wiring, the love of a steadfast partner, otherworldly protection, certain decisions and inborn traits—at one time or another, I've counted all these factors in my favor. But I also know that luck might be the most essential piece of all.

I resolved to write a real eulogy for Joseph Jr. and Carol, but I could find out nothing else about them.

THREE MONTHS AFTER my mother's death, on an afternoon in late March, I stood with my husband, daughter, youngest brother and oldest niece on the western edge of Gibbs Cemetery in Sherwood. My search was over. I'd invited everyone in my extended family to join Jim, Andrea, Josh, Jeremy, and me in our own makeshift memorial service for all our departed family members. Walter and my brother Allan's older daughter were the only ones who showed up.

I had chosen the location for its beauty, its lack of morbidity, and the feeling I had when visiting of being in a park rather than a burial site. From our spot, there was a clear view of both Mount Hood and Mount Saint Helens, snow-white and pristine against the deep blue sky. There was a border of trees and stately houses on either side of the grounds. It was a place I'd be glad to return to for the rest of my life, and after.

I'd purchased three plots. One for me when my time came, another for Jim, and one for all the remains and personal effects we would place there today. Because we were not lowering a coffin into the ground and would need nothing even close to a standard excavation, we were allowed to dig the hole on our own. We would each take a turn at this task.

It was unseasonably warm for March, the sun bright and strong in the sky. The first tender crocus and daffodil shoots were just pushing up through the grass. The trees were rustling, and there were birds overhead. It was a good day for a funeral.

I stood at the spot where we would soon break ground, cradling a box and an urn in my arms. In the box were pictures of my father, Joseph Jr., Carol, and Louie, as well as notes I had written to each of them. In the urn were my mother's ashes. My brother Allan's daughter Rachel carried the urn that held his ashes. My brother Walter had the urn that held Rick's.

For a moment, just before we began to dig, I was overcome by all I had learned about my roots, my history, and my heritage. I stood surrounded by my family and yet I was alone there on the cemetery grounds, my arms full of all that remained. I'd learned so much about my own past over the last two years, but the more I uncovered, the harder it became to distill it all into an easy or serviceable identity.

I was the American Dream.

A rags-to-riches tale. A poster girl for social advancement. An unlikely achiever and a bootstrapper. I was a feel-good story, a happy ending.

I was living proof that a child in this country can come from nothing and end up with everything. That dreams and drive and grit mean more than high birth or a fancy pedigree. I was walking evidence of equal opportunity, a testament to the possibility of transcendence.

I was an American daughter, in the most optimistic sense of the phrase.

And I was an American nightmare.

I was a child, one of millions, who fell between the cracks.

I was our failed school system. A girl who remained silent in the classroom, illiterate past the age of eight without anyone taking much notice. A kid who sat outside the school office for hours with a shattered arm and no pain relief, because my mother was in no hurry to show up and I wasn't important enough to bother about.

I was our failed child protection system. The girl who lived with her siblings on the beach for a year—alone, unschooled, and free of adult supervision, eating seaweed because we were starving—without causing any concern. The kid who went half-blind from untreated strabismus. The child returned to an incompetent and criminally negligent parent over and over and over again.

I was our failed foster care system. Placed in the home of a serial sexual predator—one of many children sent to them over God knows how many years. The sister of a boy raped in a juvenile detention home.

I was our failed legal system. The daughter of a girl-child gang-raped by upward of a dozen grown men, none of whom were sentenced to more than two months in prison. The daughter of a woman driven mad by trauma and injustice.

I was our failed healthcare system. The daughter of a woman who never once in her lifetime received adequate care for her mental illness. The daughter of a woman who was committed to countless psychiatric wards, the conditions of which were worse than any horror movie.

An American daughter.

I descend from America's foremost founding family. In my bloodline— along with the Washingtons—are the likes of the Thorntons, the Grubbs, and the Bealls. Suppliers of the Revolutionary War. Titans of industry. Men of education and intellect. Men who were among the founders of Harvard and the New York Cotton Exchange.

People so exclusive and insular they disowned their daughter for marrying outside high society.

My ancestors were the founders and builders of America, as socially prominent and blue-blooded as they come.

But I also descend from a line of women who rejected it all. From a grandmother who eloped with her chauffer. Who gave away her family's priceless heirlooms in a yard sale. A mother who burned her house to the ground, who refused her membership in the rarefied social order of her girlhood, who turned her back on safety and respectability.

I was an illegitimate child, born out of wedlock.

I'm the daughter of an Italian immigrant. A diaper salesman.

The granddaughter of a cab driver. The adopted daughter of a Latino short-order cook. The stepdaughter of a drunk and a junkie, an armed robber, a grifter, an ex-convict, and Peyote Way Church of God devotee.

My brothers and sister are Puerto Rican. My daughter is Guatemalan.

My family is the war-torn and weathered, punctured and patched-over, gilt-edged and glimmering tapestry of America.

All of it was right there, in both my hands.

MY DAUGHTER AND I, along with Jim and our niece and my youngest brother, dug a different kind of hole together.

It felt so right to turn the earth ourselves. We angled the shovel into the ground, lifting out grass and weeds and dirt. The work was hard, and sweat broke out across my forehead as I gave myself to it. When it became too arduous, Jim took over. And when we had cleared an adequate space, we gathered around it and laid our loved ones' remains inside.

I'd had a granite grave marker inscribed with their names, the years they had lived, and an epitaph reading: "They Finished Strong." My mother was beside Rick, where she had vied to be all her life. The ashes and mementoes of everyone else were nestled nearby. We played the Rolling Stones' "Gimme Shelter" on an old '70s boom box as we shoveled the turned earth back into place.

We spent hours together at the gravesite that day. We told stories. We sang some of my mother's favorite songs. We said some private prayers, and there were stretches of time where we all fell into prolonged and comfortable silence. I let the sadness of the last two years wash over me and wondered again about what allowed me to be here, aboveground and upright amidst so much wreckage.

It was just then—as if she could read my mind—that my niece Rachel leaned over and touched my arm.

"Aunt Stephanie," she said. "How did you make it through all those years with Grandma Florence? What advice would you give to kids like you and my dad? Advice for life?"

"Oh honey," I said. I'd been asked some version of that question so many times before, and yet I felt flustered to be put on the spot. "That's a good question, but let me think about it, all right? I promise I'll write something down. I'll send it to you soon."

For the rest of the afternoon I wondered what I would tell her and whether it would make sense to her.

Understand that you must make your own home in the world, however modest. It doesn't need to be rich. It just needs light, warmth, comfort, beauty, and love. Attend to these elements. Invite others in.

Find a way to be the love you didn't get. Sometimes in the course of doing this, you will need to draw a protective circle around yourself and be careful about who you let inside. Love does not preclude boundaries—sometimes it requires them.

Still, keep in mind that the most difficult people are often suffering in ways we can't fathom. It would have been so easy for me never to have learned what happened to my mother. I came so close to not ever knowing.

When I did uncover those revelations about her past, it allowed me to understand her. But it didn't restore what was lost. It didn't redeem her life. It didn't make anything okay.

So much harm had been inflicted that wasn't within my power to repair. In the wake of it all, what use was this gathering, what use was ceremony? It did nothing to diminish the tragedies at hand, and yet I had to believe it mattered.

Sometimes we can't fix what's broken. The damage can't be reversed or undone. Sometimes we don't arrive in time. But if nothing else, I could honor the lives I couldn't save. I could affirm their humanity and insist on their dignity. Gather them back from the far edges to which they'd scattered. I could hold the remnants of them close, say their names, and lay them to rest.

It was late afternoon when we felt ready to end our vigil. We felt tired and tranquil, uplifted, finished. A fiery pink light, my lifelong color of hope, was just tinting the edges of the sky. My daughter's hand was in mine, and the sun was still warm when together we rose to go home.

Acknowledgments

FIRST AND FOREMOST, I want to thank my husband, Jim Plymale, for always being there for me in every aspect of my life, including the writing and creation of every chapter of this book. He helped me relive these painful memories in order to accurately tell the story. He drove us miles to Mendocino—to the beach where it all began. Together we revisited the motel where I used to live as a child, as well as my horrid former foster home. He helped me process that long season of my life, and to him I am forever grateful.

Josh, Jeremy, and Andrea—my children. Thank you for your encouragement and belief in me. You are my teachers: You provided me with continuous inspiration and gifted me with the family I always longed for.

Thank you HarperCollins and HarperOne for choosing my memoir to publish. And for the brilliant edits, revisions, additions, and stylistic vision your team brought to the table to elevate *American Daughter*.

To my collaborator Elissa Wald and editors Sydney Rogers and Amanda Hughes, thank you for putting your hearts and souls into this book and never settling, even when dark forces tried to stop us in our tracks. Thank you all for showing up month after month to undertake the rigor of this story. And thank you for continually challenging me to bring forth the best iteration of this book.

Emma Parry, my agent. Thank you for believing in me and my story. For recognizing the potential of *American Daughter* to inspire others and for working diligently on my behalf.

Ross Cohen, my dear therapist, counselor, life coach, fill-in father, and healer. Thank you for showing up in the best way, week after week. Thank you for the unconditional belief in me that never wavered—especially at the junctures when I did not believe in myself. Above all, words cannot express my gratitude for EMDR. Without it, this book would not have happened.

My beloved staff: Kristin Sidorak, Amy White, Cara Murray, and Janis Howard. Thank you for your continual contributions to Heritage and to this book. None of it would have been possible without each of you. Janis, thank you for being so dedicated to our students and for reading every iteration of this book as it took form. Thank you, Kristin, for your help and support during the creation of this book and in the final hours of panic. You came to my rescue.

To Patty, who's been like a mother to me.

Thank you, Uncle Allan. You showed up as family for me. You are the first and last uncle I will ever have. So fun and talented you are. And to my niece Rachel, who's been unconditionally supportive of me and this book.

I'm also thankful to the Thorntons for giving me the instinct and force to continue my heritage of bringing education to generations of people.

To my cousins, Debra Panzanella, Belinda Tobacco, Connie Tobacco, and Daniela Foti, for welcoming me into the family and working vigorously with me to discover our Italian lineage.

Thank you to all of the discerning readers who took the time to read each chapter and respond with honest feedback. You know who you are. Your input has been invaluable.

For those in my family who have died and whom I have gotten to know through this book: You have been with me in spirit, guiding me in ways unseen. You have been by my side in life even when I wasn't aware. To my grandparents: It's sweet to think that I might be the apple of your eyes.

As I write this, I can recall a quote that's been with me for a long time, but which didn't fully resonate with me until I wrote this book:

I come as one, I stand as ten thousand.

—*Maya Angelou*

About the Author

STEPHANIE THORNTON PLYMALE is the CEO of Heritage School of Interior Design. Stephanie calls Portland, Oregon, home—a word with much meaning as she grew up without one. From living in a car on the beach with her siblings to isolation in the dependent unit of the state of California to a horribly abusive foster home, Stephanie never experienced a feeling of family as a child. Married at nineteen to her high school sweetheart, Stephanie held on to a desire for family roots that helped her to build a stable marriage and loving home for her three children.

From a young age, Stephanie had an insatiable desire to create a feeling of home. This incited her passion for interior design, which led to a successful career working in nearly every facet of the industry, including residential, commercial, retail curation, fabrication, and staging. After eighteen years of owning her own firm, Stephanie felt ready to pursue her next chapter. It was then that she took over Heritage School of Interior Design. Stephanie's vision was to make education accessible to all who were interested in excelling in the industry.

Stephanie has supported hundreds of students in achieving their dream careers. Many alumni have gone on to win prestigious awards and begin wildly successful businesses. She continues to balance family life with promoting Heritage, the success of its students, staff, continually growing community, and philanthropic efforts.

Though Stephanie's traumatic childhood, family life, and career are unique, she takes heart in knowing that life's lessons are universal and that everyone has a story. Her goal is to inspire others to share their stories, receive support, and feel empowered by their ability to survive, forgive, heal, transcend, and live the life of their dreams.